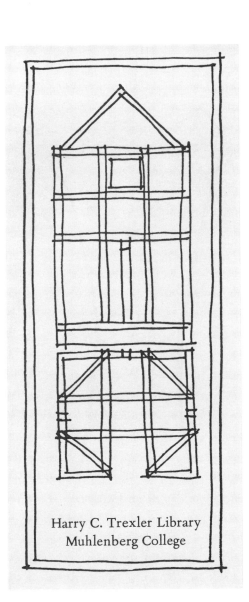

SPLIT CORPORATISM IN ISRAEL

SUNY Series in Israeli Studies
Russell Stone, Editor

A publication from the Center for the
Study and Documentation of Israeli Society,
The Hebrew University of Jerusalem

SPLIT CORPORATISM
IN ISRAEL

LEV LUIS GRINBERG

STATE UNIVERSITY OF NEW YORK PRESS

Published by
State University of New York Press, Albany

© 1991 State University of New York

Printed in the United States of America

For information, address State University of New York
Press, State University Plaza, Albany, N.Y., 12246

Production by E. Moore
Marketing by Fran Keneston

Library of Congress Cataloging-in-Publication Data

Grinberg, Lev Luis, 1953-
    Split corporatism in Israel / Lev Luis Grinberg.
        p.   cm. — (SUNY series in Israeli studies)
    Includes bibliographical references and index.
    ISBN 0-7914-0705-5 (alk. paper). — ISBN 0-7914-0706-3 (pbk. :
alk. paper)
        1. Histadrut ha-kelalit shel ha-'ovdim be-Erets-Yiśra'el.
    2. Trade-unions—Israel. 3. Industrial relations—Israel.
    I. Title. II. Series.
    HD8660.A5H583   1991
    331.88'095694—dc20   90-45047
                                                              CIP

10 9 8 7 6 5 4 3 2 1

To Yael, Michal, and Jonathan

CONTENTS

ACKNOWLEDGMENTS

I would like to thank the Sapir Center for its financial support for this research and Michael Shalev for allowing me to use material collected in a joint study. Michael Shalev deserves my special gratitude for his friendly advice, comments, and encouragement throughout all stages of my research. I also thank Yonatan Shapiro, Naomi Chazan, Yoav Peled, Nitza Berkovitz, and Ronen Shamir for their useful comments, and Jon Simons for his close work with me in writing the book in English. Special thanks are due to Baruch Kimmerling, without whose prodding and encouragement this book would not have been written.

PROLOGUE

On March 15, 1990, Shimon Peres, leader of the Israeli Labor party left his office as finance minister. He had been dismissed two days earlier by the prime minister and leader of the Likud party, Yitzhak Shamir, who claimed that Peres was manoeuvering to bring down the National Unity government, originally established in 1984 and renewed after the elections of 1988. Indeed, sixty hours after his dismissal, Peres garnered the support of enough members of the Knesset (Israel's parliament) to defeat the government in the first successful vote of no confidence in Israel's history. The issue at stake was the government's refusal to say yes to American Secretary of State Baker's proposals to convene a meeting of Israeli and Palestinian representatives in Cairo. Without a positive answer, the peace process could not progress, while the Palestinian uprising, the intifadah, was already in its third year.

When Peres left his office he knew he faced three hurdles on the way to establishing a government that could take some positive steps on the path to negotiations and perhaps a definitive solution to the Israeli-Palestinian conflict. Firstly, he needed to ensure a majority for the no confidence vote to follow in a few days. Then, should he succeed, he would have to convert that negative approval into recommendations to the president that Peres should be given the responsibility to form the new government. Finally, he would have to translate that potential support into a coalition agreement including at least sixty-one members of Knesset. Should he stumble at any of these three hurdles, not only would Peres' gamble to advance the peace process have failed, but his position as leader of the Labor Party would become extremely tenuous.

Amid all this dramatic tension and these fateful events Peres found time, but a few hours before leaving his office, to sign an agreement with the secretary-general of the General Organization of Hebrew Workers in the Land of Israel (hereafter *Histadrut*). The agreement stated that the *Histadrut's* health service (hereafter *Kupat Holim*) would receive a 100 million dollar subsidy, its pension funds were assured high and fixed interest rates, while the *Histadrut* conceded 1.3 percent of the 5.4 percent cost of living allowance payments guaranteed under existing collective agreements.

Not surprisingly, few journalists paid any attention to this agreement signed at a time of political excitement and suspense. Those that did comment on it criticized Peres and the *Histadrut* for exploiting a political crisis to hijack more funds for these institutions associated with and politically dominated by the Labor party. Treasury officials complained that the deal denied any economic logic, while the new Likud minister temporarily in charge of the Treasury expressed his regret that the *Histadrut* had agreed to forgo legally agreed wage rises for the workers it was supposed to represent.

This small event presents a puzzle, perhaps incomprehensible to foreign eyes but which accorded with what Israelis knew about their labor movement. Why does a minister belonging to what is held to be a right wing party criticize the Labor Party and trade union leader for damaging the interests of the workers? Why does the *Histadrut* agree to concede previously agreed wage rises without provoking rank and file opposition? Why does this labor organization depend on the state to subsidize its institutional and economic empire? What is the relation between the *Histadrut* and the Labor party? How does the peculiar structure of the labor movement influence the structure and functioning of the economy? What explains the signing of such an agreement at the peak of a political crisis? How do the relations of Israel's Labor party and labor organizations, together with the structure of the latter, influence the nature of Israeli politics? And what consequences, if any, does all this have for the chances of a resolution of the Israeli-Palestinian conflict? This book aims to furnish the reader with the analytical tools needed to understand these mysterious aspects of the current political economy in Israel.

THE CHALLENGE

Israel is undoubtedly a very complex society, full of contradictions and peculiarities. The most frequent reactions to this complexity are either to treat it as an "exceptional" case or to "isolate" specific manageable issues that can be dealt with according to more widely applicable concepts and theories. In both cases something is lost. If we use the "exceptionalist" approach, the analytical concepts derived from the special case will be too close to the events they are supposed to explain, and it will be impossible to draw any wider theoretical and comparative conclusions from the Israeli case. If we use the "isolating" strategy, applying existing theories and models, an understanding of Israel's idiosyncracies will not be reached. This study adopts a third strategy, containing more risks, but more useful both for comprehending Israel's peculiarity and for suggesting some conceptual conclusions relevant to general theories. This approach orients the research according to central questions proposed by general and relevant theories, analyzing peculiar Israeli phenomena in their light, without imposing a theoretical straitjacket on them. As a consequence, new concepts are formulated to analyze the specific case, and new theses and problems are contributed to the original general theories. According to this approach, theory provides guiding questions—not answers—and social phenomena provide new data for theoretical interpretation, which may demand modification of theory.

This book offers an analysis of Israel's peculiar political economy, relating both to the historical background and recent events, while examining its structural constraints and dynamic processes. The analysis of Israeli political economy is in itself a very exciting challenge. This study aims to decode a very enigmatic society, featuring a long period of Labor party rule, powerful labor organizations, together with nationalist opposition by unorganized Jewish workers increasing their support for the Likud and more extremist right wing parties.

The puzzling question is why the political labor movement, embodied in powerful institutions, is so detached from the workers? The issue to be addressed is what implications this institutional detachment has for Israeli economy and politics. This book analyzes this problem both historically and in the light of the more contemporary period of Likud rule (1977-1984) and National Unity government (1984-1987). The study focuses on the *Histadrut*, its structure and historical development. Of particular interest are its relations with workers, employers, the Labor party, and the state on both economic and political levels.

The understanding of Israel's political economy seems to be of increasing importance not only for those directly affected (Israelis and Palestinians) but also for those less directly connected to their conflict, such as Arabs and Europeans, but especially for the Americans who underwrite so much of Israel's economic and political bill.

This study offers an analysis of various questions arising from Israel's current problems. What explains the stagnation of the labor movement and the inability of the Labor party to lead Israel towards peace? Why is the labor movement so dependent on the state that it prefers to participate even in governments which fail to advance their political programs? Why is the Likud so reliant on collaboration with the Labor party in National Unity governments? In other words, why is Israeli politics so resistant to change despite tremendous transformations that have occurred in recent years all over the world in general and as regards the Palestinian national struggle in particular?

Conventional Israeli political wisdom would have it that the two big parties, representing on the Labor side a dovish tendency to territorial compromise and on the Likud side a hawkish tendency to retain those territories conquered by Israel in the 1967 War, were simply in a position of electoral deadlock. It was the parity of support for the leftist and rightist blocs (these labels being interchanged with those of dovish and hawkish) that explained the existence of the National Unity government. Moreover, given the fateful nature of the decisions and steps to be taken, at first to pull Israeli troops out of Lebanon and reign in raging inflation and then to seek a solution to the Middle East conflict, it is held that unity was necessary to preserve the national consensus. On the other hand it is argued that Labor could not progress far with peace plans without Likud support, or that withdrawal from territories would be acceptable only if a government including the Likud as a partner undertook it. On the other hand it is claimed that by sharing power with Labor the Likud could neutralize the main opposition to its policy of maintaining the status quo. Whichever conventional analysis is accepted, economics is divorced from politics.

This book proposes an alternative analysis, seeking the answers to the questions posed above in the relations between political institutions and economic structures. The action of conservative and powerful social groups and organizations aiming to maintain and expand their power explain much of the puzzle. The institutional aspects of political economy are conceptualized here on the lines of neocorporatist theory, while the structural aspects of the economy are conceived according to dual labor market theories.

The theoretical aim of this study is to combine neocorporatist concepts of institutional intermediation between capital and labor by the state, with dual labor market approaches relating to the differential power of labor groups split along national and ethnic lines. The analysis of Israeli society suggests that the combination of both theories is a better framework for analysis than the two taken separately. The intention here is to discuss the common theoretical questions to which both respond, to examine the actual, observable, practical solutions to the problems addressed by each pattern as they are manifested in Israeli society.

From the theoretical perspective Israel is a very interesting case that includes both corporatist institutional patterns and a labor market sharply segmented on national and ethnic lines. The *Histadrut* was found to be the most appropriate focus for this study as a whole because of its peculiar feature of internal institutionalized corporatist interest mediation made possible by a split labor market. The social history shaping this specific political economic structure is outlined to reveal the most salient characteristics of the *Histadrut*.

The *Histadrut* is the oldest, most durable and stable institution in Israel, having been established in 1920, and includes some economic, labor and social welfare organizations set up even earlier. The *Histadrut* controls 25 percent of the economy and employs the same percentage of the labor force. More than 80 percent of the workers are affiliated to it directly, without regard for their work place, profession, specific union membership, or salaried status. It is governed politically, its leadership being elected through periodical general and proportional elections by all the members once every four years. Members vote for lists sponsored by political parties, and the same party has governed the *Histadrut* since its inception, though over the years it has changed names and its composition several times, it now being the Labor party. The *Histadrut* provides its members with a large proportion of the social welfare services available to the majority of Israelis, particularly through *Kupat Holim* and pension funds. The whole structure, development, and changing policies of the *Histadrut* are peculiar, fascinating for both their theoretical implications and practical consequences for Israeli society.

THE RESEARCH PROGRAM
AND ITS DEVELOPMENT

The investigation itself was peculiar. It began as a small piece of research in 1984-85 when I looked at a case study of an apparent rank and file workers revolt against the *Histadrut* from 1979 to 1982, the case of the Forum of the thirteen Big Committees. At the start it was an "industrial relations" study, but as I proceeded to collect data and formulate new questions, the scope of the study widened. After theoretical concepts had been developed and the Forum test case analyzed (in my M.A. thesis), I added two new chapters based on a common research project with Michael Shalev.

In this new work, subsequent processes of economic stabilization (1984-1987) were analyzed using the same theoretical concepts in a state of development, but the whole focus of the study changed as the spotlight moved to the *Histadrut* as the pivotal institution of the Israeli political economy. This shift came about as I realized that it makes little sense to concentrate on the workers' action unless one considers it in the general context of the political economy and historical developments of its structures and institutions. For this purpose I found it useful to apply comparative methods, employing the concepts of neocorporatist political exchange and the dual labor market.

This section is an outline of the development and transformation of my research project, indicating the theoretical framework in which the research questions were formed.

Methodology

The research methodology is based on assessment of interviews, the analysis of internal documents, and the interpretation of events reported in the media.[1] Ironically, some aspects of Israel's peculiarity give it certain advantages and create a suitable climate for social research. Israel is a very small-scale society, with a few hundred members in its administrative, political and economic elite. Access to them is relatively easy, especially for academics who share common networks with them. It was not necessary to make use of more than two contacts in order to be allowed an interview with any elite person.

The intimacy stemming from Israel's smallness creates a very open and sincere climate for interviewing elite people. Information I expected to be top secret was imparted proudly with a smile and a knowing wink. The president of the Manufacturers' Association reported how he made deals with the *Histadrut* secretary-general, in secret and informal tete-a-tete negotiations, describing his sophisticated tactics for pacifying rank and file opposition by criticizing the *Histadrut* leaders severely in public while making concessions in private. The finance minister told me how they managed to keep informal negotiations secret, while in the meantime the public was informed about formal, fictitious collective wage bargaining in the private sector. The *Histadrut* secretary-general divulged that it was his initiative to create and direct internal rank and file opposition to him, in order to base demands for wage increases on their threatened action during negotiations with government and employers.

Obviously the most discrete interviews were with civil servants still in office. They also spoke frankly, but understandably, sometimes asked not to be quoted. For this reason not every piece of information learned in an interview is attributed to a specific source. Some important information, vital to this study was discovered 'in secret documents, some not to be quoted, and some quoted without revealing their source.[2]

Preliminary Questions

The interpretation of seemingly overt events was somewhat more complicated. At first it was necessary to understand the apparent rank and file revolt. The rank and file organization in question, named "the Forum of the Thirteen Big Committees" (hereafter the Forum) was active at a crucial conjuncture—the transition from prolonged Labor party hegemony (1948-1977) over both the *Histadrut* and the government, to a new constellation of forces with the Labor party controlling the *Histadrut* and the right wing Likud in government. The first research questions concerned the establishment and development of the Forum. Under what circumstances was it organized? What had the attitudes of the workers' committees been before the Forum's establishment? When did the Forum reach the peak of its power? When and why did it begin to lose influence? When did the Forum finally disintegrate? What were the Forum's achievements, what were its failures? What were the characteristics of its members? What were its relations with the *Histadrut*?

After reading the complete sequence of events it became clear that from 1980 to 1982 the Forum had a definitive influence, playing an important role in the process of collective bargaining and political exchange. The Forum's foundation coincided with the appointment of a new finance minister who initiated an aggressive antilabor policy, causing unemployment and wage erosion. Although they struck only once for twenty-four hours, they succeeded in accelerating the conclusion of a national wage framework agreement in June 1980, they prevented a wage-freeze package deal proposed by the finance minister in September-December 1980, and they were a cautionary influence on both government and *Histadrut* during collective bargaining until May 1982. The Forum disintegrated as a result of a combined effort by both the government and *Histadrut* from May to October 1982, before the new framework agreement (for 1982-1984).

The next set of questions were about political power relations. What were the sources of the Forum's strength? Why did they not use all their power to strike in order to increase wages? Why did they not mobilize and organize other workers' committees, requesting that they do so? Why did they not revolt against the *Histadrut's* restraining policy?

From remarks made in the first interviews the Forum leaders confirmed that their objective and policy was not to undermine the *Histadrut* but to reinforce it. Moreover, they brought to light a new and surprising fact—they had secret consent from the *Histadrut* secretary-general for their activity.

Neocorporatism

At this stage a general theoretical framework was necessary to analyze relationships between rank and file workers' organizations and the *Histadrut*. Previous Israeli research did not provide an explanation for the Forum case. Questions of rank and file organization were analyzed in terms of "industrial relations," out of the political and economic context. The interrelations and exchanges between the *Histadrut*, government, and Manufacturers' Association were beyond their scope. The evident connection between the Forum's establishment, the political change in 1977, and economic change in 1979 was never discussed in theoretical terms in most Israeli research.

The first theoretical advance can be seen in the work of Michael Shalev (1982, 1984 and forthcoming). He is the first Israeli scholar to apply a neocorporatist perspective to the Israeli case. This theory provides a framework to analyze rank and file organization in relation to political exchange between employers, government, and centralized monopolistic trade unions.

Social scientists have recognized the emergence of a new pattern of relations between trade unions, employers, and the state in Western Europe in the post-war period. This neocorporatist pattern (Schmitter and Lehmbruch, 1979; Lehmbruch and Schmitter, 1982; Crouch and Pizzorno, 1978; Panitch, 1977; Goldthorpe, 1984) rests on the mutual interest of trade unions, governments, and employers in combining wage restraint with foregoing the use of unemployment as a means of determining the power relations between labor and capital. Corporatism involves tripartite exchange relations among unions and employers, mediated by the state. Usually but not always this phenomenon occurs while social democratic parties are in government.

From an economic perspective, trade unions offer wage restraint in exchange for full employment. Politically, they agree to legitimize the established social order in return for recognition by employers and the government of their status as the workers' exclusive representative. It follows that trade union centralization is a precondition for corporatist exchange. Yet precisely for this reason, corporatist arrangements are inherently unstable, since there is always a tendency for rank and file workers to mobilize in opposition to the right of centralized unions to make compromises in their name. Such periodic mobilization from below presents a serious challenge to the partners in corporatist exchange.

The neocorporatist theory has remarkable advantages over classical Marxism. On the one hand it adopts two of its central assumptions—the basic contradiction between capital and labor, and the tendency to crisis brought about by the contradiction between the conflictual, antagonistic economic sphere and the democratic, egalitarian political sphere. On the other hand, neocorporatism rejects the predicted revolutionary solution to class conflict.

Neocorporatist theory provides a common framework for scholars from different perspectives to analyze political economic phenomena, both those who reject and criticize corporatism as a developed pattern for the reproduction of capitalist social relations, and those who welcome it as the most advanced form of working class influence on the political level.

Another important advantage of the neocorporatist approach is the ease with which it translates theoretical concepts into concrete operational definitions. Capital and labor are analyzed in terms of their organizations, political and economic, and their elite. There is no need to employ an intangible concept of the historical or real interest of the working class; instead, different concrete examples of their interests, expressed by trade unions and rank and file workers, are discussed. The specific combination of an "open" theory with concrete operational definitions makes the neocorporatist theory very useful.

The neocorporatist approach emphasizes institutions of capital, unions, and the state. As the *Histadrut* is a puzzling institution, corporatist theory seemed the most appropriate approach to the subject. The neocorporatist concept of state attribution of "public status" to private organizations, and the political exchange between elites, offers an explanation of the cooperation between the *Histadrut* and Likud government and allows for the possibility that the former may have used the Forum's strength for its own purposes and interests. Yet some important questions remain unanswered.

Historical Perspective

A further theoretical advance originated with my receipt of a secret document (it is an internal bank report which I am forbidden to quote). This report discusses problems of pension funds, explaining the Comprehensive Pension Agreement signed in June 1979. The report reveals the existence of a very complicated package deal between the *Histadrut* and Manufacturers' Association. The deal included a wage restraint agreement, cheap credit from the *Histadrut* bank (*Hapoalim*) to members of the Manufacturers' Association, and a complete transfer of all workers to the *Histadrut's* expanded comprehensive pension fund. This agreement is crucial not only in explaining the political conjuncture when the Forum was established, but also for an understanding of the peculiar and complex Israeli pattern of corporatist institutionalization. It involves wage restraint, taxation, and subsidy of capital investment on the economic level, along with mutual support of employers and the *Histadrut*. Yet all this was achieved without state mediation. What is more, the agreement contradicted government policy. This revealed the importance of the *Histadrut's* multiple functions, not only as a centralized trade union, but also as a quasi-state with a welfare role, and as an employer owning large economic enterprises. It became clear that the *Histadrut's* peculiar structure, containing the three elements of corporatism within it, would shape the Israeli political economy.

The basic discrepancy between the actual role of the *Histadrut* and the simpler trade union role expected of it by neocorporatist theory does not, however, remove the need to answer typically corporatist questions about centralized political bargaining. Rather, it becomes vital to develop concepts relevant to this specific phenomenon.

In order to formulate these new theoretical concepts, this study reviews the historical background of the *Histadrut* and centralized political bargaining. This historical analysis and theoretical conceptualization transform the nature of the whole study, shifting the focus of investigation from rank and file organization to the *Histadrut's* political economic structure.

From the historical survey in chapter 2, it appeared that the *Histadrut's* unique structure reflects the problems faced by Jewish workers in the pre-state period in seeking employment in the face of stiff competition from unorganized Arab labor. In return for partial control of the economy, the *Histadrut* acted to discourage the emergence of workplace based trade unions representing the material interests of specific groups of workers. Moreover, in combining representational with entrepreneurial functions, from the outset the *Histadrut* was forced to develop a viable compromise between capital and labor within its own boundaries.

Centralized wage bargaining did not emerge until relatively late, on the eve of World War II, and only after the Arab revolt of 1936 made the separation of the Jewish and Arab economies possible. The first corporatist agreements were reached during the war, but they were accom-

panied by growing labor unrest. Rank and file opposition to corporatism was expressed during the 1940s by the organization of workplace
committees and strikes, but was also channeled into a political struggle
inside the *Histadrut* between Mapai on one side and the left-Zionist
opposition (*Achdut Ha'avodah* and *Hashomer Hatzair*) on the other.

Following the creation of the state, in the 1950s trade unions were
established for professional workers and civil servants who struggled
for autonomy from the *Histadrut*. Later, in the early 1960s, a similar
trend emerged among industrial workers' committees under conditions
of rapid industrialization and a high level of demand for unskilled
labor. Israel's occupation of the West Bank and Gaza Strip following the
Six Day War provided an effective counterforce to the militancy of
industrial workers, in the form of competition from unorganized noncitizen Palestinians. However, this was not the case in the public sector,
where employment of these workers was largely precluded by legal
and security considerations or by their lack of appropriate skills. On the
contrary, the bargaining power of state employees increased, especially
among workers who were capable of inflicting damage on the economy
as a whole, such as those employed in the sectors of transportation,
communication, and electric power. Their representatives were the
leading workers' committees in the Forum established in December
1979. A pattern of differential power between labor groups emerged.

Split Labor Markets

As a result of the historical investigation, this study has abandoned a misinterpretation of neocorporatism as a "model" or "ideal
type" and replaced it with a more dialectical understanding of it as a
concrete historical pattern. A historical approach avoids the danger of
forcing social reality to fit an a priori ideal type theoretical model.

However, neocorporatism still leaves a great theoretical vacuum
in respect to labor market processes and structure, as the central question of labor groups' differential power remains unanswered. Since
labor market cleavages coincide with national and ethnic divisions, dual
labor market theories are both necessary and fruitful.

Some Israeli scholars have used such theories to investigate different phenomena: the segmented labor market after 1967 (Semyonov and
Levin-Epstein, 1987); or the origin of the Labor Zionist movement under
conditions of a split labor market at the turn of the century (Shafir,
1989). Different theories of fragmented labor markets have been applied
in this study (Piore and Doeringer, 1971; Piore and Berger, 1980; Gordon, Reich, and Edwards, 1982; Bonacich, 1979) without any a priori

preference for one over another, giving social reality the dominant role in selecting the most adequate explanation.

A central theoretical distinction between high and low priced labor is said to rest on their different bargaining strength. The theories also identify the political interest of capitalist employers in segmentation of the labor market and the division of the workers in order to control the working class. In Israel, the primary sector, usually characterized by technological sophistication and stable employment, does not meet dual theories' expectation, because this sector's industries are mainly public, not private. The Israeli variation originated in the peculiar form of capital accumulation of the Zionist enterprise, which from its beginning and to the present day has imported capital and administered it in national and public institutions.

Analytical Concepts Applicable Specifically to Israel

The combination of the unique structure of the *Histadrut*, with its origins in the labor market problem of Jewish settlers in the 1920s, and the existence of a new unorganized Palestinian labor force since 1967, explains the most distinctive feature of contemporary split corporatism in Israel, namely the contrast between the business and public sectors. In the business sector,[3] both private and *Histadrut*-owned, labor's workplace organizations are weak and wage restraint occurs as a result of both the competitive impact of the unorganized labor force and centralized control (by the Labor party) of the national unions of industrialized workers. In the public sector, however, labor relations are in a permanent state of crisis, with both national unions and workers' committees pressing for wage hikes, with or without *Histadrut* support. It emerges that in the private sector the *Histadrut* conducts a cooperative dialogue with private employers which is tantamount to corporatist exchange without state mediation.

The term private sector corporatism (PSC) was coined here to describe this peculiar Israeli pattern of centralized wage restraint, constructed and operated by the *Histadrut* and the main employers' organization. The employers are themselves powerless to assist the state in confronting public employee militancy despite their interest in preventing spillover of wage increases from the public to the private sector. The strong workers are those employed by state owned companies (civilian employees of the military, transportation, communication, and electricity workers, etc.). Split bargaining takes place when the *Histadrut* and private employers prevent the strong workers from participating in the private sector corporatist negotiations, diverting them to the public sector agreements.

Split corporatism is a term describing two different systems of collective bargaining and political exchange where well organized workers in the public sector act separately from workers in the private sector and enjoy better wage agreements. The position of the state in split corporatism is thus undermined by the strength of the *Histadrut* and private employers on the one hand, and that of organized labor on the other.

Without any premeditation the original case study of rank and file organization turned into a theoretically informed analysis of the peculiar structure and dynamics of the Israeli political economy, based on corporatist political exchange, a dual labor market economy and the institutionalized pivotal position of the *Histadrut*. This analysis serves two purposes:

a) it deepens an understanding of Israeli society by means of recent theories developed in advanced capitalism;
b) it provides these theories with feedback from the Israeli experience and thus sharpens some of their concepts.

THEORETICAL CONTRIBUTIONS

Chapter 1 discusses the theoretical compatibility of neocorporatism and dual labor market patterns. The first is characterized by the settling of political and economic rivalry through state mediation in the context of a uniform labor market. A politically organized working class, usually controlling the state through social democratic parties, is able to ensure its full employment by centralized national negotiations. The second is characterized by a segmented labor market, a weak and poorly organized working class, where the state is noninterventionist, merely providing a general framework which facilitates capitalist free enterprise.

Neocorporatism and the dual labor market are two central patterns in the political economy of late capitalism. Both patterns developed mainly after World War II as a democratic response to business cycles and the strength of workers' organizations. In his discussion of dualism and corporatism, Goldthorpe (1984) presents the two as opposing tendencies in advanced capitalist societies. This study aims to challenge Goldthorpe's interpretation of both patterns, analyzing them as systems with common features in light of the Israeli experience.

Despite his own observation that dualism and corporatism coexist in several countries and that strong trade unions even accept the situation—as in Austria (see Bauboeck and Wimmer, 1988), Germany, and

Switzerland—Goldthorpe warns against its long-term political consequences:

> the fundamental division and effective depoliticization of the
> working class, with the concomitant disappearance of any orga-
> nized challenge to the capitalist order in the name of economic
> democracy and social equality. (Goldthorpe, 1984:340)

This warning reveals an essential paradox in Goldthorpe's analysis of the phenomenon. On the one hand, his prophetic insight—confirmed by the case of Israel, if analyzed in these terms—is astounding.
As soon as the Israeli corporatist trade union and labor party accepted—and even helped create—the reality of a dual labor market, a large
proportion of workers stopped supporting labor parties and turned to
those of the right. On the other hand, Goldthorpe's warning attributes
undue importance to the political-ideological sphere in both theories,
while passing over the complex relationships between the political and
economic spheres, and the historical circumstances and special mechanisms common to both patterns. His emphasis on ideology leads
Goldthorpe to view the two patterns as incompatible, each dominated
by one of the two sides of the class conflict—corporatism by a strong
working class, and dualism by strong capitalism.

This study proposes an opposite view[4]—that both dualism and
corporatism represent partial solutions to the common problems of
advanced capitalist democracies. Not only is the synthesis of the two
patterns possible in a dynamic reality, but (paraphrasing Goldthorpe's
warning) this synthesis may become one of the most sophisticated
forms of controlling and maintaining order among the working class in
capitalist society.

These two apparently conflicting models are actually based on
concrete social formations but are defined in very static forms and
therefore do not include the dynamics and processes which create the
patterns they describe. They cannot explain crisis, instability, and
change. In other words, their static interpretation leads to the imposition
of the "model" on reality, and a failure to understand specific, complex
formations which vary from the "model." I reject this Weberian understanding of theory, mainly because it is not helpful in the present study.
The more dialectical approach proposed here raises questions about
theoretical generalizations, but only examination of concrete historical
phenomena provides complete and specific answers. This dialectical
method is in my opinion the most productive way to use the body of
theory accumulated by neocorporatist and dual labor market scholars.

The main deficiency in dual labor market theories is their neglect of political processes and an explanation of the role of the state. In contrast to corporatist theory, they divorce the economic from the political sphere. Corporatist theory complements this omission in labor market theories, so together they constitute a broad theoretical basis which is used here to analyze the peculiar dynamics and structure of Israeli society. Israel is indeed a very peculiar combination of both patterns, but not the only one. However, every society has its specific patterns, and the scholar's task is to discover its characteristics by means of questions which are based on knowledge of different societies.

OUTLINE OF THE CHAPTERS

The Israeli case is, in this sense, a very rich and exciting challenge. In spite of the comprehensible tendency to view it as an entirely unique case, it is important to analyze it in a comparative approach. During the prolonged and complicated process of research its focus changed from workers' resistance to a study of the *Histadrut's* political power relations with the state, employers and workers, based on economic interests and structures. The scheme of the book is presented below, concentrating on the substantive and theoretical questions of chapters 3-6 which deal with relatively recent events, the analysis of which is based on original information from primary sources. The historical chapter 2 is based on secondary sources interpreted along the lines of this study's theoretical approach.

Chapter 1 briefly presents the theoretical concepts of neocorporatism and the dual labor market, ending with a short discussion on features common to both which provide a basis for their fusion.

Chapter 2 is a broad and general analysis of the main historical processes and sources of political and economic structure, from the *Histadrut's* foundation in 1920 until the Likud party's ascent to power in 1977. The pre-1967 period is characterized by flux and uncertainty in the dual labor market structure, varying with both Jewish-Arab relations and Jewish immigration. The post-1967 period is structured by a fixed dual labor market within the Israeli political economy following the introduction of noncitizen workers from the occupied territories. The theoretical discussion analyzes the central patterns of the Israeli political economy and *Histadrut's* pivotal position, to be applied in later chapters: The *Histadrut's* internal corporatist capacity, split collective bargaining, the partnership of PSC through *Hevrat Ovdim* mediation, and manifestation of crises at the level of the state.

Chapter 3 discusses the rank and file's ability to prevent wage restraint policies being implemented by centralized corporatist unions and to change existing institutions and structures of the political economy. The chapter describes the establishment of the Forum in 1980, and their opposition to the employers' (including the *Histadrut* and state) aggressive policy to limit wage rises. The *Histadrut* elite's use of the Forum's action to maintain existing patterns and institutions, reinforcing their own power, is analyzed.

Chapter 4 discusses the ruling party's ability to coordinate interests through the state during 1981-1983. As the Likud was organizationally detached from labor and capital and politically divorced from the *Histadrut*, it failed to coordinate the political economy. The chapter describes the *Histadrut's* unwillingness to cooperate with the Likud government to restrain (public sector) workers strengthened by their position in the labor market, and PSC's ability to control wages in the secondary (private) sector. The inflationary and fiscal implications of this pattern, aggravated by the democratic demand for "political business cycles" are also analyzed. The PSC's detachment from government is the catalyst for a complex pattern of the political economy: split corporatism.

Chapter 5 analyzes an interim period (September 1984-May 1985) prior to the *Histadrut* elections. The large National Unity government was in power, but the partners of private sector corporatism imposed package deals on the government, thus sustaining hyperinflation and precipitating the state into a fiscal crisis. The theoretical question here is the dependence of the government on *Histadrut* cooperation and the latter's need for legitimation, to counteract its support for drastic antilabor economic policies. The state's and employers' collaboration with the *Histadrut* leadership is described, and the strong workers' exchange of legitimating the social order in return for economic rewards is conceptualized.

Chapter 6 deals with the theoretical question of state autonomy, analyzing the radical program to stem inflation, successfully reducing it in a very short period from 500 percent a year to 20 percent. This change was possible because of the state's ability to withstand political pressures from the powerful economic interests of employers and workers. The factors analyzed are the crisis conjuncture, the action of civil servants, American financial aid; and the National Unity coalition supporting the policy. The dynamics of the economic development and political events during 1985-87 are described and the maintenance of existing structures and institutions are analyzed. The dilemma discussed is how the *Histadrut* managed to maintain its pivotal position in the political economy despite the harm to *Hevrat Ovdim* enterprises and to the workers, caused by the state's economic policy.

The epilogue returns to the theoretical discussion to reintegrate it with the rich material of the Israeli case study. Corporatist and dualist patterns are analyzed in the light of the study's findings, with the aim of demonstrating that their combined application is more fruitful than each taken separately. Some analytical concepts are developed beyond the frameworks of both approaches, emphasizing the need for further theoretical development.

CHAPTER 1

CORPORATISM AND DUALISM

This chapter contains a short summary of the theoretical concepts central to this study. After the presentation of corporatist and dual labor market theory, various concepts shared by the two theories and approaches for integrating them are explored. Finally, the particularity of the Israeli case in this context is discussed.

NEOCORPORATIST THEORY

Starting in the mid-1970s, the pluralist theory many social scientists then ascribed to came under increasing criticism. This approach, its critics maintained, failed to explain several phenomena that had developed in various European countries after World War II:

a) growth of the state's scope and its involvement in economic activity;
b) the manner in which interests were represented through monopolistic organizations of workers and employers;
c) the making of central economic decisions through national negotiations between three bodies—the state, the employers, and the trade unions.

According to the neo-corporatist critics, the pluralist approach fails to explain why it is the employers and workers, rather than other groups, that become prominent interest groups; why a political economic elite arises in open democratic societies; and what the dynamics of the new political arrangement are.

Schmitter (1974) was the first to define the growth of corporatism:

> As a macrohypothesis, I suggest that the corporatization of interest representation is related to certain basic imperatives or needs of capitalism to reproduce the conditions for its existence and continually to accumulate further resources. (Schmitter, 1974:107)

Corporatism is not characteristic of Western Europe only, but exists in other countries as well. In order to distinguish between corporatism based on interest association and that in which monopolistic trade unions are imposed on the workers, Schmitter borrows the terms "societal corporatism" and "state corporatism" from J.M. Cortez Pinto and J. Pires Cardozo. This distinction has helped scholars to focus on the democratic phenomenon of societal corporatism characteristic of advanced capitalism, and distinguish it qualitatively from the authoritarian phenomena typical of developing capitalism. Crouch (1983) perceives this distinction not as a dichotomy, but rather as a continuum between two poles, with several intermediary conditions. He thus facilitates discussion of phenomena (and countries) that do not precisely fit either the pattern of societal corporatism or that of state corporatism.[1]

The new pattern of interest representation, in which the state is involved in economic activity and invites employer and worker representatives to nationwide, centralized dialogue and negotiation, has arisen within the framework of developed capitalist societies. It is this dialogue that gives the state its consensual image enabling it to tend to the public interest. This development is not a "technical understanding" of economic needs, in Keynes's terms, but rather a new balance of political power between the classes. The welfare state and its involvement in economic activity develops along with the growth of the working class's power, which, as it evolves, creates organizations to protect its interests: trade unions and political parties (Panitch, 1977). These workers' organizations constitute a threat to capitalist accumulation and its means of production. There thus arises a need to blunt the edge of the class struggle located in the production process, in the factories. The development of the welfare state has successfully achieved this goal, by offering the workers a standard of living and income not derived from wages. The working class obtains these benefits not through confrontation in the factory, but rather through social legislation, in the political-parliamentary sphere. Application of this social legislation enlarges the state's scope, institutions, and involvement in the economy. The state, furthermore, becomes one of the largest employers in the economy.

The need to determine income policy, more than any other factor, is essential to corporatism because it requires cooperation, on a national level, between the state and the trade unions. The "consensus" obtained between the state and the trade unions is the policy of "full employment," which is the heart of corporatism. For this reason, it is World War II, when political circumstances necessitated "full employment" in Europe, that marks the historical turning point toward cooperation between the state and the trade unions. Unlike other European states, Norway and Sweden had "full employment" as early as the 1930s. Therefore, corporatism developed in those two states before the war (Panitch, 1977:74).

Corporatism is not only a means of representing interests, as Schmitter maintained, but rather "a political structure within advanced capitalism which integrates organized socio-economic producer groups through a system of representation and cooperative mutual interaction at the leadership level and mobilization and social control at the mass level" (Panitch, 1981: 24).

The state involved in the economy must carry on collective bargaining with worker representatives, but encounters at the outset the opposition of the various noncentralized trade unions. By their very nature, these unions cannot cooperate and restrain their demands. The unions must first undergo a process of centralizing their authority and establishing a hierarchical structure that enables them all to conduct joint bargaining with the government.

The issue here is an internal process within the trade unions that is a necessary condition for the creation of the corporatist structure. This structure is neither a theoretical model nor a social ideal, but rather a historical phenomenon—one that arose in Europe in the middle of the twentieth century, and could conceivably disappear eventually with changes in the conditions that led to its birth.

Rather than emphasizing the centralization of unions, Maier (1984) ties corporatism to the weakness and vulnerability of certain economies after World War II, competition in the international market, and the impulse toward cooperation the shaky economies instilled in both workers and employers. Corporatism, however, as a bridge between the market and political arenas, also requires the concurrent development of social democratic parties and trade unions.

Trade Unions and Labor Parties

When worker and employer representatives conduct centralized bargaining on a national level, that does not mean all workers enjoy equal bargaining power vis-a-vis their employers. The power of the worker as an individual is essentially different from that of the capitalist. The individual nonunionized worker demanding a wage increase will be fired if his employer finds another worker who will do the same work for lower pay. Unlike the workers, who before organization act as individuals, two capital units, when joined, merge into an integrated total and form a new single unit. There lies the essential difference between labor and capital—the liquidity of capital versus the atomization of the workers. And that is the difference between the power of the worker and that of the employer. In order to improve his wage, the worker must organize, together with his fellow workers, thereby eliminating the competition that damages their common interest. The worker must forego his individuality and act in common with the other workers; the employer does not have to do so. While the worker has only one way of defending his interests, through workers' organizations, "capital has at its command three different forms of collective action to define and defend its interests, namely the firm itself, informal cooperation, and the employers or business association" (Offe and Weisenthal, 1980:75).

Another form of labor organization important for the workers' struggle is their political party. Only unions and parties, then, determine the workers' power, while the employers derive their power from their economic control. It is precisely this power gap between worker and employer that creates the conditions for corporatism. The workers' total dependence on their organizations impels them to establish parties and trade unions powerful enough to control the state. A situation is thereby created in which the workers' parties control the state and expand the scope and dimension of their activities. The class conflict thus moves from the factory, where the worker is weak, to the political arena, where he is stronger (Korpi and Shalev, 1980).

This, then, is the paradox: the worker's weakness vis a-vis the employer leads him to organize and transfer his struggle to the political arena, where he has the upper hand. However, it is in this political sphere that the representatives of the workers and their parties appropriate the worker's ability to carry on his wage struggle, dissociate themselves from him, and conduct in his name centralized bargaining in which his demands are compromised. The worker thus returns to his original state of weakness vis-a-vis his private employer, becoming once again an individual faced with a centralized system of trade unions, government, and employers.

Pizzorno (1978) draws a distinction between the structure and the essence of the trade union and the party. The trade union has at times tended to fill roles traditionally viewed as the political party's, conducting nationwide bargaining with the government. This bargaining can involve the state's entire socio-economic order. The trade unions can threaten the government in such a way that they, not the opposition party, play the most significant adversary role. Underlying these phenomena is the special power the trade union's direct connection with the workers gives it. The union can mobilize its members for strikes and other forms of struggle far more successfully than can the party.

In corporatism, the trade union becomes an autonomous element that independently determines its goals. Its achievements are measured in terms of political power—that is, its ability to continue its successes in the future.

Unemployment weakens the centralized trade unions, for as soon as there is a surplus of workers the threat of a strike becomes ineffective. Therefore, the trade union's condition for corporatist negotiation is "full employment." In exchange, the trade union promises to restrain the demands of the rank and file workers or a state of full employment prompts demands for wage increases.

Corporatist cooperation between the government and the employers on the one hand and the trade union on the other, then, is an exchange conducted in two spheres:

a) Political: The trade union offers the government legitimation, and the government, in exchange, grants the union power;
b) Economic: The employers promise the union full employment in exchange for its restraint of wage demands.

Rank and File Resistance

Groups of workers who place the authority of the centralized trade union to make wage concessions in their name in doubt can challenge the corporatist structure. Labor groups arise and organize against the corporatist elite, but, just as they arise, these groups can also disappear. The organizing of workers who oppose corporatism is an integral part of it. The class struggle can ebb and flow within corporatism itself, but we must understand that this struggle will not necessarily change the entire system (Pizzorno, 1978).

The trade union's centralization and hierarchical structure do not guarantee that the workers will accept the compromises their representatives make in their name. Economic instability occurs when the trade union is unwilling or unable to trade moderation for power, or to prevent the activity of groups of rank and file workers at the shop level. Certain political conditions make labor organization against compromise with the government worthwhile, and the union can sometimes exploit worker militancy to strengthen its bargaining power. Such conditions are usually associated with the deterioration of government economic policy, or with the fall of a government sympathetic to worker demands. In the latter instance, the unions may fear that the trade-offs conducted with the former government will cease with the new. In such a case, the union itself will encourage independent, militant activity among the rank and file (Pizzorno, 1978).

The very cooperation between the centralized trade union and the government creates factions within the union. Some of the leadership may advocate a greater degree of cooperation, while others will favor resistance and opposition to government policy. The dominant faction—usually that favoring cooperation—faces a constant threat that the advocates of opposition will solicit support among the lower echelons of worker leadership. This danger, then, constitutes an additional source of pressure for the leaders of the centralized trade union (Sabel, 1981).

The fundamental dichotomy within the working class, however, is between the national trade union leadership and the rank and file leaders. Lange (1984) discerns structural tension and even internal contradiction between the trade union leadership "who introduce concepts of capitalist growth into their wage policy" and the workers, who seek maximum advancement of their personal interest and status.

Labor organizations outside the trade union initially seek recognition by various elements in the economy. Their first bid is for the support of members, that will provide them with a public status and the ability to bargain and represent, to give and take. This objective of "recognition and identity" does not attempt to attain benefits through negotiation, but is a "demonstrative" action (Pizzorno, 1978).

The power of such groups lies more in their ability to block cooperation between the unions and the government than in their capacity to bargain and obtain actual benefits for the workers. The appearance of labor groups who reject the authority of the centralized trade union therefore temporarily puts corporatism's mediatory mechanism out of commission.

The national union leadership, then, is threatened by shop level organizations. A study of the rise of local worker committees in

England in the 1950s shows that as long as the local committees associated themselves with the national trade union, thereby strengthening the union, they were encouraged. But when the various shop level committees began associating horizontally among themselves, the trade union did its best to undermine them.

Nevertheless, the trade union and the shop are not in a state of constant conflict. They need each other, and therefore, in the long run, cooperate. This mutual dependency derives on the one hand from the union's need to mobilize the rank and file's support for the national collective agreements it hopes to attain and the local committees' ability to give the union this authority; and on the other from the committees' need for the union's economic support and judicial advice (Crouch, 1982).

Can corporatism withstand the workers' pressure? According to Panitch, corporatism works to the workers' detriment and serves to prevent the collapse of the capitalist state. The workers' best hope, he maintains, lies in the rank and file leaders organizing and opposing the corporatist system and the centralized trade union. Crouch, on the other hand, sees a tragic contradiction in the logic of collective action. The source of its power lies in the militance of the rank and file, who in order to exert their influence on a national level must establish centralized, national organizations. As a result, the rank and file lose the original power that lay in their ability to conduct decentralized, local struggles. The new organization will once again, because of its centralized nature, enter into corporatist bargaining and compromise.

Beyond their debate on the chances of changing the corporatist pattern, Panitch and Crouch agree that instability is built into that structure. This instability has two sources:

a) the rank and file workers' tendency to question the centralized trade union's authority to compromise wage demands in their name;
b) the obligation of the government and the employers—who hope to preserve the corporatist relationship with the trade union—to maintain a state of "full employment," thereby encouraging worker wage demands.

Both these factors make corporatism a dynamic pattern that changes periodically.

The Role of the State

Despite the central role that corporatist theory attributes to the state's political and economic intervention there is no consensual view or generally accepted conceptualization of the state. In her direct discussion of the issue, Skocpol (1982) claimed that the state's autonomous action should be central to macrosocial analysis. During crisis periods professional civil servants develop strategies and implement policies in spite of the opposition of powerful social groups.

In response to Skocpol's claim, Schmitter (1985) recognized that corporatist theory attributed a central role to the state without offering a proper conceptualization of this role. Schmitter rejects the idea that state intervention in the political economy is a function of the macroeconomic needs of capitalism or the manipulative-cooptive aims of civil servants. He suggests that the state's relative autonomy should be conceptualized as a structural matter, "grounded in the institutional interests of the state" and that government's and civil servants' structural and conjunctural interests should be distinguished (1985:37-41).

A key debate among students of corporatism is between those who maintain that the state is fashioned to facilitate optimal defense of capitalist interests, and others who see the state as the arena for class conflict.

Panitch (1981) and Offe (1985) perceive corporatism, in as much as it embodies interclass cooperation, as a threat to the working class. Precisely because of the discrepancy between the workers' extreme dependence on their organizations and the employers' independence (which is explained in detail below), cooperation between the centralized organizations represents a concession on the workers' part. The capitalist state thus helps the ruling class to solidify and advance its common interests.

In contrast to this approach, which incorporates the classic Marxist definition of the state, Esping-Andersen, Friedland, and Wright (1976) maintain that not only corporatist policy but also the internal structure of the capitalist state is "a product, an object, and a determinant of class conflict." In their view, the state is not simply an instrument of the capitalist class, but can also serve as the workers' means of taking control of capital. These scholars maintain that the state's structure, despite its functioning as a perfect mechanism for perpetuating capitalism and political neutralization of the working class is the result of class conflict. The structure of the state assures the continued accumulation of capital, and serves to forestall labor radicalism by making its demands congruent with the reproduction of capitalist social relations. However—and this is the key point—the political structure necessarily incorporates internal contradictions, and its solutions are never final and problem-free in terms of the class conflict. The workers' demands can never be neutralized with absolute success. The political question the working class faces, then, is not whether or not there are internal contradictions within the state's structure, but rather how powerful these contradictions are and how the workers can exploit them for their own interests.

Cameron (1978) has studied the expansion of the public sector, which is one of corporatism's clearest characteristics. He calculated the ratio of all government revenues to gross domestic product and analyzed the relative expansion of public expenditure in eighteen advanced capitalist countries, from 1960 to 1975. The results of this study point to two key factors in expansion of the public sector: social democratic or socialist governments, and foreign trade that is highly developed in relation to local production and marketing. The explanation for his findings is that small countries greatly dependent on imports and exports develop highly centralized industry. This type of industry, and the concomitant centralized collective bargaining, foster the establishment of strong workers' parties and centralized trade unions. These two elements lead to expansion of the public sector, which becomes another source of income for the worker.

To deal with the proliferation of corporatist policies at different economic levels, evolving within the framework of the state but without its direct intervention, Schmitter and Streek (1985) developed new analytical concepts. Meso-corporatism refers to institutionalized cooperation at regional and industrial level, and mini-corporatism is that taking place at the factory level.

The third concept, central to this study, is private interest government (Whose unfortunate acronym is PIG). State boundaries and influence are delimited by the existence of private organizations (PIGs) receiving state authority, which implement corporatist policies by themselves (see Schmitter's definition here in chapter 2, page 64). According to this perspective, the relative autonomy of the state is not a priori (structural) assumption but rather a matter of empirical research of (institutional) state-PIGs power interrelation, that "remains vulnerable to cyclical fluctuations" (1985:50).

DUAL LABOR MARKET THEORY

Parallel to neocorporatist theoretical development in the 1970s, social analysts in the U.S. described the existence of a dual labor market. This theory is designed to explain a different phenomenon—the fragmentation of the labor market into distinct parts, each with its own requirements and working conditions—and the resulting nonhomogeneous labor force. A concomitant phenomenon needing explanation is the correlation between various labor market requirements and the demographic characteristics of the workers.

Although various theories attempt to explain the source of the fragmented labor market,[2] all agree that the phenomenon exists and attempt to analyze it through various concepts. I shall present here the three chief approaches—the dual labor market, the segmented labor market, and the split labor market.

The first formulators of this theory were those who termed their approach "the dual labor market" (Piore and Doeringer, 1971; Piore, 1979; Piore and Berger, 1980). According to these scholars, the flux and uncertainty characteristic of the capitalist economy reveal the fundamental difference between labor and capital: capital is the fixed element in production, and labor the variable. The workers, who are immediately dismissed when economic activity ebbs, pay a disproportionate price for this flux. The corporations' primary reaction is to concentrate their capital in the stable areas of production and the workers in the unstable areas. This is the first distinction dictated by technological imperatives. But this distinction gradually penetrates the work force itself: in order to avoid the losses the dismissal of skilled and experienced workers entails, these workers are granted the same benefits accorded to capital—first and foremost, tenure. Piore thus describes the transformation of class conflict into a dichotomy among the workers:

> The original dualism in modern economics is between labor and capital. Dualism within the labor market arises when portions of the labor force begin to be insulated from uncertainty and variability in demand and their requirements begin to be anticipated in the process of planning and decision-making. They become at this point like capital, and the original dualism between capital and labor becomes a duality between that portion of the labor force which shares in some part the privileged position of capital and those other workers who continue to function as the "residual" factor of production. (Piore and Berger, 1980:24)

This division of the labor market between stable workers who belong to the primary sector and those who remain subject to economic flux in the secondary sector does not occur in a uniform manner. This process can occur within a company as part of an improvement of production methods; in the division between big, capital-rich companies and small, labor-rich companies within the same industry; or in a corporation's subcontracting work to an employer of temporary labor. This division can also occur between relatively stable industries and those in need of seasonal labor, such as agriculture or construction.

Piore, however, deals not only with demand for labor, but also with supply. What characterizes those workers employed in the variable sector of the labor market? According to Piore, these workers see themselves subjectively as nonpermanent, and do not attribute to their work the importance the more stable workers do. Those in the variable sector also have the option of other means of livelihood. In this context, Piore focuses chiefly on migrant groups. In addition to their subjective view of themselves, migrants are affected by such objective factors as the lack of skills, experience, connections, and even the language of the host country. All of these make the migrant a prime candidate for exploitation by capital as a temporary worker. Other groups—chiefly peasants, but also housewives and youth—share some of the migrants' characteristics.

The Response to Working Class Power

The segmented labor market theory (Gordon, Reich, and Edwards, 1982) maintains the emphasis of the dual market theory on technology, while stressing the problems connecting the labor processes and the labor market. Special emphasis is given to the small and large companies' differing abilities to develop new and effective methods. The approach is presented within a broad historical context, as the tendency that represents an answer to the workers' reaction to new labor processes. Segmentation of the labor market is the stage following the homogenization of the workers (1935-1945), a process that strengthened them and brought them the important gains resulting from unionization. This organization process began among employees of large corporations that had developed new labor processes and whose profits allowed them to grant their workers improved wages and working conditions.

Following this period of labor gains, the state, the corporations, and the unions began to stabilize at a new level of power balance. The next stage was segmentation:

> Segmentation depended, we shall propose, upon the successful integration of the strong national industrial unions of the 1930s into a cooperative collective bargaining system, limiting the further impact of the union movement and initiating a period of labor peace between employers and workers. (Gordon et al., 1982:11)

As was true in Western Europe, the 1930s depression and the uncertainty of the business cycle in the United States forced the government to intervene. The need to protect themselves against economic uncertainty led the workers to the political arena, within the Democratic party framework, and prompted them to consolidate their achievements through legislation. However, in this instance the state failed to become an active mediatory force between the labor organizations and the employers, but rather established a general legislative and legal framework in which negotiations could take place and class compromise be formulated.

The creation of the secondary (peripheral) sector—small companies dealing with the less stable areas of production, using older processes and reaping smaller profits—was concomitant with the rise of the large corporations' primary (core) sector. It is the primary sector that allows the secondary sector to exist—both through its lack of interest in areas that involve uncertainty and low profits, and through its ability to subcontract work to the secondary sector, thereby circumventing the unions and employing unorganized workers.

Within the primary sector itself, an additional segmentation—between independent and subordinate workers—occurred, thus creating three segments in the labor market: independent primary, subordinate primary, and secondary.

Unlike the proponents of the dualist theory, Gordon et al. saw the stabilization of workers in the secondary sector not as the result of their subjective attitude toward work, as in the case of migrants, but rather as stemming from racial and gender discrimination. A correlation between discrimination and segmentation was thus intentionally created by the employers, resulting in worker division according to both work process on the one hand and sex and race on the other. These divisions hampered the unification of the working class and the development of a unified political consciousness.

Ethnic and Racial Hostility

In contrast to the two approaches above, the "split labor market" theory (Bonacich, 1972, 1979) shifted the emphasis from the economic sphere—flux of demand, development of technology and labor processes—to that of the power balance between employees and employers. According to this approach, the labor market's nonuniformity stems from the differential bargaining power of certain labor groups. Racial, national, ethnic, and sex differences do not perpetuate themselves or intensify because of the primordial nature of these categories, but rather because the various groups receive differing rewards for their labor, due to different sets of historical and social circumstances.

While the previous approaches are confined to the microeconomic plane, or at most the macroeconomics of a single country, Bonacich's analysis is global in scope. The primary fact of capitalist development is the nonhomogeneity of the labor force and the existence of differential wage levels. These factors are associated with the nonuniform development of capitalism. In its European countries of origin, capitalism led to a rise in the workers' standard of living, the organization of trade unions, workers' political parties, and the gaining of civil and social rights. None of these benefits, however, accrued to those lands whose capitalism was an imperialist or colonialist import, where the traditional economic framework was demolished and the peasants rapidly proletarianized.

Wage differences among various labor groups are due not only to the migration of peripheral workers to advanced capitalist countries or that of European workers to developing countries, but also to the very ability of capital and products to travel from one end of the globe to another, thereby fostering competition between cheap and high-priced labor in different countries.

The fundamental structural interest of the capitalist employer is to maximize profits. Political and other conditions being equal, he will therefore choose to employ the cheapest labor available. The more expensive—that is, the more organized—workers, those with higher standard of living expectations, are under these conditions in danger of dismissal or wage cuts. The displacement of expensive labor by cheap labor occurs not only through substitution of one worker for another, but also through other means in various times and places: job dilution, maintenance of depressed pockets, competition through imported products,[3] and the transfer of factories from countries with high-priced labor to those with cheap labor (runaway shops).

The extent to which high-priced local workers can successfully combat displacement depends on their political power, but is also conditioned by the labor market. Of the two strategies available to the workers—blocking the employers' access to cheap labor or eliminating wage discrepancies by joint organization—the latter possibility is more difficult to achieve and therefore occurs less frequently. The strategy of equalizing wages is a difficult one, being not so much an ideological, cultural or political problem as it is a practical one. Low-paid workers are scattered and any attempt to organize the workers of the world would be utopian. It is far more practical to organize local well-paid workers against them. The highly paid workers' most common—and often successful—approach, therefore, is to block the employer's access to cheap labor through political pressure. Such approaches include exclusion movements and the creation of racial caste systems. Another common method is to close off certain industries occupied by highly priced labor to cheap labor.[4]

Bonacich sees no possibility of cooperation between the employer and the well-paid worker, but rather a continual state of struggle and conflict. These workers' chances of complete exclusion of cheap labor are slim, and a final balance is never reached. There exists rather a state of perpetual conflict between the employer's interest in lowering the cost of labor and the well-paid workers' interest in maintaining their status.

The fact that high-priced labor's preferred strategy is exclusion and not equalization of the cost of labor makes the reality of the split labor market rigid and resistant to change.

> In all three types of efforts to block capital's access to cheap labor, high-priced labor faces a paradox, namely, that in preventing their own displacement in the short run they also retard the economic development of cheap labor groups, thus helping to keep alive the split labor market. (Bonacich, 1979:32)

Even though the various theories of the fragmented labor market have not been unified into a single theoretical framework, it seems to me that this is more a matter of difference of emphases, deriving from the complexity of the phenomenon and the multiplicity of historical cases, than one of any essential contradiction between approaches. The chief issues pertinent to the labor market theories I shall deal with in this study are:

a) the political and technological forces that prompt the employer to fragment the labor market into various sectors;
b) the differential power of the workers in various sectors and the characteristics of wage bargaining in each sector;
c) cheap labor's threat to displace high-priced labor, and the possibility that the latter will organize to split the market to protect their status in it.

Taken together, these phenomena demonstrate amply that the labor market generates dynamic processes requiring long-term historical research.

PATTERNS AND CONCEPTS
COMMON TO BOTH THEORIES

The compatibility of corporatism and dualism is possible because both are based on a feature shared by both patterns: the need to repair the damage to labor and capital caused by the business cycle. According to Piore, the business cycle leads corporations to distinguish between production processes of products for which demand is stable and of those entailing greater risk. The labor market is thus fragmented. The corporatist theory stresses that periods of recession hurt both the worker and the employer, and that both have an interest in political exchange that will allow them to circumvent the business cycle—that is, the assurance of full employment in exchange for wage restraint. Both patterns allow for this redress through collective bargaining, the transfer of class conflict in the economic sphere to politics, and interclass compromise by means of state mediation.

The theoretical argument of this study is that corporatism and dualism are two typical solutions to the same problem: the question is how the eruption of the capital-labor contradiction inherent in the economic sphere can be prevented within the political framework of the state. The question itself contains two assumptions which both theories share: (1) The economic contradiction of labor and capital is the main conflict in every society; (2) The labor-capital conflict can be transformed within the framework of the state.

Class conflict is transformed by transferring its potentially critical focus from one sphere of political economy to another. In corporatism, labor and capital organizations compromise through political exchange and state mediation to limit the effects of the business cycle. When crisis does occur it is one of the legitimacy of the centralized trade unions in the eyes of their members, focused on relations between rank and file workers and their representative organizations (Pizzorno, 1978).

In dualism, conflict is contained by transferring the costs of economic fluctuation and uncertainty from capital to labor (Piore and Berger, 1980). Here too crisis is manifested within the working class, in the form of competition between two (or more) large groups of workers, differentiated by their strength in the labor market, the price they receive for their labor, and primordial characteristics such as nationality, ethnicity, race or sex (Bonacich, 1979).

Legitimation is a cardinal question not only for the ruling party of the state, but also for the centralized trade unions, whose elites must maintain workers support. If they fail, all negotiations and agreements are pointless. Thus public and private employers, as well as the parties linked to them, who are partners of the trade unions in collective bargaining, also have an interest in legitimation of the unions. They share with the unions' elite an awareness that legitimation of the unions is integral to the social order, which depends on an exchange of legitimation.

Even with the aid of others, centralized trade unions are only strong vis-a-vis rank and file members if capital's relative weakness is transferred to the workers in the economic sphere. So the legitimation of centralized trade unions is to some extent conditional on the workers' weakness in the economy, yet should they be too weak the unions' political power vis-a-vis the employers and the state is undermined. To achieve this balance desired by unions and employers, the Israeli case study suggests that not only a threatened recession, but also a limited group of underprivileged unorganized workers, is useful. Weakness in the labor market of atomized workers is turned into political strength by the organizations representing them.

In both patterns the trade unions bring their objectives to the political arena instead of aggravating relations within the economic sphere. Through political parties, they work toward legislation that will protect the rights of workers and unions. Since high-priced labor may aspire to block cheap labor, the political organization can be corporatist, yet the organization itself and the civil and social rights it achieves are limited to high-priced labor only.

The workers' political and legislative achievements create the framework for both dualism and corporatism: the welfare state. However, the state's role differs fundamentally in the two patterns. In dualism, the state's response to workers' lack of civil or social rights and to discrimination against them within the labor market is noninterference. In corporatism, on the other hand, the state is perceived as an active party that mediates between the worker and the employer. This is not necessarily a contradiction, for involvement in one sphere does not necessitate involvement in another.[5] The analysis of the Israeli case shows that the state can act as mediator between worker and employer in certain sectors of the labor market, and at the same time abstain from involvement in others, providing only the general framework for economic activity.

Rather than creating a new theory combining dualism and corporatism, this study uses both theoretical frameworks to analyze concrete patterns of political economy. In general, case studies will not fit one model, but constitute a complex and original pattern. It is the task of historical research to discover, describe and analyze its features.

THE ISRAELI CASE

Israel fits neither the corporatist nor the dual labor market model, although salient characteristics of both patterns can be found there. Although Israel's highly centralized trade union has, from its inception, conducted corporatist policy and maintained close ties with the Social Democratic party that has headed the government for most of the state's existence (Shalev, forthcoming), this case is a definite exception to the corporatist pattern. The two chief components of the exchange between workers and employers—wage restraint and full employment—do not exist there in their usual form.

Full Employment. There is a broad ideological consensus in Israel that Zionism requires the absorption of Jewish immigrants and their full employment. Any deviation from this policy is considered the common problem of all concerned elements—the state, the employers, and the *Histadrut*—and responsibility for full employment falls on all three. Full employment, then, is not a component in the exchange between the trade union and the employer, but rather represents a consensus among all factors.[6] This is a Zionist consensus, associated with the desire to bring Jews to the country and fear of *"yerida"* (literally, descent—Jewish emigration from Israel). In 1966 the danger inherent in recession was seen as the problem of *yerida*—that is, a delegitimation of the state, undermining its raison d'etre, and not one limited to the workers or trade unions.

Restraint of Wage Demands. The *Hevrat Ovdim* (the holding company of all *Histadrut*-linked economic enterprises) has as much interest in restraining wage demands as any other employer, public or private. Moreover, if the distinction between the private and public sector is drawn, the worker-owned company's considerations place it in the former category, because for such a company sharp wage rises do not mean a budget deficit, as they do in the public sector, but rather a drop in the company's profits, as it does for private employers. The *Histadrut* has a declared policy of wage restraint, although the emphasis is not on the interests of the *Hevrat Ovdim* but rather on those of "the economy"[7] or the state. For decades, the *Histadrut* leaders identified the worker's interest with that of the nation, the state, and "the economy." The leaders of the *Histadrut* and the *Hevrat Ovdim* still speak in these terms, with no recognition in practice of the employer's and worker's conflicting interests.

Israel's earmark is the dualism of its labor market. The cheap labor force is made up largely of "typical" workers: migrants from various ethnic groups, displaced peasants, and a "non-citizen" population (Shafir, 1989; Semyonov and Levin-Epstein, 1987). Nevertheless, certain basic elements in the analysis of the creation of the dual labor market are missing.

The Origins of Segmentization. In all the theories of the labor market, one basic datum is always clear—cheap labor seeks work, and the employer seeks cheap labor. In Israel, however, neither side participates in quite so simple or straightforward a manner. The Jewish immigrants who came to Israel were motivated not by any particular expectation of the Israeli labor market, but rather by the desire to escape the cruelty of persecution in the Diaspora. The Arab workers were thrust willy-nilly into the situation of cheap labor. Moreover, it would be difficult to identify any capitalist profit-motive as a major component of Zionism.[8] And it was certainly not the search for cheap labor that brought about the Six Day War, although the availability of cheap labor was one of that war's results.

Features of the Primary Sector. In the dualist theory, the primary sector is characterized by large corporations, technological development, and innovative production methods. In Israel, however, the primary sector is composed chiefly of public sector employees,[9] with only a small proportion of large corporation employees (who take part in the public sector's collective bargaining).

In light of these and other striking discrepancies between the Israeli case and both the corporatist and dualist patterns, we cannot discuss the Israeli structure and processes of recent years without some historical background. The issues both corporatism and dualism raise call for an examination of this historical process from the standpoint of development of the labor market, the workers' economic and political organization, evolution of collective bargaining, and corporatist exchanges.

The theoretical approach presented here leads this study to investigate specific structural and conjunctural questions about the overlap between political and economic spheres and the regulation of class conflict. The structural aspects are: (1) the split labor market that creates inequalities of power among workers; (2) the institutional mediation between labor and capital through the *Histadrut's* political economic structure; and (3) the ability of the ruling party to coordinate class interests depending on its internal composition. The most important conjunctural aspects are the economic business cycles and the political change of which party is in government.

The *Histadrut* is the focus of this study because it is related to all the structural and conjunctural questions, as will be further analyzed. It relies on a combination of corporatist political exchange and the presence of weak workers in a dual labor market. The analysis of structural and fluctuating relationships between the *Histadrut* and workers is the basis for the discussion of combined dualist and corporatist patterns of class conflict regulation. The comparative analysis of *Histadrut* cooperation with and alienation from government highlights the question of the capacities of the ruling party and the political commitment of labor institutions to it. Finally, the analysis of the fluctuating power relations between the *Histadrut* (as private interest government) and the state provide an operational definition for a discussion of the relative autonomy of the state.

CHAPTER 2

HISTORICAL BACKGROUND

The present organizational and political structure of the Israeli working class and the balance of power within it are the results of a specific historical process. As noted in the preceding chapter, corporatism and dualism are not regarded as a model, or an abstract form of relationship among the labor organizations, employers, and state, but rather as concrete historical phenomena subject to development and change. This study, therefore, must first deal with the overall, long-range processes of the workers' organization, activity, and the development of their institutions.

The historical periodization has both economic and institutional bases. The three main periods (1919-1939; 1939-1967 and post-1967) are characterized by different relations between Jews and Palestinians in labor markets: in the first period there was "free market" competition, in which the Arab workers held the advantage. During the second period there was separation between the two groups and in the third period there is a segmented labor market in which Jewish labor is protected by the state.

The subperiods are characterized by political-institutional developments as they were shaped by economic fluctuations. The relations between labor institutions, labor markets and workers, and their connection to state and employers, are analyzed in this chapter. The correlation between market processes, institutional domination, and political exchange among elites are presented within a coherent conceptual framework. The concluding section attempts to characterize the *Histadrut's* pivotal position in markets, institutions, and politics.

THE STRUGGLE FOR
JEWISH LABOR (1919-1939)

Discussing the period of the *yishuv*[1] involves two methodological problems the reader must be aware of:

a) When speaking of this period, the concept "government" is applicable to both the Zionist national institutions and the British mandatory authorities. Both performed functions defined as governmental, in the realm of economic policy and legislation as well as that of relations between employers and employees.
b) Most of the available economic data pertain to the Jewish sector, but the economic unit in fact comprised both Jews and Arabs. The Arab-Jewish conflict during that period, moreover, involved economic factors; employment, land ownership, and marketing.

The common denominator among the Jewish workers who arrived in Palestine with the earliest waves of immigration was that their labor was their sole means of support. During the years preceding World War I, these workers encountered several obstacles in their search for employment. Their first problem was competing in the labor market with the Arab worker. Their second was the absence of a well-developed Jewish economy. In response to these constraints the workers' parties developed the particular organizational and ideological structures that characterize socialist Zionism—the "unique" mode that came to be known as constructivism. Its most salient elements were:

a) a self-contained labor economy that created a demand for Jewish workers.[2]
b) the multi-function party that supplied a variety of the workers' needs, such as housing, education, and—central to this study—employment (Horowitz and Lissak, 1978).

The Histadrut *as a State Apparatus*

During 1918-1920, the British government had not yet developed a planned economic policy and unemployment appeared. The World Zionist Organization (WZO) was then debating its approach to capital investment in Palestine: American investors, headed by Judge Louis

Brandeis, advocated private enterprise, whereas WZO chairman Dr. Chaim Weizmann favored public investment as the means of creating a Jewish society and economy in Palestine (Kimmerling, 1982). This orientation led to an alliance between the workers' parties in Palestine and the WZO leadership. The workers were looking for the kind of investment that would create additional workplaces for Jews while guaranteeing the exclusion of Arab labor. Both the workers and the WZO leadership feared that private investment would favor the cheaper and more efficient Arab labor and thereby lead to unemployment among the Jews, who would then leave Palestine and effectively put an end to the Zionist enterprise. The exclusion of Arab workers from the Jewish labor market and the full employment for Jews was the political platform of the Zionist movement, agreed between labor parties and the leadership of the WZO.[3] Exclusive Jewish organizations on the political level and cooperatives on the economic level both aimed to achieve the same goal: a monopoly in the labor market.[4]

The General Organization of Hebrew Workers in the Land of Israel (the *Histadrut*) was founded in December 1920. The *Histadrut's* structure and functions have been political since it inception, establishing the bases of the future state. The *Histadrut* was designed to unite all the various workers' parties in a single body, and to centralize the various functions that the parties had been performing: employment, housing, health, and ownership of economic enterprises. *Histadrut* membership is direct to the general peak organization, and the division of power among the various parties is determined by proportional elections to a central body, the Executive Committee, which is structured according to parliamentary principles. The executive, governmental body is the Central Committee chosen by a coalition of the parties that control a majority of delegates.

The political economic structure of the *Histadrut*, known as "comprehensiveness," facilitated the two largest parties' absolute control of that body, as well as the definition of its objectives in nationalist Zionist terms—the "conquest of labor," and the provision of the workers' basic needs: education, health, housing, etc.

This structure rested on the Jewish worker's weakness vis-a-vis the Arab worker in the labor market, and of the veteran Jews vis-a-vis the new immigrants. Whenever the Jewish workers achieved stable employment, however, their improved position in the labor market led them to attempt to organize trade unions, which brought them into conflict with the *Histadrut* leadership. The *Histadrut*, on the other hand, hoped to translate this relative strength into party activity or, alternatively, economic-cooperative activity.[5]

The growth of hired labor in the early 1920s was a potential undermining of the "cooperative solution," and the exposure of the Zionist movement to the forces of the capitalist market posed two dangers for the Zionist enterprise:

a) The profit motive could once again lead to the hiring of Arab labor and a concomitant shortage of jobs for Jewish new immigrants.
b) The organization of hired workers on a workplace basis could give rise to joint Arab-Jewish trade unions that would fight for their common interest, including, conceivably, opposition to immigration as detrimental to the interests of those already working in Palestine.

The *Histadrut* leadership, therefore, opposed organization on a workplace basis (except in the government sector, where, in accordance with British policy, Jews and Arabs worked together).[6] It may be said, then, that the *Histadrut's* party political and cooperative-economic based structure originally rested on the Zionist ideals of building a Jewish society and economy. The *Histadrut* is thus different from the model corporatist centralized trade union, which transfers the employer-employee relationship from the shop-economic to the national-political in order to perpetuate both full employment and growth. The comprehensive, cooperative structure of the *Histadrut*, then, derived from the Zionist movement's need to foster both of these conditions. Financed by national funds, the *Histadrut* fulfilled such governmental functions as health, education, housing, and defense, which were in fact vital to the workers' welfare. In the absence of a Jewish state, the *Histadrut* took on functions that in advanced capitalist societies belong to the government. The first shock to this structure came with the Fourth *Aliyah*, which, unlike the previous ones, brought a great deal of capital with it.

Between Class and Nation

The years 1924-1925 saw the beginning of economic growth initiated by the influx of capital that the new Jewish immigrants had brought (5 million Palestine pounds in 1924 and 9 million in 1925). The Manufacturers' Association also began operating during this period, some twenty years after the workers had created their parties (Halevi, 1979; Shirom, 1983).

Prosperity also brought in its wake a sharp increase in the number of strikes: sixty-one in 1925 as opposed to nine in 1921. In reaction, the mandatory government appointed a fifteen-member tripartite commission comprising five *Histadrut* representatives, five Manufacturers'

Association representatives, and five representatives of the *Va'ad Ha-leumi* (National Council, the governing body of the Jewish community in Palestine during the British Mandate) and the WZO. The commission was charged with stabilizing labor relations by formulating a collective labor agreement acceptable to all parties. This first attempt at corporatist bargaining failed: the commission of fifteen was unable to reach such an agreement. Why? Part of the answer may lie in what the commission was able to resolve and what remained in dispute. Agreements were reached on wages, on management recognition of workers' committees, and on a standard procedure for arbitration and settlement of labor disputes. The manner in which labor exchanges would operate and the procedure for worker dismissal were left unresolved. The chief points at issue, then, were monopoly of the labor market and unemployment. On the one hand, the WZO could not guarantee full employment, and on the other, the private employers did not want to offer an assurance of preference for Jewish over Arab labor. During that period, the private employers did manage to restrain Jewish wage demands by flooding the labor market with a large supply of unskilled Arab labor (Sussman, 1974).

The 1926-1927 ebb in economic activity placed the *Histadrut* leadership in an awkward situation and threatened the entire system with collapse. The partnership between them and the WZO leadership had failed to produce the anticipated results. Unemployment was not averted, and the bankrupt *Hevrat Ovdim* construction company, *Solel Boneh*, did not receive the help it needed. The *Histadrut* leaders came to realize that the Zionist leadership in fact shared some of the capitalists' views and in a pinch would side with them. Therefore the two large parties, headed by then *Histadrut* Secretary-General David Ben Gurion, concluded that, in the interests of Hebrew labor and *Hevrat Ovdim*, labor must head the Zionist movement and control the investment of national funds.[7] For this purpose *Achdut Ha'avoda* and *Hapoel Hatzair* merged to form the Eretz Israel Workers Party—*Mapai*. Ben Gurion explained that only the interests of the working class were identical with those of the Zionist enterprise, since the workers' interest in Hebrew labor coincided with the national goal of establishing a Jewish society (Gorni, 1973; Ben Gurion, 1974).

Attaining leadership in the WZO, however, meant cooperating not only with Zionist leaders abroad, but also with local private sector capitalists—manufacturers, farmers, traders, and financiers. With the last two groups, the task was relatively easy. The traders and financiers supported the *Histadrut's* demand for Hebrew labor, since only the wages paid to the Jewish worker remained within the Jewish economic cycle and were used to purchase goods in the Jewish market or deposited in Jewish banks. In contrast, the Jewish money paid to Arab workers working for Jewish employers was absorbed into the Arab economy.[8]

In the private productive sector (farming and manufacturing), the situation was more difficult, due to the controversy over employment of Arab labor and its effect on the Jewish worker's employment possibilities and wages. In order to gain allies among these employers, the *Histadrut* leaders formulated a new distinction. Before the economic crisis they had differentiated between two types of capital—public and private—and had cooperated with the first while opposing the second. After the crisis, however, the distinction moved from source of capital to destination of capital—that is, who received the wages. A private employer who hired Jewish labor would be considered a nationalist, and thus worthy of the workers' cooperation.

National Segregation

The year 1932 marked the beginning of a new period characterized by cooperation between the mandatory government and the Jewish national bodies, mass *aliya*, and economic growth.

For most of its existence, the mandatory government balanced its budget. Since the Jewish sector of the economy provided most of its income, this income grew in direct proportion to the Jewish population. And a growing British budget was in the interest of the *yishuv*: investment designed to develop the country as a whole and improve its potential for economic growth benefitted the largely Jewish modern sector (Gross, 1984).

The British government opened Palestine's gates to aliya in 1932, and the deteriorating situation in Europe prompted a new wave of immigration, the Fifth *Aliya*. Palestine's Jewish population almost doubled between 1933 and 1936. These immigrants brought large quantities of capital, and this era of economic growth, *aliya*, and full employment saw also the flowering of the *Histadrut* and of *Mapai*. In the 1933 fourth *Histadrut* convention elections, *Mapai* won 82 percent of the votes. *Mapai* joined the WZO executive as a minority party in that year and in 1935 became the majority party.

In April 1936, Palestinian Arab truck drivers, traders, and laborers initiated a six-month long strike whose political objective was to force the mandatory government to halt *aliya* and the concomitant rapid growth of the Jewish community and economy. The strike did in fact accelerate a decline of the Jewish economy, a process that had begun in 1935 for financial reasons, but also brought unanticipated consequences for both the Palestine Arab national movement and Zionism.

Jewish labor responded to the strike by occupying every job vacated by the Arabs—on the railroad, in the Jaffa and Haifa ports, the Nesher quarries, the potash works at the southern end of the Dead Sea, and the private agricultural settlements. By the end of 1939 work on the agricultural settlements was being done exclusively by Jews. The structure of the Jewish labor market changed radically and led to an almost total separation between the Jewish and Arab sectors of the economy (Kimmerling, 1982).

The economic recession of this period was less problematic than that of 1926-1927, mainly for two reasons:

a) The economic infrastructure, the production apparatus, and Jewish investments had all begun to bear fruit.
b) The WZO and the Jewish Agency, now headed by Mapai, had adopted an unequivocal policy of preventing bankruptcy by intervention in the Jewish economy (Horowitz, 1948).

Unemployment was nevertheless widespread. The problem was especially severe in the areas of farming, construction, and small-scale manufacturing, while medium and large-scale industry continued to expand and absorb workers. Thus the worst damage was in those sectors vulnerable to fluctuating demand which had been dependent on cheap, casual Arab labor (Shapira, 1977; Margalit, 1976).

Mapai's achievements in the national sphere and the urban workers' inability to prevent compromises agreed in their name led to disaffection between the party leadership's representatives in the *Histadrut* and the Jewish Agency on the one hand, and urban labor on the other. The 1935 *Mapai* census already showed that only 25 percent of the urban workers, as opposed to 75 percent of the pioneering settlers, were party members. Members of the Tel Aviv *Mapai* branch grumbled increasingly against the leadership, objecting to the formation of "classes" within the *Histadrut* and the branch party's lack of influence on the local labor council. As the 1938 *Mapai* convention approached, the Tel Aviv workers formed their own faction within the party and, in coalition with representatives of *Hakibbutz Hameuhad* (the United Kibbutz Movement, the larger labor settlement organization dominated by *Mapai*), created "Faction B" (Yishai, 1978).

Nevertheless, *Mapai's* control of the *Histadrut* and of the WZO during the crisis years enabled it, through its policy of economic intervention (extension of credit and the establishment of the unemployment fund, subsidies funded from abroad) to avert any severe blow to either the workers or the industrialists. The year 1939 was marked by the signing of a collective cost-of-living increase allowance (COLA) agreement, the first of its kind, between the Tel Aviv workers' council and the Manufacturers' Association. This agreement was to become a model for the entire Jewish economic sector. The national bodies' interventionist policy and the COLA agreement mark the beginning of a corporatist process—the representation of interests and compromise through centralized agreement. Paradoxically, this process began before the inflation of World War II, while unemployment was rising. However, this period also saw three developments which outweighed the opposition of the unemployed militant workers and ensued in an agreement between the workers' representatives and the private employers:

a) the creation of a separate Jewish economy and the concomitant elimination of the Arab labor controversy which had previously blocked any collective agreement on wages and employment between the private employers and the Histadrut;
b) Mapai's control of the national bodies and the Histadrut and its efforts to implement a national income and investment policy;
c) the growing discontent of the Tel Aviv industrial workers and the concurrent need to restrain their wage demands.

Thus the 1936-1937 partition of the economy on national lines and the 1939 signing of the first corporatist agreement mark the end of the period in which wage restraint occurred because of the competition of Arab labor, and became a question of *Histadrut-Mapai*-workers relations of power.

A DUAL STATE
APPARATUS (1940-1967)

The political and economic changes of the World War II years had major repercussions for the economic structure of Palestine, also producing a new balance of power between the workers and their parties, and the institutionalization of corporatist patterns.

During World War II, Palestine became the second largest industrialized country in the Middle East (after Egypt). The proportion of workers employed in industry reached a peak never matched in all the years of Israel's existence—31 percent. This accelerated process of industrialization was the result of Britain's comprehensive wartime activities.

The Palestinian economy, until then wide open to foreign trade, was protected from competition and received raw materials according to the British government's priorities. The mandatory government kept an increasingly close watch on the economy, rationing food and raw materials. Essential foodstuffs were subsidized in order to control price rises. The restriction of imports and the growth of industry and exports altered the balance of payments, which became positive for the first time: export surplus between 1940 and 1946 reached 33 million pounds sterling (Halevi, 1979; Gross, 1984).

Initial Steps toward Corporatism

The government's centralized intervention in the economy affected other areas characteristic of the Israeli political economy.

The sectoral distribution of capital changed. The influx of private capital was relatively small while the import of public (Zionist) capital, particularly American, grew. The *Histadrut*-owned *(Hevrat Ovdim)* companies shared the industrial development and prosperity of the war years, and grew so fast in relation to private capital that they purchased some of its declining enterprises. The *Histadrut* construction company, *Solel Boneh*, also flourished, mainly purchasing private firms (Horovitz and Lissak, 1978; Dan, 1963).

The *Histadrut* underwent accelerated centralization in which responsibility for wage bargaining was placed in the hands of a new department created for that purpose in 1941, the trade union department. Strike authorization was transferred from the labor councils[9] to the *Histadrut* executive committee. Local union activity[10] ceased almost completely (Tokatly, 1979).

Wage bargaining on a centralized, national level increased. The prosperity of the war years created inflationary pressures, and prices increased during that period by 130 percent. The *Histadrut* and the Manufacturers' Association reached sporadic COLA (cost-of-living allowance) agreements from 1940 to 1941, and at the end of 1941 an automatic COLA agreement was formulated, with the participation of the mandatory government. The *Histadrut* also conducted collective bargaining for wage framework agreements (see glossary) with the Manufacturers' Association and the government (Tokatly, 1979; Halevi, 1979; Gross, 1984).

Continual industrial growth made Tel Aviv the largest and most important concentration of workers. The *Histadrut* leadership found it difficult to impose their authority over the workers. Led by the left wing opposition parties, the workers increasingly opposed the processes of economic and political centralization. The labor opposition within *Mapai*, Faction B, also grew in Tel Aviv (Tokatly, 1979; Yishai, 1978). *Mapai's* 11 percent decline in the 1941 *Histadrut* Convention elections indicated the waning of support for the party's leadership. The support of urban labor brought the largest Zionist left opposition party, *Hashomer Hatzair*,[11] gains of the same percentage.

Controversy within *Mapai* intensified in 1943. Full employment strengthened the workers' demands for wage increases and their ability to attain them. The number of unauthorized strikes organized by the left-supported workers' committees rose. No cooperation between the party leadership and Faction B occurred within *Mapai*, and in the *Histadrut* the Faction B delegates voted increasingly with the left opposition parties.

Ben Gurion's demand for new *Histadrut* elections aggravated the split. Faction B withdrew and established its own party called "*Achdut Ha'avodah*." The new elections brought the *Mapai* leadership a relative "victory"—they retained control of the *Histadrut* despite the growing strength of the opposition parties. *Mapai* won 53 percent of the votes, with 18 percent to *Achdut Ha'avodah* and 20.3 percent to the leftist bloc, led by *Hashomer Hatzair*.

The war years highlighted the *Histadrut's* structural weakness in all their severity. In the absence of an unorganized labor force, with neither Arabs nor Jewish immigrants, the *Histadrut* was unable to restrain the workers' wage increase demands during a period of full employment. However, the workers' dissatisfaction with the *Histadrut* leadership did not lead to the formation of trade unions, but was translated rather into support for the leftist parties' political opposition to *Mapai*. This can be explained by the *Histadrut's* political structure, which encourages opposition to organize into parties and thus fight for control. The establishment of *Achdut Ha'avodah* prevented the formation of trade unions based on the power of the workers within the labor market, and instead channeled this power into the party. This period saw an alliance of urban labor and the kibbutz movement, despite their disagreement on the issues of trade unions and the *Histadrut*. The kibbutz movement's influence was decisive on the leadership level and, through them, in determining party policy.

The workers developed their own instruments for their struggle, and toward 1947 workers' committees here established in 91 percent of the plants. *Achdut Ha'avodah* or *Hashomer Hatzair* had a part in most of these committees, and complete control of some (Medding, 1972; Tokatly, 1979).

At the beginning of 1948, *Hashomer Hatzair* and *Achdut Ha'avodah* joined forces to form the United Workers' Party *(Mapam)*. This new party posed a substantial threat to *Mapai's* leadership monopoly in the national bodies and even more so in the *Histadrut*. The 1948 *Histadrut* Convention elections brought *Mapam* 41 percent of the votes.

Mass Aliya

With the end of the war and the first Knesset elections that made *Mapam* the second largest parliamentary power; with twenty Knesset seats, the *Mapai* leadership began to concentrate its efforts in the political arena. Apprehensive of *Mapam's* influence over youth, the government appropriated the *Histadrut's* responsibility for education but left it jurisdiction over health services. *Kupat Holim* (the *Histadrut* sick fund) is essential to the *Histadrut's* organizational power because of its wide membership, but at the same time perpetuates the *Histadrut's* dependence on government funding.[12]

The *Histadrut* retained most of the functions it had filled as part of the "state-in-the-making." It kept its important economic and investment role through the *Hevrat Ovdim*, its settlement role through the kibbutz and *moshav*[13] movements, and its role in organizing employment through its labor exchanges. *Kupat Holim* became the main organizational tool for enlisting new members, and thus helped perpetuate the discrepancy between the *Histadrut's* need for membership and its role as a trade union.

The *Histadrut's* unchanged political and economic structure preserved its ability to control labor by creating worker dependence on it. The *Mapai* leadership managed to make the *Histadrut* its key means of mobilizing political support (Medding, 1972). The establishment of the state served to strengthen the national, governmental institutions vis-a-vis the *Histadrut*. The former controlled the public capital imports that constituted three-quarters of the total capital imports. The state also controlled the land and property abandoned by Arab refugees (Kleiman, 1967).

The *Histadrut's* retention of most of its "state" functions after the establishment of the State of Israel made *Mapai* dominant, as it controlled both institutions. It was within *Mapai* that government and *Histadrut* members conducted their bargaining. The most important political and economic decisions, including those relating to wage policy, were made in the party—as long as, of course, the workers lacked sufficient power in the labor market to fight for increases on their own.

The growing stream of *aliya* in 1949 caused a rising level of unemployment. This time, the new Jewish immigrants did not bring enough capital to generate increased consumption and economic growth. It was therefore the government that concentrated import of capital in its hands, as it was the recipient of loans and grants from abroad.

During the War of Independence (1947-49), the Arab sector ceased to function as a producer of agricultural goods, and trade with neighboring countries stopped completely. When the war ended, therefore, most investments were immediately concentrated in agriculture and the production of food for the growing population (Kleiman, 1967). Some of the Jewish African and Asian immigrants who arrived after 1948 settled, with government assistance, in *moshavim* and in lands vacated by Arab refugees. The bodies that supervised settlement—the Jewish Agency, the government, and *Mapai* as the party that dominated them—controlled the key agricultural resources: land, water, and capital.

The chief effect of that *aliya*, however, was on the make-up of the labor force. After the initial separation of Arab and Jewish economies, the prosperity of World War II crystallized it into a fixed structure. The Jewish labor market underwent a process of homogenization and wage differentials between skilled and unskilled Jewish labor decreased. This gap began to widen once again in the years 1949-1952 with the mass *aliya*, which was a condition for the restructuring of a new dual labor market. The surplus unemployed labor and the employment of many Asian and African immigrants in unskilled work widened the differentials between skilled and unskilled. During that period, the unskilled Jewish Oriental workers took on the function of the Arab labor force in the 1930s in lowering the wages of the unskilled (Baharl, 1965).

This widening of the wage gap and the creation of a government bureaucracy led to a rapid change in the composition of the working class. By mid-1954 only 8 percent of the veteran immigrants were working in unskilled jobs, as opposed to 33 percent of the new Oriental immigrants. The veteran immigrants had left their unskilled jobs in industry and construction to work in the professions, as clerks, and in administration of the *Histadrut*, the government offices, and the factories (Baharl, 1965; Rosenfeld and Carmi, 1976).

Sixteen trade unions were established during the 1950s. Until the middle of that decade, it was chiefly the professionals who aspired toward wage increases beyond what the centralized agreements offered. The establishment and strengthening of these professional unions relates to the absorption of Jewish Oriental immigrants and the corresponding change in the labor force's composition.

With the mass *aliya* of Oriental Jews, the concomitant growth of the unskilled labor force, and the drop in their wages, the power that during the World War II and early statehood years had been concentrated in the hands of the industrial workers passed, in the mid-1950s, to the professional and government employees' trade unions.

The Full Employment Crisis

This period was one of accelerated, state-encouraged industrialization, *Histadrut*-government confrontation, and its resolution within *Mapai*. Workers' committees in industry and the public sector opposed the policy of wage restraint and demanded increases. A new party model, the multiclass party, arose, and two big political blocs, the Alignment and *Gahal* (Liberal-*Herut* bloc), were formed.

In 1956, *Mapam* and *Achdut Ha'avodah*[14] were coalition partners and as such jointly responsible to their constituencies for government policy. Ben Gurion, who sought to expand the power of the state as opposed to the *Histadrut*, nominated Pinhas Lavon, a kibbutz member, as secretary-general of the *Histadrut*.[15]

In 1957, both the influx of reparation payments from Germany and the presence of unemployed labor generated accelerated industrialization. Since the reparation agreements stipulated that Israel purchase industrial equipment from Germany, the Israeli government granted industrialists cheap credit from the reparation money to finance imports of German machinery. The reparation money thus became a key factor in the growth of industrial investment and the renewed development of private capital.

The government's participation in industrialization was extensive, reaching 55 percent of the total investments in 1959. Government subsidies were channeled into industrial development in various ways—cheap credit, development budgets, and a price control policy. In 1958 the Industrial Development Bank was established, and in 1959 the government amended the Investment Encouragement Law. These two steps were designed to facilitate the allocation of government development funds to industry. Toward 1960, these government initiatives began to bear fruit—unemployment was reduced and industry had absorbed a rapidly expanding labor force (Klinov-Maloul and Halevi, 1968; Swirski and Bernstein, 1982).

The *Histadrut* tried to adjust to these new conditions. Most of its efforts were devoted to accommodating itself to the industrial expansion of the 1960s through organizational changes in the *Hevrat Ovdim* and a centralization of the wage-determination process. The *Histadrut* secretary-general played a key role in these efforts.

As the 1959 elections approached, the controversy within *Mapai* intensified. Prime Minister David Ben Gurion and his supporters criticized the kibbutz movement and the *Histadrut* leaders. Ben Gurion's state-oriented approach stressed the importance of the government bodies and negated the *Histadrut's* comprehensive political economic structure, which he called a "state-within-a-state."

Pinhas Lavon and the leftwing parties represented the opposition to Ben Gurion's position. As secretary-general of the *Histadrut* and a kibbutz member, Lavon advocated strengthening the *Histadrut's* economy and its comprehensive, centralized structure.

The debate between government and *Histadrut* representatives was most prominent in 1960. The state, by encouraging investment in industry, had made the owners of private industry dependent on its subsidies and had thereby strengthened its position in relation to them. The *Histadrut*, meanwhile, had mobilized its forces for an opposing campaign for economic growth, with the objective of competing with the private sector and maintaining its own economic power. However, industrialization and growth had also undermined the *Histadrut's* authority over the workers.

The class conflict was now transformed into a threat from rank and file "action committees" of industrial workers, which were still not unionized.[16] The low level of unionization of these workers was due to the dual labor market, while their new strength stemmed from full employment and accelerated industrialization. These committees were beyond the control of the centralist bodies and held their own strike against the *Histadrut's* decision to pay COLA to only the lower income groups, who had not received them for two years. While the new working class was largely comprised of new immigrants who had not joined the traditional labor parties, several veteran *Mapam, Achdut Ha'avodah*, and *Maki* (Israeli Communist Party) members were also among the "action committee" organizers (Tzaban, 1977).

Full employment and increasing demand for labor on the one hand and the *Histadrut's* efforts to conduct a wage restraint policy on the other led to increasingly frequent strikes—a trend that peaked in 1963, particularly in industry. These strikes usually lacked *Histadrut* authorization and were conducted in opposition to its policies. The *Histadrut*, whose political power had been based on the worker's weakness in the labor market, was seriously undermined. The industrial workers' affairs were managed by the *Histadrut's* trade union department, composed according to party proportional representation. *Mapai's* control of the *Histadrut* was threatened by the prospect of economic dissatisfaction being translated into votes against *Mapai* and for the opposition factions in the upcoming elections.

This dilemma served to heighten the controversy over *Histadrut* or state orientation. A growing faction within *Mapai*, aware that the party's immense power depended on its control of the *Histadrut*, decided to effect a political change that would avert loss of this power and legitimize it in the workers' eyes. Firstly, the *Histadrut* elections were repeatedly postponed between 1963 and 1965, and were finally announced in 1965. Secondly, *Mapai* had joined *Achdut Ha'avodah*, which had been active among the militant workers' committees to create the Labor Alignment. This step ensured their retention of control of the *Histadrut* in the next elections (Shapiro and Grinberg, 1988).

The establishment of the *Mapai-Achdut Ha'avodah* Alignment had far-reaching effects on the entire party system. Ben Gurion and his young supporters who had risen up through the defense establishment (Peres and Dayan being the best known among them) withdrew from *Mapai* and set up their own list called *Rafi* (Israeli Workers' List). They advocated eliminating the *Histadrut's* comprehensive structure and its transformation into an organization coordinating trade unions. These changes were to foster the influx of new immigrants into the trade unions and the party, and of course pave the way for his "popular young supporters'" rise to party leadership, under the aegis of the charismatic Ben Gurion.

The idea of uniting the traditional *Histadrut* workers' parties meant institutionalizing control through party and *Histadrut* apparatuses. It was also an attempt to form an interclass party that would represent the middle class, bureaucrats, salaried professionals, and nonskilled workers alike.

The rightwing parties countered the establishment of the Alignment with a similar step. The Liberal and *Herut* parties, which had for four years shared the opposition, formed an electoral bloc called *Gahal*,[17] designed to counterbalance the Alignment. While the *Histadrut* establishment and *Mapai* were seeking an approach to the new Oriental immigrant workers through *Achdut Ha'avodah*, the Liberal party was doing the same through *Herut* and its charismatic leader, Menahem Begin. *Herut* had come to terms with the victory of *Mapai*, in successfully organizing most salaried workers under the *Histadrut* framework, and decided to work toward worker support in the proportional factional elections within the *Histadrut*. *Gahal's* entrance into the *Histadrut* represents an acknowledgement of the *Histadrut* rules of the game, whereby social unrest is channeled into party, rather than economic, activity. The object was to strengthen *Gahal's* influence over the salaried workers and threaten the labor parties in their home territory. Both *Rafi* and *Gahal* favored making the *Histadrut* a "normal" trade union, establishing an industrial workers' trade union, separating the *Histadrut's* economic and political functions from the trade union department, and granting the trade unions greater independence (Shalev, 1982).[18]

The *Histadrut* and the Knesset elections were held only two months apart in 1965. The new Alignment bloc managed to retain its dominance in both. Their victory, however, had not been easy. The election timing had made 1965 a peak year for strikes and labor disputes, particularly in the public sector and more specifically among government employees and professional organizations. *Mapai* had anticipated that the Alignment would bring it the support of the new working class, but its economic policies which followed the 1960-1963 workers' rebellion in the *Histadrut* hurt that class severely and distanced them from it.

In 1966, a combination of several factors led to a severe recession of economic activity. Growth of GNP dropped to one percent and the unemployment rate rose to 7.4 percent. The government, in view of the worsening trade deficit and the 1965 rise in real wages, held back from initiating new development projects. The intention behind suspending development activity was to solve both problems—to restrain wage demands and improve the balance of payments (Klinov-Maloul and Halevi, 1968; Zandberg, 1970). This policy led to a severe recession, due to the industrial slowdown that had been apparent as early as 1964.

THE RESULTS OF
THE SIX DAY WAR:
THE SPLIT LABOR MARKET

The 1967 War was an economic and political turning point. *Rafi* and *Gahal* joined the government and *Rafi* leader Moshe Dayan, who had gained repute as chief of staff during the 1956 War, became defense minister. The euphoria of victory created a demand for unity and led to the establishment of a broad national unity government. A long period of relative industrial quiet began in 1967 and lasted until the end of the war of attrition (1969). During those years, no new wage agreements were signed, no cost-of-living increments were paid, and the growth of the real wage fell from an average of 10 percent per year in 1965-1966 to 1.3 percent in 1967-1968. The economy radically changed the expansion of local markets into the occupied territories, the significant growth of *aliya* and import of capital, and the influx of a large labor force from the conquered Arab population—were all important developments. Growth was thus regenerated, but did not reach the 1960-1965 proportions. The increased defense expenditures and arms purchases abroad caused a continual growth of the trade deficit and the national debt

(Horovitz, 1970; Arnon, 1979; Tsaban, 1977; Kimmerling, 1982).

The most dramatic change of the 1967 War was in the labor market, whose structure was transformed into a fixed split labor market, and whose dynamics fluctuated from deep-seated unemployment to full employment. It was also during this period that many Jewish workers who had been unemployed during the recession entered the labor market by moving from the secondary sector (construction, agriculture, light industry) to the primary (technological industry, primarily military) and to public service. For a number of reasons—ranging from legal and security considerations to lack of technological training—these two areas were closed to the Arab worker, both citizen and noncitizen. These workers were absorbed into the secondary sector, thus "freeing" Jewish workers for technically skilled jobs (Blumental, 1984; Portugali, 1986; Semyonov and Levin-Epstein, 1985, 1986).

This segmentation occurred almost without competition, as a transition from a period of unemployment to one of full employment, with the concomitant changes in the economic structure. "Market forces" placed the noncitizen workers in areas of employment that were less stable and paid less, and the state played a decisive role in denying that work force civil rights while maintaining discipline (Shalev, 1989).

In the absence of centralized bargaining, "market forces" determined wages. In the public sector, where budgets had greatly increased, wages rose chiefly by "crawling." In the private sector, wages rose in the large plants that sought additional skilled labor. The profitable plants took advantage to a lesser degree of the new work force among the conquered population and low wages were thus maintained. Statistics show that in the areas that absorbed Arab workers from the territories, wages either remained stable (as in industry) or fell (as in construction) (Klinov, 1976; Semyonov and Levin-Epstein, 1987). This distinction helps us understand another phenomenon: after 1967, the industrial and construction workers lost the power and ability to organize that had been rooted in the homogenization of the labor market in the early 1960s, and no more action committees were formed in these areas.

"Democratization" of the Unions
and Imposed Corporatism in the Secondary Sector

The power structure of labor changed in 1967: workers exposed to Palestinian competition in factories never organized again horizontally in rank and file associations. Strength was maintained among jobs closed to Palestinian labor: professionals, employees of the government and of large government-owned companies—the ports, the seamen, the airports, El Al (the national airline), and the electric company.

As the 1969 Knesset and *Histadrut* elections approached, the Alignment had made no change in the *Histadrut* political structure that would allow the entry of the rank and file from the Oriental working class, but tried to exploit the post-war uplift and renewed economic boom to buttress its position. The Alignment merged the traditional labor parties (*Mapai, Achdut Ha'avodah, Rafi* and *Mapam*) into a single election list. The 1969 elections gave the Alignment a large victory over its chief opponent, *Gahal*.

In the early 1970s, the *Histadrut* leadership initiated the establishment of trade unions for those industrial workers who had been weakened by the segmented labor market: the Association of Metal, Electrical and Electronics Workers, the Food Workers' Association, and the Textile Workers' Association. The initiative came from the top without rank and file pressure, at an easy conjuncture for *Histadrut* leadership. All were organized according to the *Histadrut* model of proportional elections, with no direct workplace representation. In all the party-based elections, the Alignment won by large majorities. The professional unions, on the other hand, became more independent: the Association of Social Science and Humanities Graduates, the pharmacists, the microbiologists, the jurists, the psychologists, and the social workers, all held personal elections (Tokatly, 1979). It is to be noted that all these skilled workers were organized in nationwide unions outside of the industrial workers' organizations, on the basis of profession and regardless of employer.

Trade union "democratization" was an organizational rearrangement reflecting the new power structure based on the fragmented labor market: there was a great distinction between the professional workers whose position in the market improved after the segmentation and the unskilled industrial workers weakened by it.

The war of attrition led to the reestablishment of the national unity government after the 1969 elections. Toward the beginning of 1970, after four years during which wage agreements had not been renewed and the gap between actual wages and those stipulated in the existing wage agreements grew, the strong trade unions and workers' committees anticipated high wage increases. Full employment and shortage of skilled labor buttressed their bargaining power and allowed them to make large demands. However, the post-war boom had created new economic problems; the immense growth of imports neutralized renewed export growth and within a few months the foreign currency reserves fell by 50 percent. With the declared intention of restraining wage demands, the government turned to the *Histadrut* and the *Lishkat Hateum* (the coordinating bureau of economic organizations), initiating tripartite bargaining whose objective was a wage, price, and tax agreement.

The government had a double interest in such an agreement—as the employer of the large public sector whose wage demands were rising rapidly, and as the body responsible for the economy as a whole. The government's goals were to reduce demands, halt inflation, and decrease imports. The *Lishkat Hateum* was interested in a uniform wage agreement that would prevent its members from competing for labor through unregulated wage increases. The *Histadrut*, for its part, sought to regain the role of representing the workers in national, centralized wage bargaining, to replace the plant level agreements which had been made during the preceding two years.

The negotiations ended in an agreement that gave the workers a 4 percent COLA and 4 percent in wage increments to be paid in bonds during the next five years. Three joint commissions for each of the three negotiating parties were established to supervise implementation of the agreement: (1) labor agreements renewal; (2) productivity and efficiency; (3) prevention of price and wage rises. The government agreed to keep tax increases as low as possible, and the private employers to avoid raising prices (Galin and Taub, 1971; Zandberg, 1970) .

This "package deal" was the most open and explicit corporatist agreement the government, the *Lishkat Hateum* and the *Histadrut* had cooperated in. However, despite the government's and *Lishkat Hateum's* hopes that the agreement would put an end to labor's demands, they both agreed to the *Histadrut's* demand to embark on branch and plant level negotiations on working conditions other than wage rises. These "other conditions"—changes in salary scales, seniority systems, and other payments—involved changes in income. The *Histadrut* thus hoped to avert conflict with strong labor groups by giving them a proper framework for expressing their bargaining power in a differential manner (Tokatly, 1979; Galin and Taub, 1971).

The "package deal" did indeed restrain wages in those areas where the workers had been weakened by the segmented labor market, but most labor groups able to attain increments through their bargaining power engaged in labor disputes and broke through the limitations of the framework agreement. After the end of the war of attrition in mid-1970, a wave of labor disputes began that made that year a peak one for strikes and lost work days, most of them in the public sector (Galin and Taub, 1971). No partner of the package deal was able to restrain strong workers' organizations, especially the

Histadrut, whose political structure distanced it from the workers.

The framework agreement thus became a minimum increase won by the *Histadrut* for the workers whose wage would have been continually eroded otherwise.

In order to prevent a drop in foreign currency reserves, the government began in 1970 to step up its mobilization of capital abroad, particularly in the U.S. At this point a structural deficiency of the Israeli economy that was to intensify with the growth of defense spending was revealed. The large amount of foreign aid and the surplus of imports resulted in a growing demand for nonnegotiable goods and services and created a lopsided economic structure in which the service branches are too large and the production branches relatively small. This structure strengthened the bargaining power of the public sector workers, whose wage increments derived from budgetary increases, as opposed to wage increments in the private sector, which depended on increased production (Leviatan, 1978; Ofer, 1976).[19]

After signing the "package deal," the *Histadrut's* ability to restrain the wage demands of these powerful labor groups diminished considerably. The secretary-general was caught between growing labor demands and government pressure to restrain them. Between 1971 and 1973 the consumer price index rose by 12 to 20 percent and labor disputes continued.

The 1972-1974 framework agreements in the public sector, which stipulated a 6 percent wage increase and 8 percent COLA, were also violated. The trade unions delayed signing agreements and waited for the opportunity to achieve large increases, assuming that the later they signed, the greater their increments. Indeed, while the 1972 increments did not exceed 30 percent, the engineers won a 35 percent increase in May 1973. Their agreement brought in its wake increases for the professionals, journalists, and teachers. The nurses then struck and received a 42 percent increase, followed by the doctors who received 45 percent. The Ashdod port workers, who had already received a 40 percent increase in early 1973, were exceptions (Tokatly, 1979).

Despite its loss of authority over the workers, the Alignment did better in the 1973 *Histadrut* elections than in the previous ones. This was due in no small part to the Alignment's popular candidate for secretary-general, Yitzhak Ben Aharon, who lacked any real power to act but never ceased his criticism of government policy vis-a-vis the workers. After the elections Ben Aharon decided to resign, in view of the difficulty he faced in continuing to act as secretary-general in accordance with his socialist views.

The pattern of the 1960s in which labor parties supported the workers in labor disputes disappeared in 1967, giving way to trade unions with no political support. Ben Aharon, seeking a labor movement approach to the worker's hearts, established a forum of Labor party workers' committees designed to exert pressure within the party without violating party discipline and without operating outside the party (INT-AS). More powerful, however, were the *Histadrut* and Alignment functionaries who created a tie of organizational dependency with the workers, primarily through the *Histadrut's* sick fund, labor councils, *Hevrat Ovdim*, pension funds, and strike fund.[20] The Yom Kippur War marked the end of the period of prosperity and the political capacity to distribute material benefits. The Alignment's ability to control both the *Histadrut* and the government was thus endangered.

The Decline of the Labor Party and its Fall from Power

The post-1973 period saw the beginnings of recession and the development of acute *Histadrut*-government disagreement on how to overcome the economic crisis. The widening dispute brought dissolution within the ruling party and a serious defeat in the 1977 Knesset elections.

The trend that had already been clear in 1965—the transfer of support from the Alignment to the Likud among the low income groups, Oriental immigrants living in disadvantaged neighborhoods and development towns—reached decisive dimensions in the elections (Weiss, 1979). While the continuation of partial economic growth allowed the Alignment supporters to see the government-*Histadrut* conflict as marginal, thus averting a crisis and an even greater loss of Alignment votes; those labor groups who had not received their share of the growing GNP because of their organizational weakness transferred their support to the large opposition party.

This was the beginning of a trend that peaked in the late 1970s and early 1980s, in which Alignment supporters were characterized by European origin and a high educational level and Likud supporters by Asian and African origin and a low educational level (Peres and Shemer, 1984). This political phenomenon's relation to the differential status of ethnic groups in the labor market and the role of the *Histadrut* and the Alignment in creating this reality have yet to be studied, but those issues are beyond the scope of the present work.

It became clear, after the 1973 elections, that there was now a viable alternative to Labor-based government, in the form of the Likud. Both the Alignment and the Likud had diverse social bases that included members of the middle and upper as well as working class (Weiss,

HA. 25/9/74). Such "class parties" as *Mapam* in 1948 and the Liberal party of 1961 disappeared. The multiclass party structure brought class contradiction into the two large political blocs themselves, becoming especially acute when either is in power and has to make decisions. The problems of the multiclass party were particularly apparent during the internal Alignment disputes and the government-*Histadrut* conflicts of 1974-1977. The Likud engaged in much populist rhetoric during that period,[21] but when it rose to power had to switch finance ministers and economic policy three times within its first four years of office in its efforts to resolve internal class differences (Ben Porat, 1982).

The Yom Kippur War not only stopped the modest growth that had begun in 1967, but also accelerated negative economic processes that had also started then: the balance of payments deteriorated; defense expenditure, import of capital, and defense loans all rose sharply; and the structural deficiency of the public sector's ever-expanding part in the economy and in the GNP intensified. Inflation reached 30-40 percent yearly—this time not because of large demand, but because of increased spending. Reduction of *aliya*, the greater number of Israelis leaving the country, and the energy crisis all contributed to the halt of growth. Capital imports from the U.S., restricted from the outset to specific defense products, exacerbated the problem of funding public and civil services. The government tried to maintain the scope of its budget and services through taxation and the reduction of basic product subsidies, while the proportion of GNP soaked up by taxes rose from 36.3 percent in 1972 to 47 percent in 1975 (Rosenberg, 1980; Ofer, 1976; Leviatan, 1978).

In an effort to stop the balance of payments deterioration and to finance new security expenses, the government initiated a policy of creeping devaluation in order to promote export and diminish private consumption. The ensuing inflation, viewed as "functional" to state purposes (INT-RA, see chapter 6), significantly enhanced the value of the capital subsidy embodied in unlinked development loans, and industrialists thus received additional support. The third objective of this policy was wage erosion, evading the institutionalized pattern of collective bargaining (Rosenberg, 1980; Sussman and Zakai, 1983; Brodet, 1979; INT-RA).

The rise in taxes, the recessionary trends, and the intent to lower wages all placed the workers on the defensive. 1974 saw a sharp drop in wage increases and labor disputes. The workers' committees demanded that the *Histadrut* fight the government's wage restraint and price-raising policies. The *Histadrut* tried to mobilize the workers' committees and thereby signal that the Alignment policies, which hurt the workers and their wages, created a problem for the *Histadrut* leaders who were about to lose the workers' confidence (Tzaban, 1977; Tokatly, 1979).

Despite these expressions of protest, the *Histadrut* leadership moved towards compromise and in August 1975 signed a new four-year COLA agreement with the *Lishkat Hateum*. The agreement stipulated that compensation could be paid twice yearly and cover only 70 percent of the rise in the price index. The introduction of the partial COLA represents an additional refinement in the use of COLA as a tool for lowering existing general wage levels.[22]

A growing drift in wages in the form of various increments and promotions on the branch, office, department, and personal levels was occurring alongside government and *Histadrut* attempts to check wage rises in the public sector through centralized policy. The drift in wages, which intensified greatly after 1974, continued to widen the gaps among labor groups and create dissatisfaction among the disadvantaged ones.

The frequent *Histadrut*-government disputes made the party in power both the arena for conflict between them and a stabilizing and policy-shaping force. For this purpose, the Alignment formed a party resolution committee comprising seven representatives of the government, seven of the *Histadrut*, and seven of the party (Harel and Galin, 1978).

Heavier taxes, reduced public and private consumption, and reduction of investments as well as import surplus marked 1976. Two months before the private sector wage agreements expired, the *Histadrut* and the *Lishkat Hateum* signed a collective wage agreement granting an increment ceiling of 3 percent for 1976 and 3 percent for 1977. In the public sector, however, wage demands were much higher, and it was difficult to restrain them, particularly in view of the approaching elections. Agreements that deviated from the framework agreement were signed with the nurses, doctors, and taxation workers; and a labor court ruling allowed the engineers "education compensation." In early January 1977, the government passed, on its first reading, a mandatory arbitration law that could severely injure the workers, and especially the *Histadrut* as their representative. This move was the most grave and obvious indication of the *Histadrut*-government confrontation and evidence of the party's inability to serve as a bridge between them. Under the threat of the mandatory arbitration law, Prime Minister Yitzhak Rabin and the *Histadrut* secretary-general signed a "package deal" that froze prices, profits, taxes, and wage agreements (Dror, 1983; Sussman and Zakai, 1983; Reshef, 1981).

In the 1977 Knesset elections many votes of the low income salaried Oriental Jews were transferred from the Alignment to the Likud, primarily in the development towns that in 1973 had still been firmly under the influence of the ruling party (Weiss, 1979). After its defeat and first expulsion from government, the Alignment's leadership set about saving its skin in the next *Histadrut* elections. Through immense organizational effort, most *Histadrut* members, including those who had voted Likud in the Knesset elections, were convinced that the anticipated Likud government and Liberal finance minister's decrees made it imperative that the opposition Alignment control the *Histadrut* and lead the workers' struggle. The Alignment's campaign brought results surprisingly better than they had expected. For the first time, the Alignment won more votes in the *Histadrut* than in the Knesset—523,000 as opposed to 430,000 (Bahat, 1979).[23]

CONCLUSION: THE HISTADRUT PIVOTAL POSITION IN THE POLITICAL ECONOMY

The idiosyncrasies of Israel's political economy are rooted in a historical process in which the development of the labor force and the accumulation of capital were always contingent upon external circumstances: the early twentieth century East European pogroms, the Polish economic decrees of 1924, the Nazis' rise to power in Germany in 1933, the blockage of immigration during World War II, the increase of American contributions, the immigration of Oriental Jews during the 1950s, and reparation payments from Germany. All of these had far-reaching effects on the structure and composition of Jewish capital and labor.

The second factor that makes the Israeli case "unique" is the continual conflict between the Jewish society and the Arab-Palestinian society and economy. During the period of the *yishuv* this economic confrontation took the form of competition for work, land, and the marketing of produce; during Israel's statehood it has taken the form of growing defense expenditure. Since 1967 the conquest of the West Bank and Gaza and the effects of their integration into the Israeli economy have been decisive.

All these factors produced a specific economic and political structure that differs from those of the capitalist societies in which the corporatist and dualist approaches developed. The main features of Israel's peculiarity are as follows:

a) the special structure of the Histadrut, whose representatives are elected by political party and which also performs functions of employer and state;

b) the broad scope of the state's involvement in the economy and the large dimensions of the public sector;
c) the relative weakness of private capital, and the extent of its dependence on government subsidy;
d) the structure of the workers' differential power. Power is concentrated in the professional workers' unions and other public sector organizations, in contrast to the relative weakness of the industrial workers.

The *Histadrut* was originally created as an "autonomous workers' authority," that is, a body that would absorb moneyless Jewish immigrants into Palestine. The *Histadrut's* structure is the result of the Jewish laborer's weakness in competition with the local Arab workers and new immigrants, and the Jewish employer's desire to maximize his profits. Prior to the state, the *Histadrut* represented the Jewish community's means of achieving its Zionist objectives and constituted the labor parties' power base, enabling them to control national institutions as well.

In other words, the exigencies of the Jewish workers' situation in pre-state Palestine explain why the *Histadrut* was structured not as a centralized trade union but rather as a corporatist body in itself, responsible for the functions of both state and employer too. This form of organization was made possible by the WZO,[24] which accepted the *Histadrut* leadership's contention that private Jewish capital, whose profit motive would always dictate its employment of Arab labor, could not build a new Jewish society.

The *Histadrut* leaders, who identified the interests of Zionism with the workers' need for employment, drew their power also from the fundamental difference between Zionist capital and Zionist labor. While the worker had to immigrate to Palestine in order to work there, the capitalist could send his money from afar.[25] For this reason, the leaders of socialist Zionism headed not only labor organizations but also the national, governing institutions, while the leaders of "General Zionism," the capitalists, remained abroad.

The Histadrut's Political Structure

The organization of Jewish labor institutions, first the political parties, and later the *Histadrut*, was determined by two principal factors: the split labor market and the aim of Zionism to create an independent Jewish state. Jewish workers' weakness in the economic arena was transformed by labor institutions into strength in the political arena. The political structure is based on the direct membership, proportional elections and services members receive.

The special membership system, in which membership does not depend on employment or trade union affiliation, creates a kind of "citizenship" in the *Histadrut*. People join the *Histadrut* mainly to receive health and other services, without any relation to their working or salaried status. Competition for *Histadrut* membership comes from other health insurance funds.

The internal election system is proportional, with votes being cast for party based lists, and not individual candidates, just as in the Knesset elections. Every group may present its own list of candidates, even if there are no workers among them, though they must formally be members of the *Histadrut*. In contrast, large groups of workers seeking representation in *Histadrut* institutions must form an electoral list like a political group.

Both these features make the labor functionary who begins in the local workers' committee and seeks to climb the *Histadrut* ladder dependent on his party status and independent of his local labor constituents.

The chief service a "citizen" of the *Histadrut* receives, health insurance, was crucial in an immigration society. Most new immigrants relied on the *Histadrut* health services and thus became members. Until 1959, the labor exchanges were also under *Histadrut* control, and another important service the *Histadrut* offered were pension funds. These services the *Histadrut* "citizen" receives loosen the ties between the workers and their representatives even further. The member wants to continue receiving his services regardless of the *Histadrut's* trade union policy.

The *Histadrut's* political structure prevented direct worker representation, without party mediation, in the workplace. The nonrepresentative *Histadrut* trade union department is similar in this sense to the state-imposed union, located in the democratic-autocratic continuum proposed by Crouch (1983) close to the autocratic pole. The rank and file are prevented from organizing on a shop basis, and a political appointee is imposed on them. This system works only when the workers are at such a disadvantage in the labor market that they are dependent on the agreements the *Histadrut* signs, as was the case in the pre-state era.

The establishment of the state and the subsequent division of functions between the government and the *Histadrut* exacerbated the latter's problems. *Mapai's* decision to leave the *Hevrat Ovdim*, health and employment functions in the *Histadrut's* hands was in effect a decision to retain the *Histadrut's* political structure. This decision fragmented the state's functions between the government and the *Histadrut*, leaving *Mapai* as the supreme decision-making body in both. This fragmentation of the state, however, bore the seeds of structural tension and rift. The *Histadrut* has constituted since 1948 the most salient "private interest government," as defined by Schmitter: "a non-state association (that) allocates goods, services or statuses that are monopolistic in nature and indispensable for members; it is therefore capable of affecting and potentially controlling their behavior, and does so with the specific encouragement, license or subsidiation of the state, thus imposing certain public standards and responsibilities on the behavior of the association" (1985:47).

The early 1960s rebellion of the industrial workers' committees occurred at a time of industrial growth, full employment, and homogenization of the work force. While in the advanced capitalist corporatist pattern the labor organizations undergo a process of centralization and move toward bargaining on a national level, under these conditions the Israeli workers' committees acted separately or on a local basis, like those of the Dan (Tel Aviv) area. The whole political structure was under a tremendous threat. Prevention of structural change in labor organization depends on the channeling of workers' protest into the opposition parties, a viable solution from the *Histadrut's* conservative point of view. The channeling of workers' protest to political action diverts workers from organizing independent trade unions at the economic level, which would challenge the *Histadrut's* structure. Political action appears to be a viable option because of the *Histadrut's* electoral system, allowing much space for internal opposition within its structure.

The *Histadrut's* structure hampered its ability to meet the demand for uniform wage restraint. The party representation system distanced the *Histadrut* leadership from the rank and file—both the workers themselves and the workers' committees and trade unions elected through direct, nonparty elections. In order to avert confrontation between strong labor groups and the *Histadrut* leadership, the latter developed wage determination mechanisms that allow for expression of the workers' differential power and discourage them from leaving the *Histadrut*. These mechanisms were: (1) starting in the 1950s, the drift in wages in the public sector; (2) in 1970, dividing the bargaining process into three levels: national, branch, and plant. These mechanisms entailed the evolution of split collective bargaining.

The Emergence of Split Collective Bargaining

Differing levels of unionization and differing degrees of party and *Histadrut* involvement in electing labor representatives are indications of the differential bargaining power, determined by the market, of various labor groups.

In the 1950s the professional workers formed their own independent trade unions and conducted direct, personal elections. They also demanded significant wage increases, thereby widening the differentials between themselves and the unskilled workers. The relative power of these workers can be explained by the new circumstances: the scarcity of their manpower force in relation to the large supply of unskilled labor; capital concentration in the hands of the state, their principal employer; and their membership in the dominant ethnic group in the state, the *Histadrut*, and the economy.

All of the above support Bonacich's contention (1979) that the wage differentials between cheap and expensive labor derive from differences in their bargaining power, ability to organize, political influence, and historical background.

The industrialization and full employment of the 1960s led to rank and file organization in industry, but even then no one was able to establish country-wide trade unions, like those of the professionals, for industrial workers. The *Histadrut*, with the involvement of political parties, established the industrial workers' trade unions only in the 1970s, when those workers were weakened by competition with nonorganized labor.

The logic behind labor organization is that, in its absence, job competition among workers leads them to minimize wage demands. The logic of the *Histadrut's* industrial trade unions in the 1970s, however, reflected its political economic structure. The *Histadrut* sought to maintain its organizational power by preventing the formation of independent trade unions, whose representatives would be directly elected by members. The *Histadrut's* political control of weak labor trade unions was made possible by the competition with Palestinian nonorganized labor that helped to curb wage demands. This is the only explanation for the *Histadrut's* paradoxical failure to organize the noncitizen workers on the one hand and its failure to protect its members by limiting their access to the labor market (as in the Hebrew labor struggle during the pre-state period) on the other (Shalev, 1989).

The complex structure of labor organizations includes two levels—the work committees and trade unions. Work committees are elected directly by the workers in one specific company, and include local and national committees. National work committees usually exist when there is a large employer, and if it is the government they have a status similar to trade unions in the collective bargaining, while local committees are included in trade unions and have no independent authority on the national level. Trade unions are mainly of two kinds, the most representative being those whose leadership is elected directly without party mediation, and whose membership consists of strong, professional and skilled workers. The unions representing employees of industries and the local committees, who have a weak market position are formally governed by party representatives elected in proportional elections.

The *Histadrut's* comprehensive, direct-membership structure allows strong labor groups to act independently while remaining in the *Histadrut* and continuing to enjoy its services. It is important to stress that not only does the *Histadrut* supply its social services and mediate between workers and employers like a state, but it also plays the role of the centralized corporatist trade union by providing such services as legal and economic advice and strike funds for labor groups. This is another reason for the strong labor organizations' desire to act independently but without splitting entirely from the *Histadrut*.

The 1970 package deal embodies a paradox of Israeli corporatism. The agreement incorporates both a tripartite (government, *Histadrut*, private employers) bargaining framework for wage demand restraint and a framework allowing the "strong groups" independent operation. Ben Aharon explained the "logic" of dividing negotiations into three levels: "to divert worker unrest and anger from the *Histadrut* toward the employer, and to channel the power that builds up in the various levels of the organization." Nevertheless, during the 1966 "great recession," the workers' anger was directed toward the *Histadrut* for having cooperated with the government's unemployment policies (Tokatly, 1979).

The wage restraint process, then, takes place not only on three levels—national, branch, and plant—but is also split into two circles: the private sector and the public sector. The two sectors are differentiated by the degree of *Histadrut* involvement in their negotiating process, by the extent of the *Histadrut's* ability to restrain their wage demands, and by their level of worker organization.

This distinction between the private and public sectors helps define the area in which it is difficult to restrain the wage demands of various public sector labor organizations. This distinction also reflects the desire of the private sector partners in the *Lishkat Hateum* and *Histadrut* to disconnect one negotiating process from the other. They wish to prevent the strong public sector unions from imposing wage increases on the private sector above what would be obtained if the two sectors were not differentiated.

The private sector workers' organizations are distinct from the "strong" organizations, the professionals and workers' committees in government enterprises. This detachment helped the *Histadrut* and the private employers to direct the strong labor groups' high wage demands toward the government, thereby splitting the collective bargaining process. Wage restraint in the private sector is achieved as noted, through national, centralized negotiation between the *Histadrut* and the *Lishkat Hateum*. These two bodies also usually determine the COLA agreements for the entire economy, according to their ability to restrain demands within the private sector.

An examination of wage levels in the economy shows that the distinction between the private and public sectors, and not between branches, explains most of the trends in wage structure such as gaps and differences (Gross, 1983; Shteier and Levin- Epstein, 1988). During the 1970s, the private sector's collective bargaining partners learned to conclude their bargaining before that of the public sector. They needed, and were able to achieve, a more restrained agreement, wishing to avoid the influence of the strong public sector workers achievements.

Since 1970, the private sector has managed to restrain wage demands through centralized framework agreements based on the weakness of the secondary sector workers. This was made possible by a series of developments, mainly the appearance of a nonorganized noncitizen labor force which made it difficult for the Israeli workers to fight for wage increases. The government, in contrast to the private sector, faced a double crisis: (1) defense expenditure was growing and expanding the trade deficit and the budget; (2) the public sector did not employ noncitizen labor which could help to lower its wage expenses.

Corporatist Exchange in the Private Sector[26]

The private sector does contain a type of exchange similar to that of corporatism, but the element of state mediation is missing. The *Histadrut* agrees to wage restraint in centralized, national bargaining with the *Lishkat Hateum*, and in exchange the private employers give the *Histadrut* political power by recognizing it as the sole representative of labor, not questioning its authority. This *Histadrut-Lishkat Hateum* exchange, conducted through centralized negotiation of comprehensive wage policy, is referred to as private sector corporatism (PSC). The internal corporatist structure of the *Histadrut*, as trade union and employer, allows the PSC partners to pursue a centralized policy without government intervention, and sometimes even despite government opposition, as was the case between 1980 and 1982, to be analyzed in chapters 3 and 4.

The profit motive is common to both the private and *Histadrut*-owned plants. Due to the competition between them, they affect each others' wage levels in both acquiescence to and restraint of wage demands. Wage increases in one plant generate pressure to raise wages to a similar level in the others.

Horizontal organization of rank and file workers' committees naturally hurts the private sector employers, both private and *Histadrut*. The private sector workers are not directly represented in centralized negotiations. On the branch and plant levels, the National Committees and the plant workers' committees are involved, but they have little freedom of action on this level while the local labor councils and the *Histadrut* trade union department are very active. The workers' committees are highly dependent on both the plant administration and the *Histadrut* bodies.

The private sector framework agreements, by restraining demands and the workers' committees' ability to attain wage increments outside the agreement, give the *Histadrut* and the private employers a basis for negotiation and agreed wage policy. The workers' capability in this sector depends on business considerations: successful plants will give their workers increments (due also to the employers' interest in industrial quiet); less profitable enterprises give the workers only those increments stipulated in the private sector framework agreements. The 1970 "package deal" greatly extended *Lishkat Hateum-Histadrut* cooperation far beyond what could be achieved in the public sector, and made possible maximal wage restraint within the private sector.

While the *Histadrut's* political economic structure creates an "understanding" between capital and labor through political mediation, this understanding is reached in the context of the private sector. The *Hevrat Ovdim* does not conduct its own collective bargaining, but adopts the results of the bargaining between the *Histadrut* and the *Lishkat Hateum*. If not for the private sector bargaining, the *Hevrat Ovdim* might have more trouble restraining wage demands than the private employers. Due to its higher concentration of capital, the *Hevrat Ovdim* employs a higher proportion of technologically-skilled labor (in the primary sector), and the *Hevrat Ovdim* also hires less Arab labor due to its original commitment to create jobs for Jews. Moreover, the *Hevrat Ovdim* is formally owned by the entire *Histadrut* membership, and its ideology requires at least some form of lip service to the workers' cause.

The workers in whose name the *Histadrut* conducts centralized negotiations are those weakened by the split labor market. At best, they are organized in unions controlled by the party that dominates the *Histadrut*, without direct representation. In the case of the noncitizen workers, they are not organized at all. The trade unions that represent the strong public sector workers in the labor market or the professional workers (such as engineers) in the private sector are not included in the centralized private sector framework agreements. Instead, these groups conduct their own collective branch bargaining in the public sector. The fact that the strong, organized workers are not included in the private sector corporatist collective agreements is extremely important in understanding the *Histadrut's* restraining ability, which derives chiefly from the market's segmentation, and not from the processes of representation and centralization that characterize West European democratic corporatism.

The key elements of corporatism exist in this private sector political exchange: (1) there is a public body interested in centralized wage restraint agreements and labor-employer mediation; (2) the workers receive services from a public (quasi-state) body; (3) certain standard of living "increments" are the results not of labor-employer relations on the economic level, but rather from *Histadrut* political mediation; (4) there is a public body able to subsidize both sides of the exchange.

All four of these elements exist in Israel, as we shall presently show, thanks to the *Histadrut's* peculiar political economic structure. The state is not actively involved, but rather provides the legal framework.

Beyond its business interest in wage restraint, however, *Hevrat Ovdim* becomes, structurally, a central element in mediating the interests of the *Histadrut* and those of the *Lishkat Hateum* and on the informal level sometimes intervenes actively. The following factors give *Hevrat Ovdim* this mediatory role:

a) Hevrat Ovdim shares the Histadrut's general goals and its desire for political power and authority among the workers, so that its legitimization rests on these shared objectives.
b) Hevrat Ovdim identifies with the Manufacturers' Association's overall goals of developing production and export and enhancing their profitability.
c) Hevrat Ovdim presents the Histadrut leadership with the private sector's arguments in its determination of wage policy, and expresses the limits of wage increases possible while maintaining profitability.
d) Hevrat Ovdim maintains wide-ranging and varied ties with the private economy, and seeks to expand these ties.

In addition to *Hevrat Ovdim's* central role in creating common policies in private sector corporatism and its informal activity, the *Histadrut* has formal organizational instruments for mediation of interests: the party controlling the *Histadrut*, the trade union branch, the union and committee "portfolio holders," the labor councils, and others.

These formal mediatory elements' contacts with both the rank and file and the private and *Histadrut* employers allow the *Histadrut* to play a crucial role in formulating the corporatist compromise and avoid excessive friction with the private sector workers.

The Histadrut and Public Sector Labor Organizations

In the public sector, it is much harder for the *Histadrut* to control the workers and reach moderate wage agreements. This is due to the relative independence of the labor organizations in this sector (engineers, doctors, and other professionals, nurses, government enterprise committees, etc.); to the size of the organizations, each of which represents thousands of workers; to the direct elections of their committees and union representatives; and to the state's ability to "pay the bill"— whether by raising taxation, through loans, import of capital, or printing money.

The fact that it is harder for the *Histadrut* to restrain wage demands in the public sector does not mean that it has no interest in doing so. The gains of some of the public sector trade unions—such as professionals or technicians—influence the wage of their colleagues in the private sector. Moreover, the results of bargaining with the doctors or nurses, for example, affects the budget of *Kupat Holim*, the *Histadrut's* largest employer. The *Histadrut* is more able to control wages of the public sector's weaker groups, such as some of the civil servants, the clerks' association, the technicians' association, and those organizations that are chosen by party elections and thus more directly influenced by the trade union department.[27]

As noted, a characteristic form of raising salaries in the public sector is the drift in wages. This process, difficult for the *Histadrut* to control, involves raising wages without collective agreement, but rather through agreements with individuals or labor groups whose wage is raised by promotion, calculation of seniority increments, overtime, and special wage increments. The drift in wages began with the strengthening of the professional workers organizations—doctors, veterinarians, and engineers—in the mid-1950s, a process that paralleled the demand for personal and independent elections to their professional organizations. Between the Yom Kippur War and the next economic crisis, there was an attempt to check wage demands through collective, wage agreements, but the drifting wage system, which grew by 50 percent between

1974 and 1978, doomed these efforts to failure (Sussman and Zakai, 1983).

The main weakness of collective bargaining split between the private and public sectors, is that certain groups of workers are able to hurt all the employers together. There are two such groups:

a) the engineers, professionals, and technicians who enjoy the best of both worlds—the conditions attained on the plant level in the private sector and those obtained from the government in collective bargaining;
b) the government enterprise workers who supply services vital to production and to import-export marketing.

The first group of workers is employed in both sectors, but their collective bargaining for framework agreements is conducted in the public sector. As part of their policy of avoiding the private sector's involvement in their collective bargaining, these unions wage their strikes only in the public service areas. However, when a collective agreement is formulated, it obligates the granting of wage increases to members of the same profession in both sectors. In other words, their strikes affect only the public sector, while their wage increases affect the entire economy. The opposite is true of the second group of workers. Their negotiations are on a plant level, and the wage increases they receive affect only the government, but their strikes affect the entire economy.

The *Histadrut* maintains very close contact with both groups in a complicated relationship of cooperation, power competition, mediation and struggle. The fluctuation of *Histadrut*-public workers relations is connected both with labor market flux and political conjunctures, as will be analyzed in the following chapters.

The State: The Sphere of Crisis

Despite the fact that private sector corporatist partners are independent of the state's political mediation between labor and capital, they have an interest in state subsidization of both. On this issue the *Histadrut* and *Lishkat Hateum* negotiate with the government from a position of strength: the subsidies demanded from the state are earmarked for the attainment of their "classical" common goals of growth, export, and investment.

In the overall balance of power between state and society there is an advantage to the latter. This structural imbalance in the Israeli political economy originated in the pre-state period when the Zionist movement subsidized labor and capital in order to create a Jewish economy (Kimmerling, 1982:30-37). The political consequence of this subsidy was to empower the *Histadrut's* political economic structure and *Mapai's* role as a nation building party. In 1948 *Mapai* established the structural mutual dependence between the dual state apparatuses—the state and *Histadrut*—intending to remain in control of both institutions and the key factor in relations between them. *Mapai* feared, understandably, that a structural change of the *Histadrut*—converting it into a "normal" trade union—would totally demolish the party's social foundations.

Since 1967 the Israeli political economy has been in a trap: the state faces PSC demands to continue subsidizing capital, thus increasing its expenditure from one side, and public sector wage demands on the other side. The state has no trade union partner with which to exchange wage restraint for other attainments, while capital does not hold itself responsible for the fiscal crisis of the state. Thus since 1967 the crises of class conflict have been manifested in the sphere of the state, whose only means of retaining its relative autonomy was to boost capital import.

The Israeli dual labor market and dual state apparatuses prevent the coordination of wage agreements in the public and private sectors through homogeneous corporatist bargaining and tripartite government-trade union-private employer political exchange. The potential of private sector corporatism to function without the state's help developed beginning with the 1970 package deal. The Likud's success in the 1977 elections created a new conjuncture in which the *Histadrut* was no longer politically committed to the ruling party and therefore felt no obligation to restrain public workers' demands.

Since 1977 the *Histadrut* has been transformed into the central body coordinating the interests of capital, parties, the state, and labor. Obviously the specific form of coordination suits the *Histadrut's* interest in maintaining its political structure. The Histadrut has a pivotal position which is expressed differently on each level: there is a political exchange with the Manufacturers' Association including wage restraint and mutual legitimation; it mediates between labor organizations and government in public sector wage negotiations; it controls weak workers by means of politically imposed unions; it negotiates national economic policy with the state, discussing prices, the subsidy of capital and labor, health budget, pension policies, and investment plans.

In separate research interviews, representatives of the *Histadrut*, *Hevrat Ovdim*, and of the *Lishkat Hateum* expressed their awareness and understanding of PSC, and its relations with the state. Three excerpts from these interviews follow:

A. Shavit, chairman of the Manufacturers' Association and the *Lishkat Hateum*:

The Histadrut is not a trade union in the negative sense we know abroad . . . I see the Histadrut as a kind of comprehensive government, that has the whole economy in view . . . The Histadrut should be understood as a state. Levinson was the Finance Minister, the secretary of Hevrat Ovdim was Minister of Industry. They have a foreign relations division, the Agriculture Center is the Ministry of Agriculture, Shikun Ovdim is the Housing Ministry, Mishkan and Mivtahim (pension funds) are Welfare and National Insurance. Kupat Holim is the Health Ministry; they have more control and know what's going on more than the Health Ministry. All these are residues of what existed prior to statehood. The managers of Hevrat Ovdim became exactly like industrialists, even the kibbutzniks I meet act like employers in every way.

Naftali Blumental, *Hevrat Ovdim*:

Relations between the manufacturers and the *Histadrut* are characterized not by conflict of interest but rather by dialogue. Both sides have the same interest, in the same way the buyer and the seller do. There aren't two separate world views, but rather a single view shared by both. The commonality of interests is very great, and both view the government as a foreign element—both as a cow to be milked and also as a body to be feared lest it hand down undesirable decrees. When a manufacturer works in partnership with the *Histadrut,* they both have equal status, while the government has the power to dictate and we therefore fear it together.

Yeruham Meshel, *Histadrut* Secretary-General:

The *Histadrut* economy has helped us in private sector bargaining more than once . . . When I wanted to present an economic policy plan (to the government), I always tried to come with accepted economic conceptions on employment, COLA, growth. Then the *Hevrat Ovdim* representatives who came with me to the meeting could report that they had reached an agreement (on the plan) with the private sector, so thus it often happened that I represented the interests of all three (*Hevrat Ovdim*, the Manufacturers'

Association, and the trade union—L.G.). I always tried not to stand alone before the government, but with the manufacturers as a second front.

The following chapters will describe and analyze the changes in these political economic patterns within the fluctuating market conditions and power relations. They will analyze the influence of the new political configurations on state-society relations, private corporatist exchange, and economic crisis and stabilization.

CHAPTER 3

THE STATE'S FAILURE TO
CREATE HOMOGENEOUS CORPORATISM

This chapter focuses on the period of office of the second Likud Finance Minister, Yigael Horowitz, between October 1979 and January 1981. Horowitz, a former Labor party member, was aware of the vital importance of government dialogue with the *Histadrut* to obtain consent for his policies. He also understood and exploited the vulnerability of the *Histadrut* because of its internal capital-labor contradiction and its dependence on state subsidies for *Kupat Holim* and *Hevrat Ovdim*. During this period class conflict threatened to erupt, and strong labor organizations organized to oppose both overtly procapital government policies and the *Histadrut's* eventual compromise in their name.

The theoretical issue discussed here is that of the relations between a centralized trade union and rank and file resistance to corporatist agreements. To what extent was the labor elite in real danger, and was it able to use the workers protest for its own benefit? This is a classic question of corporatist literature, but this chapter adds to it the problematic of the labor market structure. From this perspective the questions are also related to the relations between peak unions and different groups of workers, based on their power in the labor market.

The particular event to be analyzed is the apparent revolt of strong work committees that coordinated their actions under the umbrella of what they called the Forum of the thirteen Big Committees (hereafter the Forum). The Forum was established at a time of open and deep conflict between capital and labor, when the state was collaborating with private and *Histadrut* employers with the aim of changing economic structures. This new policy threatened both the strength of certain workers in the market and of the *Histadrut* in the political structure. In the course of this chapter the structural weaknesses of the *Histadrut* which became very obvious in this period are examined. The organization, composition and activities of the Forum are discussed, the argument being that the Forum was a temporary solution to the *Histadrut's* lack of powerful organization representing labor.

The Forum's influence was conservative: it helped *Histadrut* to preserve its structure and pivotal position in the political economy. In other words, it played a role in thwarting the eruption of open class conflict. This was achieved by prohibiting "weak workers" from joining the organization, while steering clear from any attempt to neutralize the *Histadrut's* monopolistic role in collective bargaining. Thus the Forum aided the *Histadrut* to maintain existing split labor markets structures along with different degrees of labor organization among correspondent groups of workers. As in the past strong workers had benefited from their privileged position in the labor market and their collaboration with the *Histadrut* leadership, they had no intention of altering the system. For its part, the *Histadrut* used the Forum to compensate for its own shortcomings.

It should be made clear that there is no functionalist argument underlying the analysis here. There are no forces compelling people and institutions to fill vacuums and conserve the stability of an integrated system in which each social actor has its function to perform. All these events can be explained as a matter of power struggles and constellations of interests. In other words, there are social conflicts whose outcome need not necessarily be conservative. As we shall see in the coming chapters, effects of instability and change are contingent on different balances of power.

The Failure of the First Liberal Finance Minister

When the first Likud government was established, the *Histadrut* leadership, not unexpectedly, anticipated with trepidation possible problems in conducting a dialogue with the new government. This anxiety intensified when the new finance minister, Simcha Erlich, announced his "revolutionary" economic policy in November 1977. This movement toward "liberal" free market policies cancelled currency control that had characterized the Alignment's "social-democratic" state-interventionist economics.

Declaration of the new economic policy led to worker protest, particularly among those close to the *Histadrut* leadership, notably the Haifa and Ashdod port workers. The private sector framework agreement was signed in March. This agreement stipulated a 12.5 percent wage increase, as well as October 1978 and April 1979 wage adjustments in accordance with inflation that would maintain the real wage.

The public sector, however, presented the greatest problem. In order to withstand worker demands, *Histadrut* Secretary-General Meshel and Erlich engaged in discussions that resulted in a "package deal" that stipulated restraint of wage demands and price increases for half a year. COLA increments were paid only in April and October 1978. This "package deal," however, failed to satisfy the public sector workers, and in June the *Histadrut* representatives and the Civil Service Commission agreed on a 15 percent pay advance in exchange for industrial quiet for the ensuing months, during which framework agreement negotiations were to be continued. Toward the end of the six-month period, public sector wage demands arose once more, and Meshel and Erlich reached an agreement whereby negotiation and raises would occur on two levels—branch and sector. In exchange for this agreement, the *Histadrut* promised to constrain irregular wage demands.

In February 1979, when the *Histadrut* refused to support the Engineers' Association demands, they bypassed it and turned directly to the government. Negotiations resulted in the government's accession to the engineers' demands and the signing of a separate, irregular wage agreement with them, followed by a series of other irregular agreements. Thus the government, by its own act, "put an end to negotiations" through the *Histadrut,* as Meshel put it, and cancelled the centralized bargaining policy in the public sector (Tokatly, 1979; Reshef, 1981).

The rate of price rises accelerated sharply between January and March 1979, threatening the erosion of wages. Aware of the bitterness that was accumulating among the workers, the *Histadrut* announced a four-hour warning strike against government policy. Participation in the strike was almost total.

In an effort to check inflation the government curtailed its expenditure and in May linked development loans to industry to the price rise rate, thus effectively cancelling the subsidy these loans had offered. This decision led to a sharp drop in private sector investments (Razin, 1979).

During the economic crisis, the *Histadrut* found in the *Lishkat Hateum* a partner with which to run the national economy. In order to prevent wage erosion caused by accelerating price increases, both sides agreed de facto to pay COLA advances each month between January and October 1979 (Leviatan, 1982). During those months, the credit problem was aggravated considerably by certain steps the finance minister was taking. The Manufacturers' Association began negotiating with insurance companies and with Bank Hapoalim to establish a comprehensive pension fund .

The pension funds episode furnishes a vital insight into the *Hevrat Ovdim's* ability to subsidize capital through its special ties with the trade union and the role it played in private sector corporatist intermediation. In June 1979, a tripartite arrangement was entered into by the Manufacturers' Association, the trade union department and *Hevrat Ovdim* (in the form of Bank Hapoalim and the *Mivtahim* pension fund). Under this arrangement, known as the collective agreement on comprehensive pensions, all the Manufacturers' Association employers transferred their employees to the *Histadrut* pension fund, and in exchange Bank Hapoalim promised to expand the volume of cheap credit for these employers. It was grounded in a historical arrangement between *Histadrut* and government reached in the 1950s (Grinberg, forthcoming). These special arrangements gave the *Hevrat Ovdim* control over 50 percent of the pension money, which they used to grant cheap investment credit (INT-BN, SA, and HY; Dror, 1983).[1] In a research interview, Horowitz maintained that *Hevrat Ovdim's* rights to use the pension money caused the failure of government efforts to restrain credit. As he put it, "Levinson (chairman of Bank Hapoalim) was the (real) Finance Minister."

This exchange of a comprehensive pension agreement for credit expressed the common interest of the *Histadrut* and the Manufacturers' Association in conducting coordinated economic policy, as well as the structural ability of these two organizations to enact such policy. Both *Hevrat Ovdim's* privileges and the *Histadrut's* political structure were established by the party that controlled the government from 1948 to 1977. It was precisely this party's loss of governmental power that highlighted the "common fate" of the *Histadrut* and the *Lishkat Hateum* and the extent of the cooperation between them. The Alignment's downfall may have even served to solidify further the private sector corporatist pattern.

The threat to private sector corporatism could come from two directions; firstly, from the government, which could undermine legitimation by curtailing the comprehensive structure of the *Histadrut* through legislation; secondly, from organized labor groups that could disrupt the collective wage agreement. Both PSC-state and PSC-strong workers relations went into turmoil during the 1980 economic recession.

This chapter firstly describes and then analyzes the developments of these two sets of relationships in the critical atmosphere of the eruption of open conflict between labor and capital.

The Government's Exploitation of Histadrut Contradiction

After two and a half years of Finance Minister Simcha Erlich's economic policy, a serious economic crisis developed. The annual inflation rate rose from 35 percent to 110 percent. The financial market was buoyant, but production had slowed, the real wage had dropped, unemployment threatened, and there were serious difficulties in mobilizing credit for industry. The *Histadrut* and the *Lishkat Hateum* attempted to initiate policies that would avert economic collapse, but the third partner—the government—was missing.

Under these circumstances Erlich resigned, but the appointment of a new finance minister, Yigael Horowitz, did not reverse the recessionary trend in production. The employers expectations from Horowitz were to halt the growth of the public sector and of government spending while alleviating the recession in the private sector. Horowitz's new policies were intended to shift economic emphasis from services to production and avert the uncontrolled growth of government expenditure and the fall of production that had already begun.

The absence of coordination between public and private sectors made the crisis particularly difficult. Demand, imports, and private consumption all rose, while investment was blocked. The entire private sector, both *Histadrut* and private employers, had an interest in checking both wages and employment in the public sector, and the *Histadrut* had the additional interest of bringing rebellious labor groups back into the fold. The government understood that continuing its policy of full employment in the public sector could become self defeating by leading to a deep economic crisis. In order to resynchronize economic processes and its budget, the government initiated restraining policies that intensified the recession already existing in the private sector and the situation became dire.

Horowitz's first two steps—cutting subsidies of basic commodities and freezing free credit—were designed to reduce consumption. In order to complete his economic program, he had to restrain wages in both the public and private sectors significantly. In the public sector this would reduce government expenditure and in the private sector it would improve production and export profitability that had been impaired in recent months. In order to achieve these goals, Horowitz had to first win the cooperation of both the private employers and the

Histadrut, whose relations with the government had deteriorated considerably during the preceding months.

Horowitz, as soon as he was appointed, had made the head of the Manufacturers' Association, "Buma" Shavit, privy to his plans. Since his policies were designed to aid manufacturing and export, Horowitz anticipated the cooperation of the Manufacturers' Association, but he also asked Shavit to help restrain public sector wages.

As Shavit later reported in a research interview, Horowitz asked him to take one group of public sector workers and prove that it was possible to restrain their wage. Shavit answered: "There are three sectors in which we can be 'macho' and let the workers strike for three years without harming the economy—(a) the universities; (b) the Broadcasting Authority; (c) El Al (Israeli Airlines)." That conversation resulted in Horowitz making Shavit manager of El Al, and in intense collaboration between them in the whole political economy.

On 18 November 1979, the new El Al management council chairman Buma Shavit announced, after consultation with the finance minister, a freeze of new contract negotiations with the company's ground crews. On the evening of 19 November 1979, Horowitz convened a press conference and announced his economic policies: cancelling basic commodity subsidies, freezing industrial credit, cutting the government budget, and freezing wage agreements. The goal of these policies was to reduce the trade deficit, effect a transfer of workers from service to production, and halt inflation (*YA.* 4-19-20/11/79.

Under great pressure from shopfloor workers' committees, particularly in production, the *Histadrut* leadership called a twenty-four-hour general strike for 27 November 1979.[2] This decision was inconsistent with the *Histadrut's* past activity and with its balanced, responsible, moderate policies, and ran counter to the interests of the *Hevrat Ovdim,* which would also be hurt by the strike. The two other large employers —the government and the Manufacturers' Association—immediately mobilized to cancel the strike.

The *Histadrut* faced a difficult dilemma. On the one hand, the embittered workers were pressing for a general strike which would, in all likelihood, be successful. Calling off the strike could well lead to a rank and file revolt. On the other hand, the *Histadrut* had recently developed a good relationship with the Manufacturers' Association, and the problem of the government's noncooperation seemed close to solution. The new finance minister had declared his intention of working together with the *Histadrut.* A strike could damage relations with the government and the private employers; cancellation of the strike could cause worker hostility to the *Histadrut* leadership.

After pressure from the government, which accused the *Histadrut* of planning a "political strike" organized by the opposition as a weapon against the government, and the Manufacturers' Association's accusation before the labor court that the *Histadrut* had failed to announce a labor dispute as required by law, the *Histadrut* called off the strike.

The factors that led to both the declaration and the cancellation of the strike point to the *Histadrut's* main structural weaknesses, salient in the new conjuncture:

a) *The Histadrut's distance from the rank and file:* The Central Committee announced the general strike only after it had sensed the bitterness in the workplace, and revoked its call to strike without having determined the workers' position. The strike was cancelled in a highly centralized manner, with even the Central Committee endorsing its cancellation after the fact.

b) *Party representation in Histadrut bodies:* The charge that the strike was a politically motivated move against the Likud government was plausible only in view of the party system by which representatives were elected to the *Histadrut* bodies. It was thus possible to claim that those workers who supported the Likud opposed the strike. The *Histadrut* had no institutional means of refuting such a charge, even though some of the workers' committees that were disappointed at the strike's cancellation included Likud supporters and leaders.

c) *The economic interests of Hevrat Ovdim:* The two largest employers, the government and the Manufacturers' Association, had worked to have the strike call rescinded. It is impossible to determine whether the heads of *Hevrat Ovdim* had also acted informally for the strike's cancellation, but there is no doubt that the strike was intended to hurt the *Hevrat Ovdim* as much as the other employers—a clear contradiction of the "labor economy" concept.

In the past, the *Histadrut* had usually been able to overcome these structural weaknesses—by mediation between workers and employers, by depriving labor groups that rejected the *Histadrut's* proposals of its protection, or by supporting those groups of workers whose demands seemed reasonable to the *Histadrut*. The conditions that prevailed in November and December of 1979, however, made all these methods ineffective. The common interest of all employers, including the *Hevrat Ovdim*, was wage restraint, and the workers demanded a struggle against this objective.

The *Histadrut's* chief problem was the internal contradiction between its roles: as the workers' representative on the one hand, and employer and supplier of services on the other. In an irregular meeting of the *Hevrat Ovdim* Executive Committee and the *Histadrut* Central Committee in early December, the *Hevrat Ovdim* representatives explained that business considerations dictated dismissal of workers, which is what the *Hevrat Ovdim* would do, they said. In the heat of the debate, Secretary-General Meshel succinctly defined the *Histadrut's* structural problem: "There's a contradiction within the *Histadrut* . . . finding a common denominator within the *Histadrut* is harder than finding one against government policy . . ." (*CC.-LA.* 2/12/79). In other words, it was possible to engage all the workers—but not the *Hevrat Ovdim*—in a struggle against all the employers' demand for recession. This logic led Meshel to a very complex strategy: a mixture of collaboration with government and encouraging rank and file workers' opposition.

On 11 December 1979, Finance Minister Yigael Horowitz met with the Central Committee at the *Histadrut* Executive Committee headquarters. They discussed the January COLA, the updating of tax grades, the new wage agreements that were to be signed in April 1980, the danger of unemployment, and the *Histadrut's* suggestions for planning alternative employment. At this meeting, the head of the *Histadrut* trade union division, Israel Keisar, expressed the *Histadrut's* responsible approach, and its desire to cooperate with the government and the employers despite worker dissatisfaction: "Our approach . . . stems from one factor . . . the *Histadrut* is not only a trade union—it has an economy and a complex of services. Even if it wanted to act irresponsibly, it couldn't. So you (addressing the finance minister), if you wish to recognize this basis, there is certainly a way to extricate the state from the quagmire, and we are definitely partners in that task" (*CC.-LA.* 11/12/79).

The *Histadrut*-Finance Ministry negotiations on the COLA lasted two weeks. On 26 December 1979 they reached an agreement whereby a COLA at the rate of 100 percent of the level of inflation would be paid to low-waged workers.

The renewed strength of the government vis-a-vis the *Histadrut* was based on the conjuncture of the economic crisis and the new minister's awareness and willingness to use it to the detriment of the *Histadrut*. The structural contradiction between labor and capital exists all the time, but precisely during a crisis *Hevrat Ovdim* agreed to an extensive capital-state collaboration in spite of the dangers this posed to the *Histadrut* as an institution. As Schmitter (1985:49) argues, the state may limit the autonomy of private interest governments through the maintenance of an "adversarial relationship between the privileged interest; incorporated within them." If government had failed to do so in the past, during this crisis, all employers cooperated extensively to restrain labor's wages and neutralize the *Histadrut's* ability to mediate segmented corporatism.

The Establishment of the Forum of the Thirteen Big Committees

The *Histadrut's* inability to find an internal compromise between the interests of labor and capital weakened its status and power, and prevented it from acting for either one side or the other. Meshel understood that only a labor group operating on its own initiative and responsibility could fill the vacuum that was created and truly represent the workers' interests. The leaders of some strong workers' committees understood that the *Histadrut* was incapable of confronting the government and the private employers for two reasons: fear that the *Kupat Holim* budget would be cut, and fear that the *Histadrut's* status as the workers' representative organization would be damaged. The *Histadrut* was also apprehensive of the harm a strike would cause the *Hevrat Ovdim* plants, and was not sure the workers would strike. The weakness of the *Histadrut* as an institution under these conditions had a deleterious affect on the workers' power.

The way to remedy the workers' disability was by their own horizontal organization. Such organization would have to express the workers' needs directly, to represent them without political party mediation. Participation of both Alignment and Likud-oriented workers' committees was therefore necessary. In order to direct the struggle against the finance minister and not spread it over the entire economy and all the employers, it was crucial for this mobilization of workers to be based on public service and government enterprise workers' committees, and not on those of private or *Histadrut* enterprises. It would thus be possible to engage the *Histadrut* in the struggle and thereby fill the vacuum created in representing the workers' interests.

The workers feared not only unemployment but also a decrease in wages—through both erosion and direct steps. Toward the end of December, however, El Al became the chief focus of wage-lowering threats and the starting point of strong committees' organization. Shavit presented the ground crews with an ultimatum: if they failed to sign an agreement by 5:00 PM on 30 December 1979, the management council would meet at that time and decide to dismantle the company.

As zero hour approached, El Al workers' committee member Eli Ben Menahem asked the heads of workers' committees to back them in their anticipated struggle against their management. Negotiations went into high gear when, forty-eight hours before the deadline the *Histadrut* trade union department jumped into the breach, and brought about a compromise at midnight, 29 December 1979 (YA. 23-30/12/79).

The first meeting of the big workers' committees, scheduled for 30 December 1979, took place nevertheless.[3] At this meeting, it became apparent that all the committees were afraid the finance minister would do to them what Shavit had done to the El Al workers. The members of the other committees saw the El Al agreement, signed under the threat of closure of the company, as a bad omen. The threat of dismissal to force workers to sign employer-dictated agreements could be wielded in all the other enterprises, particularly in the government sector, since it was the finance minister who had urged Shavit to take harsh measures against the workers (YA. 31/12/79).

Fear of the finance minister's aggressive policies vis-a-vis government enterprise workers was a key factor in deciding which committees would be invited to the first meeting on 30 December 1979 of what was later called the Forum of the Thirteen Big Committees . Eli Ben Menahem said he decided to forego quantity and invite a small group of strong committees that had already proven their power in plant struggles. He consciously decided to omit the private industry committees "because they are dependent on *Histadrut* endorsement,"[4] as well as the service sector committees, which "speak a different language." The organizers also wished to prove that they did not oppose the finance minister's attempt to transfer workers from service to production (INT-BME). The thirteen committees were from the aircraft industry, the electric company, El Al ground crews, post office engineers, television employees, the Dead Sea Chemical Company, airports' authority, civilian naval officers, graded seamen, port workers, civil aviation company and x-ray technicians.

The composition of the Forum can be characterized as follows:

a) Except for the x-ray technicians and post office engineers, all members were government employees, most in government enterprises, that were directly employed by a government ministry (such as health or communications).

b) Except for the x-ray technicians and television employees, all were connected with production and considered blue collar workers. Most committees were involved in key services the government gives to production and export, including all forms of transport to the outside world—shipping, aviation, air and sea ports—and such vital services as electricity and post office engineers. Two large production plants—the aircraft industry and the Dead Sea works—were also included.

c) Most members had branch status in wage bargaining, except the post office engineers who were then included in the government employees' organization labor agreement. In other words, after the public sector framework agreement was signed, there was no trade union above these committees that could conduct wage bargaining instead of them or in their name. The committees, even local committees, conducted branch and plant negotiations themselves. Some of the committees, such as aviation and shipping, were not even bound by framework agreements.

d) Election to the committees was direct, without party intervention. Of the thirteen committees, six were local, four were national—the electric company, television employees, post office engineers , and airports' authority, while three were trade unions—the naval officers, graded seamen, and x-ray technicians. The common denominator for all, however, was direct elections. (On this subject see chapter 2 pp. 101-102).

e) Party affiliation was varied. Some were led by Alignment members—the electric company, port workers, and graded seamen; some Likud—the Dead Sea works, airports' authority, and civil aviation; some were mixed—El Al and the aircraft industry; and some were nonparty—the x-ray technicians and the television employees.

f) The members' wage levels ranged from average to high. There were no committees representing the lowest wage earners, such as private industry or construction workers. Average wage earners were among the port workers, post office engineers, and El Al employees, while the economy's highest wage earners were represented in the electric company engineers, aircraft industry employees, post office engineers, and naval officers.

g) Since they were employed in government enterprises, most labor groups represented in the Forum had security classification. For that reason the vast majority were by necessity Jewish—a fact that limited the employers' ability to restrain wages by means of a competitive unorganized labor force .

The key power source of the workers represented by the Forum was their vital role in production and world marketing. The two exceptions were the x-ray technicians and the television employees. The former were apparently invited through personal connections. The television employees were invited later, after they had declared a labor dispute, because of the centralized power of this monopolistic electronic medium.[5] The Forum's greatest threat, however, was to exports, and thus indirectly to the three largest employers at once: the government, the private industrialists, and *Hevrat Ovdim*.

As long as the Forum did not challenge the *Histadrut* legitimacy as the organization representing the workers, and the economic situation united the employers in their demand for wage restraint, the Forum filled a functional vacuum and indirectly strengthened the *Histadrut*. The *Histadrut* secretary-general could therefore count on the existence of the Forum to solve some of the *Histadrut's* structural problems. On the one hand, the Forum gave the *Histadrut* a rear guard of rank and file workers who opposed government policy without forcing the *Histadrut* to make structural changes and give these workers a voice in its bodies and decisions. On the other hand, the *Histadrut* was free of partnership in and responsibility for these workers' militant stance. The Forum's committees had direct ties with the workers, represented the two large parties, and were free of association with or obligation to the *Hevrat Ovdim*. In other words, the way in which the Forum was organized answered the *Histadrut's* needs, both as a group responsible for the entire economy, and primarily for the *Hevrat Ovdim*, and as a centralized body responsible to the government. Chapter 1 dealt with the centralist corporatist trade union's possible use of rank and file workers' organization to enhance their own power (Pizzorno, 1978; Sabel, 1981). The relationship between the *Histadrut* and the Forum was of this nature throughout 1980, as both the members and the secretary-general who supported the Forum, were aware (INT-BME, AS, AM, OY, and MY).

In a research interview, Meshel maintained that he had established the Forum on his own initiative, without the knowledge of his *Histadrut* and party colleagues. While this contention may be somewhat exaggerated, it is clear that Meshel gave the Forum his blessings and was aware of its potential benefit for the *Histadrut*. The Forum could help consolidate workers' opposition to Finance Ministry policy and avert an internal rift within the *Histadrut* over its contradictory roles as employer and the workers' representative, thereby helping to extricate the *Histadrut* from its difficulties and preventing the delegitimization of its structure at a particularly problematic historical juncture.

Early January 1980 was a time of unrest in the plants. Partial strikes occurred in various locations, particularly development towns. In a newspaper interview, Finance Ministry director-general Professor Ne'eman confirmed the workers' fears. "The first steps have already been taken," he said, "in the 19 November 1979 announcement of economic policy and in lowering the wage in El Al." The rest would follow, he added, "in what would happen afterwards to the wages of the rest of the public service workers" (*YA*. 1-3/1/80; *MA*. 23/1/80).

The Forum's first act was a twenty-four-hour general strike on

27 January 1980. On the face of it, the Forum's demands were identical to those of the *Histadrut*—renegotiating the framework agreements in April, updating tax grades, maintaining the real wage, and averting unemployment. The Forum struck and thus paralyzed Israel's expert activity and her air and sea connections with the rest of the world. Its leaders rejected Keisar's request to strike separately, a different committee each day. This was the *Histadrut's* style of struggle, according to which many labor councils received permission to protest government economic policy separately, each in its time and place. The Forum's strike, however, was essentially different, and its power was decidedly felt. But this strike, as noted, was designed to achieve not immediate fulfillment of demands but rather the symbolic objectives of recognition and identity. These objectives were in fact attained, to such an extent that the Forum never had to strike again during the entire period of its existence. From the 27 January 1980 strike on, the Forum's mere declaration of its intention to strike was a threat taken extremely seriously by the employers (*YA, MA.* 23-28/1/80).

After the Forum strike, Israel Keisar announced that the *Histadrut* was not asked to endorse the strike, but understands the workers' motives" (*MA.*, 27/1/80). This was the essence of the *Histadrut's* official attitude toward the Forum during its early days. The *Histadrut* was not responsible for the Forum's actions, which nevertheless expressed the working class's feelings. The *Histadrut* also had to serve as a voice for these feelings and for workers demands.

Strengthening the Histadrut

The Forum did not oppose the *Histadrut*-government dialogue that had been renewed with Yigael Horowitz's appointment as finance minister. Horowitz had asked the *Histadrut* to present its own suggestions for economic policy, including the prevention of unemployment. The fact that the *Histadrut's* memorandum to the government was formulated with *Hevrat Ovdim* participation is not incidental. Throughout his entire period of office, Horowitz attempted to exploit the *Hevrat Ovdim's* influence in the trade union department's wage demand discussions (INT-HY).

The *Histadrut's* corporatist status attributed by the state generated expectations of cooperative policies with government, but the question remained of how the negotiations between them would reflect the shifting balance of power. The weaker the *Histadrut*, the worse the compromise reached by the two sides for the workers; and the stronger the workers' pressure on the *Histadrut* to fight the government, the stronger

the *Histadrut's* position vis-a-vis the government as a vital factor for stabilizing economy, and the better the compromise for the workers. It was
in these terms that the workers' committees argued that the *Histadrut*
was weak and had to be strengthened.

The Forum, then, was not designed to compete with the *Histadrut*.
The Forum's intent, furthermore, was not to prevent *Histadrut*-govern-
ment dialogue but rather to fill the labor representation vacuum created
by the *Histadrut's* internal labor-capital contradiction, rendering it impo-
tent in the current economic crisis.

The first results of the government-*Histadrut* negotiations were the
agreements to pay COLA advances in January and March 1980. The
Histadrut maintained a complex relationship with the Finance Ministry,
conducting negotiations whose object was wage restraint, with the
cooperation of the *Lishkat Hateum*, on the practical plane, while at the
same time publicly attacking the finance minister for economic policies
that generated unemployment.

The 1980 May Day demonstration was a salient expression of this
complex *Histadrut* policy. The *Histadrut* had avoided organizing mass
May Day demonstrations for many years, and none have been held
since 1980. In May 1980, however, as wage agreement bargaining
approached and the finance minister opposed any wage increments
whatever, the *Histadrut* organized antigovernment demonstrations that
numbered, according to various estimates, between 100,000 and 250,000
(*YA., MA., D.* 2/5/80). The *Histadrut* was thus able to avert the outbreak
of strikes and channel the workers' anger and protest toward support
for the *Histadrut* and its demands in the coming negotiations.

This period saw a process like the one Pizzorno described, in
which the trade union becomes the spearhead of the opposition—a role
traditionally reserved for political parties. The *Histadrut's* advantage
over the Alignment parties was obvious: the *Histadrut's* various bodies
gave it direct access to the workplace, whether through labor councils
and through them to workers' committees, or through the trade unions.
The activities of the Forum, created to strengthen the *Histadrut* without
partisan considerations, also gave the *Histadrut* an advantage over the
Alignment as opposition. The May Day 1980 mobilization relied on all
these elements together, and the tens of thousands of marching workers
undoubtedly included Likud supporters. Indirectly, however, the fact
that the *Histadrut* leadership was pro-Alignment led to an upsurge of
that party's popularity in public opinion polls, which increased at an
astonishing rate despite the election defeat three years earlier, in May
1977.[6]

The May Day demonstration brought the *Histadrut* a double boost of power, in relation to both the workers and the government. The *Histadrut* was thus able to negotiate about the entire social order, compromise in the workers' name, and restrain wage demands in the framework of collective wage agreements in both the public and private sectors.

The bargaining on wage framework agreements was conducted formally between the *Histadrut* and the *Lishkat Hateum*—that is, as a private sector corporatist agreement—but in fact government representatives also participated, informally, in order to set uniform wage increases and thus moderate the anticipated high wage demands in the public sector (INT-HY).

The agreement was a compromise: an 11 percent increase (as the *Lishkat Hateum* had requested) was accepted, but the increase would be divided into two payments—the first, at 7.5 percent (below the Finance Ministry's request), to be paid the following month, and the second to be determined by the *Histadrut* and the *Lishkat Hateum* according to the inflation rate during the ensuing months. This agreement was signed on 1 July, officially for the private sector only. The finance minister, however, immediately announced his approval of the agreement and adopted it for the public sector. Thus the *Histadrut* and the government succeeded in imposing a restraining wage agreement on the strong public sector worker organizations without their participation in the negotiations. This achievement, however, was not to last long (*MA., YA.* 1-11/7/80, 15-30/6/80).

The results of the framework agreement negotiations express the balance of power among the partners in the political economy. After Horowitz and the employers attacked the workers with demands for wage restraint in December 1979, the workers organized to pressure the *Histadrut* and avert a compromise in their name. This organization was essential to restore the *Histadrut's* pivotal position. In May, the *Histadrut* mobilized the workers in a large demonstration of support, and by the end of June a well-coordinated collective wage agreement between the *Histadrut,* the government, and private employers was signed. The Forum heads then contended that the *Histadrut* had "taken care of the weak;" the agreement was good for weak workers but not for them.

While this outcome was the Forum's very goal and raison d'etre, after the framework agreements were signed each committee, especially the strong ones, hoped to reach plant level agreements. This expectation was based on a tacit understanding between the strong workers and the *Histadrut*—that the workers would rescue the *Histadrut* from its institutional crisis in exchange for a return to the previous system of wage bargaining split between strong and weak workers. The Forum had helped the *Histadrut* mobilize worker support, thereby strengthening the *Histadrut's* bargaining power vis-a-vis the employers in national, centralized negotiations. The *Histadrut* sought to avoid a rift with the workers and therefore accepted the Forum's assistance gladly. This restored the *Histadrut's* pivotal position and paved the way for its support for fragmented wage demands. Although the *Histadrut* enhanced its position as a result of its complex strategy, in July the government was still able to impose moderate wage agreements because the overall strength of labor was undermined by the threat of a downward turn in the business cycle. From July onwards, this change of attitude by private and *Histadrut* employers weakened the position of labor. After signing a restrained wage agreement, the private sector corporatist partners resumed behaving according to their former common structural interest in splitting the collective bargaining process. Their intention was to evade the strength of public sector workers, who stood to gain from the forthcoming political business cycle caused by the 1981 elections.

Failure of the Policy of Restraint

Days after the wage agreements were signed, the Finance Ministry announced a broad reduction of basic commodity subsidies, thereby driving the prices of these commodities sharply upwards. The real wage, which had shrunk during the first half of 1980, grew between July and September. Agreed wage increments swelled demand, which had been checked during the first half of the year; private consumption grew; the downturn in production halted; and there were even signs of economic growth, including more employment in the private sector. At the same time, however, unemployment rose, reaching a rate of 4.9 percent in the third quarter of the year and 5.2 percent in the last quarter. Expansion of economic activity led to a growth of imports, and the trade deficit began to deteriorate, in contrast to the marked improvement of the first half of the year. Improving the balance of payments, a goal the finance minister had designated as more important even than braking inflation, was becoming an unattainable objective. Economic expansion, growth of demand, the large quantities of money the salaried workers had at their disposal after the July wage agreement payments, and the reduction of basic commodity subsidies all accelerated the rate of price rises, which had been checked during the first half of the year. The peak 131 percent inflation of 1980 was due in no small measure to the spiral of the last quarter, when the annual rate reached 180 percent (Razin, 1982; *MA.* 11/7/80; *BI.* 31).

The effects of the July wage payments and climbing prices led the finance minister to call on the Manufacturers' Association and the *Histadrut* to negotiate an economic "package deal" that would halt the rise of wages, prices, and taxes. Toward the end of September, it became apparent that no agreement on the package deal would be reached. The Bank of Israel, viewing with trepidation the cash flow which the COLA and other imminent wage increments would entail, continued to pressure the *Histadrut* and the manufacturers to jointly propose a package deal. The Bank warned that if no package deal were signed it would have to limit credit and thereby damage exports. This warning was to no avail, and after further increases in basic commodity prices, *Histadrut* and Manufacturers' Association representatives met and agreed on a timetable for paying the second half of the wage increases the framework agreements required, at a rate of 7.5 percent within a month (*MA.* 8-15/9/80).

The finance minister's failure to gain the cooperation of his partners in corporatist negotiations stemmed from imbalance between the two sides' demands. Horowitz wanted restraint of wage demands, while the private sector was interested in the subsidization of capital investments under the banner of reducing unemployment. Budgetary difficulties prevented Horowitz from agreeing to expand government subsidization of capital, and the danger of a true revolt of both strong and weak workers prevented the *Histadrut* from granting wage restraint.

After the *Histadrut* and the Manufacturers' Association ignored the Bank of Israel's and Finance Ministry's repeated pleas to avoid paying the second half of the COLA, the Finance Ministry adopted a far-reaching measure. Horowitz cancelled the money-holding privileges the *Hevrat Ovdim* pension funds had enjoyed. This financial step, that was to place 1.3 billion Israeli shekels in the government treasury within a year, damaged what at that time was the economy's chief source of investment credit (*INT-BN.* and *HY.*). The arrangement in question was the "*Hevrat Ovdim* Program" that had been implemented during the Alignment government. According to this arrangement, 92 percent of regular pension fund assets had to be deposited with the accountant-general, whereas the *Histadrut* was allowed to deposit only half of its funds. The remaining pension fund monies allowed Bank *Hapoalim* to grant cheap credit to the entire private sector and not only to *Hevrat Ovdim* (*INT-BN.*; *MA.* 24/10/80).

The cancellation of the *Hevrat Ovdim* Program was, by all accounts, of great economic significance. The finance minister wished to limit Bank *Hapoalim's* ability to provide credit in defiance of his policies, and to control demand (*INT-HY*). This step hurt both private sector corporatist partners, the *Histadrut*, and the Manufacturers' Association. The cooperation between them had been extended in the June 1979 comprehensive pension agreement, whereby the manufacturers received cheap credit in exchange for expansion of the *Histadrut* pension funds. At that time, national negotiations on the entire economy's investment and pension policy had been conducted. From the beginning of 1979, it will be remembered, the *Histadrut* and the *Lishkat Hateum* had embarked on a new COLA and wage policy. In the wake of the controversy over wage and credit policy, Horowitz dealt a blow to what he saw as the basis for *Histadrut*-manufacturer cooperation—the ability to use the workers' money for granting credit (INT-HY).

By October 1980, Horowitz had despaired of winning his two partners' cooperation, the cornerstone of his policies since his appointment. Having expected strong opposition from the *Histadrut*, Horowitz was surprised by the subdued response to his financial step (INT-HY). Even though there was no immediate response to Horowitz' step, it was undoubtedly a radical change in the structure of state-*Histadrut* relationships instigating greater intervention of the state in capital markets. The long range impact of Horowitz' step was felt some years later.

The *Histadrut's* nonresponse to cancellation of the *Hevrat Ovdim* Program was unrelated to the effect this step had on the *Histadrut* as a business enterprise, but had to do rather with the *Histadrut's* difficulty in assenting to Horowitz's request to continue wage restraint. The *Histadrut*, hoping to avoid confrontation with the Forum and the public sector trade unions, blamed the government and the finance minister for the absence of wage increments. This was a continuation of the stance the *Histadrut* had maintained since the finance minister's appointment—cooperation along with public criticism. In addition, the *Histadrut's* strategy regarding the public sector wage demands it could not control had, since 1970, been to direct those demands toward the employer, namely the government.

The *Histadrut* and the private employers knew that any additional attempt to lower wages could lead to rebellion and loss of control over the workers. It should be recalled that the severe restraint of the real wage during the first half of 1980 and a price increase rate that accelerated to an annual level of 180 percent toward the end of that year lay behind the workers' bitterness. This is consistent with corporatist theory, which posits that it is precisely the anticipated power of the organized rank and file that prevents the centralized trade union from perpetuating wage restraint. The workers are not usually able to obtain high wage increases on a national level, but they can prevent the national centralized organization from agreeing to corporatist compromise in their name in national negotiations. Such was the Forum's position in November and December 1980. The Forum did not call a strike because it lacked the power to win the wage agreements the workers expected, but it was able to prevent a wage-restraining corporatist compromise between the government and the *Histadrut*. This is what Horowitz meant when he said that "the *Histadrut* understood the economic situation, but was drawn after the workers" (INT-HY).

During the last third of 1980, the *Histadrut* and the *Lishkat Hateum* again developed a centralized economic policy without the government, as they had during the second half of 1979. The private sector corporatist partners were doubly disappointed with the government: it failed to continue its encouragement of production and export, and yet at the same time asked the *Histadrut* to go on helping it restrain wages though it was beyond its abilities. The *Lishkat Hateum* recognized the *Histadrut's* needs to avoid conflict with strong workers' organizations and collaborated with it through *Hevrat Ovdim* in reaching segmented agreements .

By the end of December, the finance minister's lack of control of the economy had reached a nadir. Prices were spiralling upward and eroding wages, unemployment had reached a new high, and the credit situation was deteriorating. The *Histadrut* and the Manufacturers' Association had opposed the finance minister since the cancellation of the *Hevrat Ovdim* Program. The salaried workers, and the Forum in an organized manner, opposed any wage restraint and demanded increases. January 1981 public opinion polls showed the Likud's lowest level of popularity. Had elections been held at that time, the Alignment would have won 44 percent of the votes and Likud 19 percent (*MA*. 16/3/81).

Under these conditions, the finance minister's dismissal was only a matter of time. His failure lay in his inability to win support for wage restraint in the public sector, and the immediate reason for his resignation was the controversy over teachers' salaries with the prime minister (*MA*. 5-12/1/81).

Summing up the second half of 1980, it appears that the *Histadrut* faced contradictory demands from the workers and the government, the former calling for wage increases and the latter seeking further wage restraints. The *Histadrut* responded with a policy of abstention. While trying to prevent deterioration of the economy's labor relations and to calm the workers, the *Histadrut* opposed the Finance Ministry's proposed package deal. The PSC-*Histadrut*-*Lishkat Teum* partnership proved itself, both in its effort to keep wages from falling below the limit the strong workers would tolerate, and in the manufacturers' concern as employers over both diminishing profitability of production and the deteriorating export and credit situation. The *Histadrut's* stance allowed it to appear as the workers' representative, and even enhanced its popularity among them. Thanks to the *Histadrut*, the Alignment continued to enjoy its status as chief opposition and natural candidate for replacing the Likud government. This support, however, was based on a certain economic situation that had increased in severity between mid-1979 and the end of 1980. Changes in the economic situation, therefore, could undo the basis of the *Histadrut* and Alignment popularity and thus significantly alter the political balance. This indeed happened, when the extremely pro-employer finance minister Horowitz was replaced with Aridor. Inertia kept the Forum in existence, but as it was no longer necessary for political exchange in the new political and economic situation and lacked the support of its constituencies in its action, it soon disintegrated.

Discussion: Workers' Resistance-Structure and Dynamics

The 1980 economic recession was one of the clearest manifestations of conflict between labor and capital. State and private employers cooperated to decrease wages generally and those of strong public sector workers specifically. Under these conditions, the political economic pattern of regulation of class conflict, in which the *Histadrut* has a pivotal position, was in grave danger.

During the new low ebb of the business cycle, the working class and its position within the *Histadrut* were weakened. The *Histadrut* as an institution faced two different dangerous processes: (1) horizontal association of workers' committees threatening revolt; (2) state autonomous procapital policies. The subjects of this analysis are the tactical and strategic reactions to cyclical changes of the workers, *Histadrut*, employers and state, and their struggle to maintain their position within the existing structures.

The *Histadrut* managed to transform the deep class conflict into a reinforced alliance with its PSC employer partner, directing workers anger against the Likud government. As was remarked in chapter 2, the *Histadrut's* political structure is derived from the segmented structure of the labor market. Both structures survived the temporary storm of economic recession. A possible explanation of this success is that the labor market recession, which provided the basis for capital's offensive, was only a temporary contingency.

The rank and file workers' militancy was not intended to change structures. This study suggests that the stability of economic and political structures should be understood in relation to the backing they receive from social and political groups connected to and empowered by them. If structural factors are based on strong, organized groups, then the spontaneous organizations and forces thrown up by the fluctuating processes are usually not powerful enough to change them. This was the case of the Forum.

The contradiction of labor and capital prevented the *Histadrut* from coordinating the interests of each. The managers in the *Hevrat Ovdim* supported the government and private employers' policy of dismissals, whereas the labor representatives demanded full employment and wage increases. In the absence of representative trade unions and exclusive working class parties, and under conditions of a split labor market, the general weakness of the working class affected strong labor groups too.

This was the first time these groups had been directly threatened by employers. Yet the Forum rejected a strategy to change structures. It is true that they considered establishing representative, independent trade unions under their leadership for all workers, and that the formation of a "'work committee' list," including both Labor and Likud members for the 1981 elections, was debated. Nevertheless, their realistic political sense led them to adopt a defensive strategy. They organized separately from the weak labor groups, while supporting general working class demands and pressurizing the *Histadrut* in its internal process of inter-class mediation.

The Forum organized at a time of economic recession, when the Likud faced a legitimation crisis as the governing party and the Labor party had the same problem in the *Histadrut*. The tension between labor and capital was evident, open and could potentially erupt into organized class conflict. Against this background, the establishment of the Forum and its action was a pseudorevolt.

As their strategy was defensive, once the conjuncture causing the recession crisis was over, the Forum became redundant and each workers' committee returned to its previous, strong position in split wage bargaining. They left intact the former structures which their strength originated in, as well as the political forces supporting them: the dual structure of the state, the dual labor market, the *Histadrut*-private employers political exchange pattern embodied in PSC, and the Likud and Labor parties. These are all the forces which might be expected to react against the Forum, were it to attempt to change the existing structure.

It seems that the thirteen strongest committees were able to defeat these forces in a few battles, but were unable to defeat them in a war. Awareness of this meant that the strategy chosen by the Forum was pragmatic, and the most suitable for their interests: to maintain their separate workers' committee strength. It also explains why the *Histadrut* secretary-general regarded the Forum as a positive initiative: he saw its potential for extracting the *Histadrut* from its legitimation crisis and rescuing it from its internal contradiction. That is precisely what the Forum did.

Corporatist scholars (Pizzorno, 1978; Sabel, 1981) emphasize the interdependence of centralized trade unions and rank and file militants. The Israeli case confirms this claim. The theoretical conceptualization proposed here is that when class conflict erupts the corporatist unions temporarily lose the power of deterrence they needed, because of their tendency to negotiate and consent without struggle. Rank and file militancy restores the unions' role as mediator between labor and employers, reinforcing their bargaining position.

The specific pattern of workers militancy should be analyzed within the specific structure of the labor market, the degree of organization and strength of labor, and their relationship with centralized trade unions. A dual labor market may have two different influences on worker-union relations. If the unions are actually afraid of a workers' revolt and complete delegitimation of their representative role, the weak and unorganized workers might assist employers and unions in their common goal of defeating rank and file opposition. In other cases, such as Israel, the strong workers receive a "payment" for their consent to the splitting of labor, which leaves segments of them in complete dependence on the centralized trade unions. This "payment" for the maintenance of a split labor market must be made with the employers' collaboration, on the basis of a sophisticated pattern of political exchange.

This analysis has led to an investigation of the power structure of labor organization in Israel. The two different strong labor groups (professionals and employees of state-owned companies) are "channeled" into bargaining in the public sector, but the bases of their struggles differ, as the previous chapter explained. The shift from reliance on the Forum to reliance on the trade unions represents a change from fragmented corporatism, operating in the private sector only, to a split corporatist pattern. That change will be discussed in the following chapter.

The political consent between private sector corporatist partners is based on the tacit agreement to make the state "pay the bill" for the splitting of strong from weak workers, and for maintenance of the dual labor market. The state was able to take some autonomous (from PSC) procapital initiatives in a situation of internal rivalry between labor and capital. The Israeli case confirms Schmitter's (1985:49) claim, while application of his conceptualization of the state as an institution to it was found to be useful.

The state formed a political coalition with the employers, from November 1979 to July 1980. After that private employers and *Hevrat Ovdim* returned to the stable private sector corporatist coalition with the *Histadrut*. They helped the *Histadrut* overcome threats from workers and the state, thus reinstating it in its pivotal position in the political economy. This realignment was due also to the Likud's abandonment of Horowitz's policies, because of fear of their unpopularity as the 1981 elections approached. The role of the ruling party and the political business cycle in the political economic pattern are the subject of the next chapter.

CHAPTER 4

THE DYNAMICS OF SPLIT CORPORATISM: GOVERNMENT VERSUS PRIVATE SECTOR CORPORATISM

This chapter discusses a lengthy period of power struggles between the state and PSC partners, from January 1981 to January 1983. At the beginning of this period the ruling party's (the Likud's) economic policy, was designed to benefit the public so that the Likud would win the elections in July 1981. The Likud's previous institutional detachment from private sector corporatism was aggravated after the elections as the government had to recoup the money it had poured into the economy, a need characteristic of any political business cycle. The high expectations of strong workers and the political rivalry of the *Histadrut* with the Likud government made it impossible to reach a corporatist understanding, and encouraged the development of a very sophisticated split corporatist agreement at the end of this period. The government-PSC confrontation was echoed by an internal struggle within the *Histadrut* between those seeking an agreement with the government, led by Secretary-general Meshel, and those supporting split negotiations, led by the head of the trade union department Keisar.

The theoretical question of this chapter is that of the ruling party's ability to coordinate the interests of capital and labor. Corporatism is an institutional approach which does not assume an a priori structural commitment of the state to either side in class conflict. Thus the government's behavior as an institution becomes an empirical question. This chapter deals with the ruling party's attempts to mediate class conflict and its failure given the Likud's lack of organizational means to aggregate labor and capital interests.

At the end of the period covered by this chapter a quadripartite agreement between the *Histadrut*, private employers, public trade unions and the state was signed after complicated and secret negotiations. This agreement embodies the central analytical concept of this book—the split corporatist pattern of the political economy. Split corporatism controls class conflict by means of the *Histadrut's* political mediation, discrimination against weak workers and external subsidy of the state (in effect, by the U.S.A.). In this political economic pattern there are two different levels of collective bargaining in the private and public sector, both mediated by the *Histadrut*. Until 1982 split corporatism was put into effect by the *Histadrut* and private employers for their own interests, with the tacit approval of public workers and the state. But the example of split corporatism examined here was a deal consented to directly by all sides, except workers in the private sector.

Split corporatism has two structural features—the split labor market and the *Histadrut's* representation of both labor and capital. The complete development of the pattern was possible only after the Likud's ascent to power, and the concomitant political divorce between the state and *Histadrut*. This chapter demonstrates that it was only after the Likud undertook a policy of "election economics" in order to be reelected that the full significance of the Likud's detachment from labor and capital was revealed. Immediately after the elections the political business cycle dictated the extraction of resources previously distributed, but the Likud government was unable to find partners prepared to collaborate in stabilizing the economy.

The Re-Election Policy

Even before Yoram Aridor was appointed finance minister,[1] the government had begun its campaign for early elections. The policy known as "election economics" was not new either in Israel or elsewhere; many studies have demonstrated the existence of a "political" business cycle (Ben Porat, 1975; Temkin and Ben Hanan, 1986). According to this cycle, the ruling party offers the public numerous benefits in an election year, raising standards of living through a generous economic policy. However Aridor's policies differed from the "normal" political business cycle in several respects:

a) Just before his resignation, Horowitz was explicitly attacked by his party colleagues for failing to take re-election into account.
b) Aridor's appointment was simultaneous with the government's announcement of its intention to hold early elections, within five months.
c) Aridor completely reversed Horowitz's economic policies: from reduction of government spending, demand, and subsidies to their expansion; from preference for exports to preference for imports; and halting devaluation.
d) After Horowitz had resigned over wage problems, warning of the dire consequences of breaking the framework agreements, many plant and branch level wage agreements that exceeded the ceiling stipulated in the collective agreements were signed, between January and June 1981.
e) Aridor unilaterally raised the amount of disposable income by changing the income tax grades.

The Likud, which had lost support from its working class constituents in 1979-1980, had to win them back during a relatively short election campaign and tried to do so through a series of clear and rapid changes. As soon as he was appointed, Aridor announced his intention of paying full COLAs which would compensate the salaried workers for rising prices. The government enterprise employees demanded 30 percent plant increments and most of them (the first being the electric company workers) declared separate labor disputes soon afterwards (*MA.* 12/2/81, 20-26/1/81).

The *Histadrut* secretary-general initiated talks with the new finance minister. The two discussed economic plans and ways to compensate the workers for rising prices. These negotiations were conducted in secret due to Aridor's chief demand: to revoke the COLA agreement that had been signed between the *Histadrut* and the *Lishkat Hateum* and to sign instead a *Histadrut*-government agreement that would provide a monthly COLA payment of 100 percent of the consumer price index rise. The *Histadrut* did not accept this proposal immediately, and hinged its agreement on the monthly updating of tax grades, child allowances, and tax credit points.[2] At the same time, the *Histadrut* was also conducting secret negotiations with the Manufacturers' Association on compensating workers for salary erosion (*MA.* 12/2/81, 22-29/1/81).

In mid-February 1981, the *Histadrut* signed an agreement with the private employers according to which a 5 percent advance would be paid in March as compensation for wage erosion. Aridor accused the manufacturers of signing that agreement in order to sabotage his attempts to reach an agreement that would provide full COLA payment every month. According to the manufacturers, such an agreement would raise the real wage by 10 percent. The Finance Ministry was forced to accept the *Histadrut*-Manufacturers' Association agreement as a fait accompli, and extended its application to the public sector as well (*MA*. 15-17/2/81).

The opposing positions of the Finance Ministry which demanded a 100 percent COLA, and the Manufacturers' Association, which rejected such a payment out of hand, forced the *Histadrut* to choose one of the two potential partners. The decision was to continue the policy that had taken shape toward the end of Horowitz's period of office: private sector corporatism in which the *Histadrut* and the Manufacturers' Association jointly operated a wage restraint policy, while the demands of the public sector workers were directed toward the government. Ever since the government's decision to give the teachers increments beyond those stipulated in the framework agreements, the *Histadrut* had stopped trying to restrain the public sector workers' wages and instead supported their demands.

The 5 percent compensation did not satisfy the public sector workers, who had been waiting since the end of December for the results of the teachers' dispute in order to demand increases that exceeded the framework agreements. The signing of the agreement between the *Histadrut* and the private employers initiated a period of public sector labor disputes which involved the teachers, university academic staff, kindergarten teachers, engineers, and government employees (*MA*. 2/3/81, 17-24/2/81). The Likud, as the party in power, had come to recognize the positive role the *Histadrut* played vis-a-vis the workers, and avoided impairing its structure and comprehensiveness. After a brief threat to pass a state health service law in February 1981, Aridor returned to the tried and true method employed by all previous Israeli governments—pressuring the *Histadrut* through the *Kupat Holim* budget (INT-BN; *MA*. 10-11/2/81).

After he failed to reach a COLA agreement with the *Histadrut*, Aridor implemented unilateral increases of the real wage. The first and most significant increase took effect on 3 March 1981, when purchase and income taxes were lowered and property and inheritance taxes were rescinded. This policy lowered the prices of household consumer items by 10-15 percent, while lowering the income tax rate by changing tax grades. As a result, all salaried workers paid significantly lower taxes. The Bank of Israel reacted to these steps with surprise, accused the Finance Ministry of not consulting the bank, and expressed doubt as to whether the budget could be put into effect after the tax cuts (*MA.*, *YA.* 3/3/81).

Between March and June 1981 government expenses grew significantly, especially through subsidy supports and wage raises. The real wage rose 11.5 percent compared with the second half of 1980, and disposable income rose even more due to the easing of taxes. Generous wage agreements on the branch and plant levels raised public sector wage increases above those of the private sector. At the same time, private consumption grew, and the larger subsidies of basic products ensured a relatively low price level compared to the second half of 1980 (*BI.* 32).

After the Likud was re-elected, a number of economic changes began that damaged relations between the three parties to the corporatist agreements. Although the economic figures for 1981 show a rise of 9.8 percent in the real wage, 14 percent in disposable income, and 10.5 percent in private consumption, the figures for each half of the year reveal a change of trend during the second half.

The COLA controversy between the government and the *Lishkat Hateum* was renewed, this time against the background of accelerating inflation and slowed production growth. The Finance Ministry suggested the COLA agreement it had originally proposed to the *Histadrut*, whereby a 100 percent increment would be paid every month and tax grades would be adjusted accordingly. The Finance Ministry laid down a condition, however: cancellation of the wage increase agreement the *Histadrut* had signed with the *Lishkat Hateum* (*MA.* 3-13/8/81). In other words, the Finance Ministry's proposed agreement included wage restraint but also a political condition, ending the intimate cooperation between the *Histadrut* and the private employers. The *Histadrut* hesitated until the beginning of October, when it signed a COLA agreement with the *Lishkat Hateum* according to the previously agreed upon formula (*MA.* 2-3/10/81).

Erosion of the real wage continued into November, while labor disputes and demands for wage increases proliferated. The elections were over and the finance minister now sought restraint. The dispute that commanded the most attention, however, was in El Al, where eighteen flight engineers had received letters of dismissal. Since the ensuing two-week strike in El Al represented a turning point in government-*Histadrut*-private employer relations, it is worth considering some of its features.

The strike was called at the initiative of the workers' committees, assisted by the Forum, which supported them without announcing any intention to strike. The El Al workers were also supported by two cabinet ministers—David Levy and Yoram Aridor. The *Histadrut* failed in its attempt to mediate between the El Al workers and their management. The *Histadrut*, moreover, was unwilling to support the workers' struggle and contended that it was designed, at the ministers' instigation, to depose the company's chairman.

Two events in the course of the dispute lit a red light for the *Histadrut* heads. The first was a meeting in which the Forum and the finance minister discussed the economic situation. This meeting aroused some suspicion of "prior coordination" between those Forum members who were Likud activists in the *Histadrut* and the finance minister. The second event was a Forum meeting in which the Likud members demanded that David Levy be congratulated for his intervention on the workers' behalf. At that meeting, party divisions within the Forum became apparent (INT-OY, *BME*; *MA*. 18-20/11/81).

In the wake of the dispute over the El Al flight engineers, the *Histadrut* rescinded its recognition of the Forum. Israel Keisar announced publicly that as far as the *Histadrut* was concerned "there was no such body." He also accused the finance minister of trying to cause a rift between the *Histadrut* and the Manufacturers' Association (*MA*. 22-29/11/81).

The deterioration of Forum-*Histadrut* relations and the Forum's internal party division were the results of far-reaching changes in the economic situation. The finance minister had bypassed the *Histadrut* and granted the workers increases beyond what the *Histadrut* had demanded. The 1981 real wage rose, in contrast to its 1980 drop. The worker-employer confrontation that had characterized 1980 was replaced by one between the government, which was offering wage increases, and the private sector employers, who opposed increases and were trying to use the *Histadrut* to achieve wage restraint in their sector.

These circumstances destroyed the workers' common interest, who therefore split between the strong public sector committees and the private sector workers with weak market capacities. The strong committees were able to obtain increases on their own from the government, which was generous to them during the first half of 1981. The common interest that had united the Forum committees and served as the basis for their solidaristic action disappeared along with that of the workers. In the absence of such a clear common interest, internal controversy over the Forum's methods and its relationship with both the *Histadrut* and the government grew. The strong body that had voiced the workers' resistance to lowered wages in 1980 and supported the *Histadrut's* demand to open the framework agreements became, in 1981, a group with no clear function and whose ability to act in concert or mobilize the workers was questionable.

The Histadrut between Two Strategies:
Homogeneous or Split Corporatism

The large government expenditure of 1981 left the public with considerable monetary assets and led to a stock market boom. This explains the growth of private consumption despite the 1982 drop in the real wage. The financial boom and the growth of imports allowed the government to increase its income despite other factors: the reduction of industrial production and exports, reduced employment in the productive sector, and the growth of unemployment. The Finance Ministry thus had the opportunity, which it exploited in full measure, to carry out national economic policy without its traditional partners, the *Histadrut* and the manufacturers. Instead of cooperating with the productive sector, the finance minister relied on cooperation with the banks; instead of conducting a centralized wage policy together with the *Histadrut,* he tried to make the Forum a collective bargaining participant (INT-AS; *BI.* 34).

After the November 1981 El Al flight engineers episode, a struggle developed between two conflicting camps within the *Histadrut,* one represented by Secretary-general Yeruham Meshel and the other by trade union department chairman Israel Keisar. Both agreed that the continued existence of the Forum endangered the *Histadrut,* weakening rather than strengthening it under the new conditions of economic prosperity. However, the two adopted radically differing strategies. Meshel hoped for tripartite government-*Histadrut*-private employer talks, as in the days of Horowitz's restraining policies, on the clear condition that the *Histadrut's* exclusive right to conduct wage bargaining in the workers' name be recognized. In exchange for this recognition, the *Histadrut* was to propose wage restraint. Meshel's objective could be defined as homogeneous corporatism—a government-employer-centralized trade union exchange—in which the union agrees to restrain wages in exchange for recognition as the workers' sole representative.

Keisar worked on two fronts: (1) centralization of the trade union department's control of the public sector workers. This centralized policy was intended on the one hand to create a body that would replace the Forum as the "vanguard of the workers' struggle" and the *Histadrut's* "front line troops" and on the other hand to reinstate the *Histadrut* as the centralized union capable of delivering wage restraint to the government if it agreed to joint negotiations; (2) centralized bargaining with the *Lishkat Hateum* toward wage restraint in the private sector.

This plan of action led to the dissolution of the Forum in May

1982, the strengthening of the *Histadrut's* status in relation to both the workers and the government, and the reinforcement of private sector corporatism. In effect, what was being developed was a more sophisticated version of the *Histadrut's* traditional pivotal position. Keisar's tactical moves, taken together, took the form of a well-planned alternative strategy to Meshel's plan, a strategy called split corporatism in this study. One effect of Keisar's moves bore personal significance. His position was strengthened while Meshel's was weakened.

The clash between Meshel and Keisar was not whether to sign wage agreements at all or whether to restrain the workers' demands, but rather the larger question of whether a homogeneous corporatist bargain like that of June 1980 was needed under conditions of Aridor-style economic prosperity. The 1980 agreement restrained all wages in both the public and private sectors. This was accomplished through tripartite bargaining and through the *Histadrut's* control of the demands of the public sector workers, thereby assisting the government. This restraining agreement was violated by the government during the election campaign. The internal discussion was about whether the *Histadrut* should do the "dirty work" of curbing strong public sector workers' demands.

At the heart of the government-*Histadrut* controversy was the question of wage restraint in the public sector. Keisar knew that the expectations of the strong public sector unions were much higher than what could be obtained in the private sector, and that his ability to keep the public sector demands within bounds was limited. He therefore worked for a detachment of the bargaining process into two parts and two separate agreements. This would allow a restraining agreement in the private sector while the public sector unions flexed their muscles. In order to prevent the resurgence of the Forum as a group able to act militantly, strike, and paralyze production in a possible confrontation with the finance minister over public sector framework agreements, Keisar established an organization of public sector trade unions that would act according to the *Histadrut's* principle of responsibility, under the supervision of the trade union department.

Thus at the end of April 1982, after the finance minister had refused to pay erosion compensation, an announcement in the name of the "thirteen biggest trade unions in the country" stated that they would begin protest meetings against the non-payment of compensation in the public and private sectors. The unions included were the organization of civil servants, clerical workers, engineers, technicians, social workers, biochemists, microbiologists, pharmacists, jurists, journalists, and civilian employees of the Israel Defense Forces. Common to all these unions was their participation in the public sector's collective bargaining process. The choice of the number thirteen and the name "big trade unions" revealed the purpose of the organization for which Keisar had worked from the end of December 1981—a positive, responsible, and controllable alternative to the Forum, which continued flirting with the Finance Ministry (*MA*. 29/4/82).

At the same time, relations between the *Histadrut* and the private employers were coming along well. They were holding talks nearing their conclusion on new wage and COLA agreements, in which both Meshel and Keisar participated (*MA*. 4-6/5/82).

The finance minister's failure to make the Forum the workers' representative, as well as the renewal of talks between the *Histadrut* and the private employers, became an almost total fiasco when his confrontations caused controversy with his senior staff members. While Aridor was visiting the U.S., Finance Ministry Director-general Ezra Sadan and Keisar signed an agreement according to which the ministry would pay 5 percent erosion compensation for the duration of the wage negotiations. This had been the *Histadrut's* original demand. When he returned, Aridor declared the agreement invalid and announced his intention to meet with the Forum. His two senior assistants, the director-general and the staff member responsible for the wage negotiations rejected both steps (*MA*. 10-17/5/82).

Aridor did meet with Forum representatives, but both sides had less impact on the collective bargaining than the other two parties—the *Histadrut* and the private employers (*MA*. 18/5/82). These two partners were already close to a separate collective agreement in the private sector, without government participation and without consideration of the public sector wage. The public sector trade unions, in coordination with the *Histadrut*, had organized for a prolonged struggle entailing strikes and sanctions designed to produce results better than those of the private sector.

When the Israeli ambassador in London was shot and the Israel Defense Forces invaded Lebanon on 6 June 1982, the confrontation between the government and the *Histadrut* was at its height. The trade unions had declared labor disputes, while the *Histadrut* and *Lishkat Hateum* had set 9 June 1982 as the date for signing the private sector framework agreement. Under these conditions, the government, with no role in any of the negotiations, was powerless. Labor disputes and strikes threatened to break out in the public sector (*MA*. 3-4/6/82).

The scheduled 9 June *Histadrut-Lishkat Hateum* meeting did in fact take place, at the height of the war, and two agreements were signed. The first stipulated a 10 percent wage increase for 1982-1984 in the private sector; the second, a flexible 80-90 percent COLA for that period, to be paid four times yearly according to the inflation rate. The finance minister's reaction to both these agreements was vehement. He protested both his nonparticipation in the discussions and decisions and the rise of the real wage entailed by the private sector agreement (*MA*. 9-10/6/82).

These agreements were actually a reflection of the Finance Ministry-*Histadrut* power balance that had prevailed during May. The private sector corporatist partners had improved their cooperative relationship through a step that exacerbated labor relations in the public sector while decentralizing the authority to conduct a labor dispute to the trade union level. But by 9 June the state was involved in a war whose economic and political significance was great, and what was the case for May was not necessarily so in June. The finance minister responded by threatening the agreement with unilateral steps that would absorb the wage increases deriving from the private sector framework agreements and COLA arrangement. This threat consisted of levying taxes (*MA*. 10-22/6/82).

There is no doubt that at the beginning of the war the workers were quite ready to back the government with a consensus and pay the price that entailed. The sense of national emergency also gave Aridor's call for wage restraint new legitimacy,[3] and the *Histadrut* and private employers were responsive to his demand for tripartite talks on a wage, tax, and price package deal.

Despite the controversy over the private sector agreement, the three sides entered package deal negotiations and two weeks later, on 22 July 1982, an agreement was reached. Despite its title, this was not a true "package deal" since the government had the authority to act unilaterally on the clauses included. The tripartite agreement stipulated that a compulsory "Peace in the Galilee" loan would be imposed and the subsidies for basic products reduced to a rate of 25-50 percent of the producer's cost. The agreement did not cover the wage and price restraint policy, the COLA, and other crucial issues. In other words, the *Histadrut* did not grant the government the wage restraint it had sought but rather a legitimization of tax and price increases under conditions the war had created—the need to impose the "Peace in the Galilee" loan and raise the prices of basic products (*MA*. 23/7/82).

A New Package Deal: Split Corporatism

When exports fell and imports grew, the service sector expanded with the financial boom. Production was curtailed, and the government was left with few means of bringing its corporatist private sector partners into discussions of a nationwide, centralized arrangement that could limit its own wage costs. In July and August of 1982, however, the *Histadrut* encouraged the public sector workers to prove their strength. For this reason, the Finance Ministry chose El Al as an arena in which it would be difficult for the *Histadrut* to maintain its policies.

The Finance Ministry's objective in the El Al dispute was to subject the *Histadrut* to pressures from two groups of workers that it had encouraged to act under its supervision. One comprised those trade unions interested in accelerating negotiations on the 1982-1984 framework agreements, which had expired in April; the other, the Forum committees that had joined the *Histadrut* in defending the El Al workers and demanded a militant struggle (Friedman, 1982; *MA.* 1/9/82; *HA.* 28/11/82).

The El Al management responded to the workers' action by announcing a lock-out: the company would open only when the workers accepted a series of conditions that included dismissals, closing the company on the Sabbath, discipline, and abstention from future labor disputes or joint organization with other workers (*MA.* 17/9/82-3/10/82). It was hard to convince the public sector workers that their chief concern should be defending their El Al colleagues when their actual worry was over the erosion of their wages. Inflation was spiralling and there was no framework agreement for the coming two years. Along with the *Histadrut,* these workers were engaged in a struggle whose chances of success were slim.

The government fully backed the El Al management's closure of the company. This effort to discipline the workers and restrict the workers' committees' right to strike while campaigning publicly was clearly intended to curtail their central role in the Forum and in the public sector as a whole.

The most significant aspect of the collective bargaining that led to the 1982-1984 public sector framework agreement was the trade unions' participation. As noted, Israel Keisar had established a joint public sector trade union organization as an alternative to the Forum. During negotiations this organization became a centralized trade union itself, playing a role in split corporatism. They entered into collective bargaining and helped to restrain wages. The bargaining was split, however, in that the wage restraint granted was not necessarily or principally among the workers it represented, but rather among others who did not participate in the negotiations. This phenomenon is central to split corporatism.

Since September, the public sector workers had been receiving the

10 percent wage increase stipulated in the intermediary agreement signed by the Finance Ministry and the *Histadrut* leadership. This increase was equal to that received by the private sector workers, but far from satisfied the public sector employees. Scoring a major achievement, the trade union department chairman had been able to convince all the union representatives to agree on uniform wage demands for the purpose of collective bargaining. At the heart of these demands was the redefinition of wage scales. The lower levels were to be eliminated, and all levels would receive increases, ranging from 45 percent for the lower levels to a minimum of 22 percent for the intermediary and 30-35 percent for the high levels (*HA*. 28/11/82, 7, 9, 12, 14, 17, 31/12/82, 3/1/83).

This was the first time all the unions had ever forged a common stance. Since 1970, the framework agreements had stipulated only the minimum wage for all workers. Each union and workers' committee later negotiated its own plant and branch increments beyond this minimum basis.

At the end of 1982, after the El Al workers had been defeated and the Forum had dissolved, the time was ripe for convincing the unions of the need for responsible, restrained, centralized bargaining.[4] For that purpose, the *Histadrut* left a gap between the private sector agreement, signed in June, and the beginning of public sector bargaining in October. This allowed the unions to start with higher bargaining positions and lessened chances of comparison between the two sectors.

The finance minister, however, did not share the *Histadrut's* intent and attacked it for having signed a separate agreement in June, without his participation. Not only was the government excluded from private sector corporatism, but the COLA agreement had also been signed without its participation, though it was expected that the finance minister would honor the agreement and pay the COLA in the public sector as well, to avoid conflict with the public sector workers.[5]

Since his assumption of office, Aridor had sought to participate in the COLA negotiations and even wished to replace the framework agreements with the COLA as an exclusive wage policy instrument. This position became a bone of contention between Aridor and the private sector corporatist partners, who wished to maintain their exclusive authority over the COLA, as well as the separation of the public and private sectors in negotiating the biennial framework agreements. The common need of the government and the *Histadrut* to conclude a public sector framework agreement led Aridor to seek joint centralized national negotiations on the wage policy as a whole. He did this through his request to reach a new COLA agreement together with the *Histadrut*, and made that a condition for his signing the public sector wage agreement (*HA*. 15-19/11/82, 6/12/82).

However, the public sector trade union organization contended, with *Histadrut* backing, that the finance minister was not a party to the collective COLA negotiations and refused to bargain with him on that subject. Moreover, they refused to compromise on the COLA in exchange for the wage increases they wanted, as the Finance Ministry had requested. The *Histadrut* proposed a compromise between the Finance Ministry and the unions, which would divide the bargaining process between two groups. One would discuss the public sector framework agreements and include Finance Ministry, *Histadrut*, and trade union representatives; the other would discuss the COLA agreement and comprise the Finance Ministry, the *Histadrut*, and the *Lishkat Hateum*.

The Finance Ministry and the unions accepted this proposal, but the government regarded the division as a technicality, whereas the *Histadrut* considered it essential. Or rather they presented it publicly as a significant move, but the reality behind the scenes shows that they did consider it as a technical play. Aridor succeeded in imposing on the *Histadrut* his condition of tying the two agreements together, but his failure to unify the centralized wage policy making processes gave the *Histadrut* the upper hand. It was during these negotiations that the split corporatist pattern took shape (*HA*. 6, 15, 23/12/82).

The finance minister had demanded a different system of calculating the COLA, one that would not fan the inflationary fires as did the existing system. He proposed paying the COLA every month at the rate of inflation programmed in advance by his Ministry—5 percent per month.[6]

But the *Histadrut* "had made an offer they couldn't refuse" (as Ministry officials said): COLA would be paid every three months at a rate of 80 percent of the increase in the price rise index, instead of 85 percent, and the January index would be excluded from calculations.[7] According to this method of calculation, the degree of restraint was unquestionably greater than that the Finance Ministry had proposed. The agreement was initialled in secret, as was the accord that the public signing would be postponed until after the public sector wage agreement was signed (*HA*. 16, 24, 31/12/82; 3/1/83; *YA*. 9/1/83).

Immediately after this positive outcome of the COLA negotiations, a public sector wage agreement whose generosity surprised even the militant unions was reached. The new wage scales included 45 percent increments for the lower levels and up to 40 percent for the higher levels; the intermediary levels received the minimum increments of 22 percent. Fifteen days after the public sector wage agreements were signed, the new COLA agreement was ratified in a public ceremony. It was only then that the true nature of the split package deal that had been secretly signed under *Histadrut* direction was revealed. The January 1983 COLA would in fact be paid according to the old agreement, at a rate of 21 percent, as the workers had expected, but starting in April payments would be calculated according to the new agreement and wage restraint would thus be intensified (*HA*. 31/12/82, 3, 9, 10/1/83).

Wage curbs would be achieved in the public sector by lowering the April COLA payment from an estimated 18 percent to 13 percent, thus closing the 5 percent disparity between the Finance Ministry's and the unions' proposals. Restraint in the private sector would be attained by effectively lowering the workers' wages in April by 5 percent through the COLA restrictions, thus detracting from their 10 percent pay increase.

This four sided (*Histadrut*-state-employers-public sector unions) political exchange constitutes a complex political economic pattern, here called split corporatism. The agreement in question is corporatist in that it was centrally negotiated by the government, the employers, and the *Histadrut* and determines wage policies for the entire economy. The agreement is split insofar as the strong trade unions take part in it and receive wage increases in exchange for their willingness to lower the wages of the weak workers.

Discussion: The Likud's Inability to Coordinate Interests

Split corporatism is a phenomenon characteristic of Israeli political economy which developed in a very peculiar historical process. This pattern is based on the structure of a labor market split along ethnic and national lines, and the institutionalized mediation between capital and labor, without state intervention, resulting from the *Histadrut's* political economic structure. The differential power of workers in the labor market motivates weak workers' employers to make collective wage agreements separately. Strong workers' organizations are also interested in this separation, but need some organizational body able to coordinate this latent collaboration with employers. This is the *Histadrut's* central role.

The *Histadrut's* structure facilitates the coordination of interests with private employers and strong labor organizations. In the split corporatist pattern there are two levels of labor-capital mediation and compromise. The private employers negotiate their sectoral agreements for the weak workers with the *Histadrut,* on the basis of private sector corporatist partnership. Strong workers' organizations (including private sector employees) are diverted to public sector bargaining with the government, mediated by the *Histadrut.* The *Histadrut* is the only entity involved in the two levels of class conflict regulation, which is essential to its pivotal position in the political economy.

The state as a structure found itself isolated from capital and labor, which may be connected with it institutionally through their representation in the ruling party. Such an institutional link prevailed while the Labor party ruled both *Histadrut* and state until 1977, but was then seriously damaged by the Likud's ascent to power. The whole political economic pattern was threatened, and the Likud's ability to coordinate interests and regulate class conflict was in question.

The change in government in Israel in 1977 illustrates the inability of the ruling party of the state to impose its policy on the *Histadrut,* and the distinct dynamics operating when different parties are in government. The Likud's political manifesto before 1977 declared its intention to transform the *Histadrut* from a comprehensive, quasi-state institution to a "normal" trade union. According to this study, the Likud government did not effect this change because it recognized that the *Histadrut's* policies were responsible and cooperative, as it depended on the state for subsidies. Additionally, the Likud's ideological commitment to continue the occupation, left intact the two central bases of split corporatism. The Likud's maintenance of the *Histadrut's* political structure and split labor market, without a reciprocal commitment from labor to the ruling party, encouraged the partners of PSC to develop their own autonomous policies and the complex split corporatist pattern.

The January 1983 public sector wage agreement embodies split corporatism. The wage increases demanded by the public sector unions were obtained in exchange for restraint of the wages of the private sector workers. Lowering the private sector wages was in the interests of *Hevrat Ovdim* and of the private employers, and could help the Finance Ministry in its macroeconomic policies, but not as an employer. The private sector workers, weakened by the split labor market, had no power to oppose the lowering of their wages, which was brought about by a clandestine agreement of the public sector workers, who received large increases in exchange (*HA.* 14/12/82, 3/1/83).

This was the first collective agreement Finance Minister Aridor signed with the private sector corporatist partners. More than anything else, this agreement expressed the government's dependence on the *Histadrut* for wage restraint, and the advantage the private sector employers derive from this dependence. In split corporatism there are both winners and losers. The chief winners are the private sector employers, and indirectly the public sector workers. One loser is the government, for which the price for dependence on the *Histadrut* is high increments to government employees. But the chief losers are undoubtedly the weak private sector workers. Restraining their wages becomes the main objective of every agreement, and presents no problem for the strong workers who are split from them in the public sector.

The pivotal institution in split corporatism is not the government but the *Histadrut*, which supports the strong unions' high demands in return for their willingness to split away from the weak workers. The *Histadrut* restrains wages in the private sector in separate centralized bargaining with the *Lishkat Teum*, and mediates between the government and the unions in the public sector. The *Histadrut* formulates a political exchange in which the government benefits from restraint of the unions' wage demands in exchange for agreeing to allow the partners of private sector corporatism to limit wages as best it can in separate negotiations.

The most significant difference between the periods of Likud and Labor rule, apart from the peace agreement with Egypt, was the rate of inflation. The difference can be explained by the social composition of each party, and their internal structure of interest representation and articulation. The organizational differences have produced varying political processes and economic outcomes.

Both Likud and the Alignment represent labor as well as capitalist interests, supporting subsidies from state resources for what is considered the national interest. The distinction between them is in the institutionalized coordination of these interests. In the Alignment, labor and capital are organized groups, represented in the *Histadrut's* system of interclass mediation and compromise. *Histadrut* "civil servants" are appointed by the labor party, the source of their power is the party, and their struggle to represent capital and labor take place within the party as well in the *Histadrut*.

Labor's and capital's interests are not institutionally mediated in the Likud, which expresses them directly, sometimes in populist forms. While in opposition, the Likud based its electoral appeal on the leader's (Begin) symbolic message to the masses without a mediating party apparatus (Shapiro, 1989). As a result, the Likud's legitimation as the governing party was far more costly. The external subsidy was not large enough to cover the Likud's legitimation costs, requiring even more American aid. In addition the government increased its budget deficit, and the overall result was a higher level of inflation.

Thus it seems that the political economy of inflation is (among other factors) a result of the ruling party's institutional ability to mediate labor and capital interests. This mediation need not necessarily occur within the party. The state as an institution may perform this role, but it becomes difficult to do so when the party controlling it is divorced organizationally from labor and capital. This is the reason why social democratic parties are those that usually develop patterns of corporatist mediation by the state.

If legitimation "costs the state money" and the situation is aggravated by the ruling party's detachment from labor and capital, then the additional price of re-election becomes this party's Achilles' heel. The Likud survived only one re-election period, but even this was at the expense of the deepest crisis the Israeli economy has ever known. After this experience the Likud did not undertake sole rule of the state again. In the run up to the 1981 elections the Likud developed a short and aggressive re-election economy (Temkin and Ben Hanan, 1986) in an effort to erase the memory of their economic failures in office.

The problems began to surface after the elections, when the newly elected government wanted to recoup the money it had poured into the economy. The Likud succeeded in being re-elected, but at the cost of losing control of the economy. Without political economic partners the Likud was unable to govern. Neither the *Histadrut* nor the *Lishkat Teum* was prepared to collaborate with the government to pull in the reins on the economy. Strong workers expectations were so inflamed that the *Histadrut* was afraid to confront them, while profits from inflation were so high that employers had no interest in restraining them either.

The overt capital-labor class conflict of 1980 (analyzed in chapter 3) was transformed into a double crisis of the state after the 1981 elections. There was a political crisis because of the state's inability to cooperate with organizations representing private interests, and control the economy through consent. There was also a fiscal crisis due to the state's obligations to continue subsidizing labor and capital through budget allocations.

These developments are due to three structural aspects of Israeli political economy. Two of these, the *Histadrut's* political structure and the split labor market, were analyzed in former chapters. The purpose of this chapter was to explain the importance of the third structure—the political party's mode of interest coordination. The (Likud's) ruling party's organizational detachment from representatives of labor and capital, coupled with political and organizational contacts between the private sector corporatist partners and the opposition (Labor) party, were the basis for an economic crisis. The next two chapters discuss the two parties' collaboration to halt inflation and restore the state's autonomous capacities.

The Israeli case study suggests that elections and their concomitant political business cycles should be conceptualized as a structural feature of democratic states. The periodical need of ruling parties to receive mass support for the legitimation of their policies is in itself a motivation for ruling parties to use state intervention in the economy for their own benefit. But, moreover, in order to recoup monetary resources after elections, governments committed not to use the business cycle weapon must negotiate restraint with capital and labor. This aspect of the political business cycle makes the question of ruling party ability to coordinate interests a very relevant one. This specific inability of the Likud ruling party, due to its institutional detachment from interest organizations, caused the 1978-1980 jump in inflation, and the economic crisis subsequent to the 1981 elections.

Trade unions elites, unlike capital, also need electoral legitimization. Certain organizational features may push them to engage in peculiar political business cycles, negotiating economic demands with governments and employers, in order to obtain legitimacy in the eyes of rank and file. The *Histadrut's* political structure explains the logic behind its demand to the state and employers to provide it with economic gains as its leadership faced elections in 1985. This is the subject of the next chapter.

CHAPTER 5

THE LEGITIMATION OF
THE *HISTADRUT* LEADERSHIP

This chapter discusses the period between the Knesset elections in July 1984 and the *Histadrut* elections in May 1985. The serious economic crisis in which the country found itself, aggravated by an "elections economy," was alleviated several times by package deals which curbed salaries and prices. Yet, with no parallel steps taken by the government, these measures only damaged the balance of payments and the foreign currency reserves of the state more seriously. The economic situation inherited from seven years of Likud government led to the establishment of a broad cabinet. During this period, all the partners of corporatism waited for the results of the *Histadrut* elections, before the Emergency Economic Stabilization Plan (EESP, discussed further in the following chapter) was put into practice.

The theoretical issue standing at the center of this chapter is the sense of common misfortune among the state's, the employers' and the *Histadrut's* elite. Cooperation by the government and the employers to ensure the re-election of the current leadership of the *Histadrut*, and the common measures taken in the sphere of wages, prices and macroeconomy policy to assure the preservation of the *Histadrut's* political structure and the validity of its leadership, will be first described and then analyzed.

The National Unity government is discussed, perceived as having been the common interest of both the Likud and Labor party, and to have been essential to the success of the disinflation program. Although this coalition would have legitimized rigorous policies from its establishment in September 1984, these policies were not implemented until later. This apparent anomaly reveals the importance of the centralized trade unions for the bargaining process and legitimation of state policies.

The nature of the *Histadrut's* political structure, in which the leadership is elected periodically on party lines, obliged the state to wait until the leadership received a new mandate in the *Histadrut* elections to compromise in the name of the workers. The deal that groups of strong workers can make, offering political legitimacy in return for higher wages, is conceptualized in the discussion as a "political economic labor exchange." In this light, the tactic of the strong workers in the *Histadrut* election campaign is perceived as a threat to delegitimize policies unless wage agreements were improved. In this process trade union elites collaborated with private and state employers because only they could underwrite wage agreements. What trade union elites provide in their mediation between employers and workers is both legitimacy and a framework for wage negotiations. Although, as will be shown below, legitimation provided by the *Histadrut* in this period had an inflationary impact, it subsequently enabled political forces to restrain inflation as discussed in chapter 6.

Economic Background

After 1981, the gap between the local uses of the economy and the resources at its disposal expanded, expressed by a constant increase in the balance of payments deficit. As a result of the bank shares crisis which cut the capital available in the private sector severely, the government successfully reduced its subsidies of basic products while increasing the prices of imported products. This policy fueled inflation and unemployment, but also improved the balance of payments (*BI*. 37:5). Towards the elections, a change in the direction of growth in individual consumption and real wages took place, yet with no improvement in the employment situation. After the elections this trend continued because of expectations of a policy of wage and price restraint once the government was established, yet the prices of basic and imported products continued to rise, while purchases of foreign currency seriously damaged the reserves (*BI*. 37:6).

The failure of Finance Minister Aridor to initiate a policy of restraint was a consequence, as seen in the previous chapter, of the *Histadrut's* lack of interest and inability to confront the stronger groups of employees (mainly of the public sector) and silence their demands, which were fed by high expectations created by the elections economy. Lacking a political mechanism for restraint, on the heels of a most generous policy in the elections of 1981, the state's recoupment of resources took the uncontrolled shape of the bank shares crisis in October 1983, at the cost of a most serious crisis of confidence in the government's economic policy.[1]

The main conclusion to be drawn from these developments is that the political difficulty of the Likud administration in cooperating with the *Histadrut* became an obstacle, because of the need of the governing party to receive legitimacy by running an elections economy. That is to say, a political business cycle, which demands "giving before the elections and taking afterwards" every four years, exposes the deficiency of the Likud's structural detachment from the trade unions. The Likud administration was hurled into an economic spiral which it had created in order to be re-elected, yet now, because it could not escape the results of its own action, became dependent on the *Histadrut*. The progress made towards solving economic problems after the second election campaign of the Likud as a ruling party in 1984 was possible only thanks to political cooperation with the *Histadrut*, requiring the participation of the Labor Party in the government.

In an historical perspective, it seems that the *Histadrut*, as the pivot of the split corporatist political economy, stabilized its position because of the 1967 occupation and the 1977 Likud party administration, and in 1984 it was about time to express its actual power. Since 1967, the unorganized noncitizen cheap labor has helped the *Histadrut* to reinforce its control over the weak workers in industry, construction and agriculture. When the Likud won the elections in 1977, the *Histadrut* was freed from its constant confrontations with the powerful workers in the public sector as it no longer had a political commitment to the ruling party. Yet as the Likud government lacked a regulatory mechanism, political or economic, having neither corporatist exchange with the trade unions nor a dual labor market to divide the public workers employed by it, the fiscal crisis of the state and the economic situation grew worse. Nevertheless this also damaged capital and labor, pushing the *Histadrut* to resume political responsibility towards the state. So in 1984, seven years after severing the political commitment of private sector corporatism towards the state, the *Histadrut* was forced, once again, to cooperate, as a result of its dependence on government subsidy, now endangered by the deepening crisis.

The Results of the Knesset Elections:
The National Unity Government

Defining the results of the elections as a "stalemate" does not accord with the objective data of the number of mandates won by the two major parties,[2] but rather points to their subjective preference to establish a national unity government. With enough political will, the two parties could each have formed a government without the partnership of the other.

The National Unity government (henceforth NUG) was a political formula which simultaneously promised legitimacy and control to the ruling parties, while being a condition for the implementation of a drastic economic plan needed to bring down inflation. The *Histadrut* contributed its ability to mediate with the trade unions to the NUG, which the Likud government lacked, while the Likud provided legitimacy to the government's policy by neutralizing the opposition, which a Labor government could not have done.

This bizarre political form with two prime ministers, two policies, and an "opposition" within the cabinet, is not a result of the "stalemate" in the elections, nor of the proportional representation system. This phenomenon can be explained with reference to the structure defined in Chapter 2 as private sector corporatism, which entails a paradox of at once demanding government subsidy, while at the same time remaining independent from the government's political mediation. Yet the economic crisis of the state and its inability to continue subsidizing became a threat to the whole political structure. Thus, the NUG was not merely a formula which suggested a possible solution for the Israeli economy. It also gave the *Histadrut* a new mechanism for maintaining its own political structure. The *Histadrut* leaders not only had their concern for "the national economy" in mind at the time of the establishment of the NUG, but also their own "private" economy, which had been damaged by the economic crisis, by suspension of the special pension fund for *Hevrat Ovdim* (by Horowitz, see chapter 3), and by the damage done to Bank Hapoalim in the shares crisis, including threatened nationalization (INT). It would be no exaggeration to state that it is not clear who brought whom to the NUG—the Labor party the *Histadrut* or vice versa.[3]

Immediately after its establishment, the new government decided to take a series of steps to put a stop to the drain on foreign currency reserves: a devaluation of the NIS, raising prices of imported products, oil and subsidized products; reduction of the sum allowed for foreign travel; limitation on the use of credit cards abroad, and stipulation that the import of cars and investment equipment be conditional on receiving credit from the suppliers. These moves contributed to a rise in inflation and erosion of real wages. Furthermore, the new government agreed to reduce the one billion dollar budget (which it did not do), and declared its intention to freeze prices and to abolish the COLA (*BI*.37:7; *HB*. 16-17/9/84).

In fact, this was the first move taken in the implementation of an over-all economic plan which was formulated during 1984 by groups of economists who worked for the Ministry of Finance, Bank of Israel, and the Labor party. A central figure connected to all of these groups was the economist, Professor Michael Bruno.

The essential feature of this plan was a combined operation to reduce inflation and improve the balance of payments by cutting the government budget significantly, and a new fixing of the relation between the prices of wages and goods, and the exchange rate. The goal of this plan was to create a structural change in both the sphere of employment, and in the capital market which would enable the release of resources to the private sector, to be followed by economic growth (INT). Notwithstanding the economic "theory," there is still the question of putting it into practice, its timing, and the bargaining process which can illustrate the political power relationships explaining both the successes and failures of the program.

Package Deal "A": The Histadrut Delays Radical Plans

In the months of September and October 1984 inflation reached a record annual rate of 1000 percent. The deficit in the budget grew because of the reduction of net tax receipts, causing monetary expansion and unemployment increased (*BI*. 37:5; *HB*. 3, 5, 8/10/84). During October negotiations were held between the government, the *Histadrut* and the *Lishkat Hateum*. The main point of conflict was over the necessity of implementing all the economic moves immediately, against the possibility of introducing, as a first stage, a policy of wage and price restraint alone, which would not effect employment too severely. A significant bargaining card held by the *Histadrut* was the pressure on it from embittered workers (*HB*. 24-25/10/84). But this time, in contrast to the case of the Forum, where collaboration with Meshel was discreet (see chapter 3), the cooperation of the committees with the *Histadrut* secretary-general was completely overt.

It seems that the pressure of the rank and file workers influenced the negotiations between the *Histadrut* and the government, resulting in acceptance of the basic elements of the proposal made by the *Histadrut* for a package deal. The proposal was drawn up by former governors of the Bank of Israel Arnon Gafni and Moshe Zanbar, and was amended by the *Histadrut* (Neubach, 1986:26). This package deal which was later called "A," as it was followed by a series of package deals, was fixed for a period of three months from November 1984 to February 1985. Wages, prices, profits, and taxes were frozen. During the first two months, the workers gave up part of the wage increase they were due because of wage erosion. Pay was to be raised later, partially by means of the COLA agreement, and partially by the government foregoing 5 percent of income tax, which was to be granted as a concession to waged workers (starting in February for three months). The employers froze prices, while the government maintained the same levels of subsidies on basic products. Dividend rates were also frozen for a period of three months. The government promised the industrialists that it would continue to subsidize exports according to an agreement existing between them, thereby ensuring the profitability of exports at the same level. The Bank of Israel stated its intention to slow down the nominal devaluation of the NIS to preserve its real value. The government announced a policy to reduce income tax on the waged workers, and to attain full employment (*BI.* 37:7; Gatenio, 1986: 61-63).

Perhaps the most significant aspect of this ongoing collaboration was the establishment of a joint committee in which the government, the *Histadrut* and the *Lishkat Hateum* participated, whose aim was to ensure the implementation of the agreement. After package deal "A" was signed, tripartite consultations and negotiations became institutionalized, the central figure in all of them being the prime minister Shimon Peres, who was familiar with both the secretary-general of the *Histadrut* and the chairman of the *Lishkat Hateum* (INT-NA, BU, and GS).

In order to comprehend the economic consequences of the package deal, it is also worthwhile to look carefully at what is not in this plan: there is no agreement about decreasing subsidies of basic products and to the exporters. There is also no agreement on dismissals in the public sector. This suited the private sector corporatist partners, but deepened rather than alleviated the fiscal crisis of the state, increasing the budget deficit.

Both the bargaining over the agreement and its content serve as illuminating examples of the way in which PSC works, when the *Histadrut* coordinates the moves of the *Lishkat Hateum* with the actions of the strong workers, with detrimental consequences for the weak workers and the fiscal situation of the state. At this stage, the logic behind the timing of the plan was not completely clear, but it became so during the following months, when everybody was waiting for the *Histadrut* elections.

Keisar developed a highly efficient negotiation strategy. Exploiting the workers' resentment, he mobilized their support, so that he became a key factor in the negotiations, while enabling him to go along with economic plans which were harmful to the workers, though presented as a "compromise."

Keisar also employed a sophisticated election strategy, emphasizing repeatedly that his essential loyalty was not to the Labor party but to the workers. This reduced the suspicion that the participation of the Labor party in the government would politically oblige him to yield on issues important to the workers. Following this reasoning Keisar prevented the establishment of a decision making body in the Labor party, the initiative of the Secretary-general Bar'am, in which both party representatives in the *Histadrut* and the government would have equal weight (INT-BU).

Keisar ran for the elections in a difficult and dangerous position, in which he attempted to express the protests of the workers while also acquiescing to package deals eroding their wages. He was given the backing of powerful workers' committees to help him stand up to the pressure to accept drastic reforms. Yet this complex policy could not have worked without the understanding of the government and *Lishkat Hateum* elites that they must wait for the *Histadrut* elections before pressing on. The decision to cooperate with Keisar during the period of the package deals was, in fact, preferable to the probable consequences of a direct confrontation, which would have forced Keisar, willy-nilly, to lead a campaign of strikes and wage demands, which would very likely earn him much electoral support. Should this have happened, the damage to the deteriorating economy would have been severe, while the election campaign would probably have enhanced the labor organizations' power and organizing capabilities, making the negotiations afterwards even more difficult.

The postponement of radical measures until after the *Histadrut* elections was dictated by Keisar, out of fear of possible damage to his status if these moves were made before his re-election. The secretary-general of the Labor party, Uzi Bar'am, stated in an interview for this research that "in all of the conversations held, he (Keisar) was saying that there is absolutely no sense in discussing the implementation of any plan until the *Histadrut* elections take place. Peres waited, and began at the first moment he could (to implement the EESP). Suppose Peres wanted to bring it up at the meeting of the heads of the party, they would have killed him. Not only Keisar, the whole party would have killed him." But this was not merely an internal party understanding. All sides understood that without powerful leadership in the

Histadrut, no plan would have succeeded (INT-MM, MI, BM, NA, and BU). Yet the difficulties arising during this six months' waiting period before the *Histadrut* elections were held, were extremely serious. They demanded a response for which there were insufficient administrative means.

The Deterioration of Price Control

It is fair to state that the major achievement of package deal "A" was the proof that cooperation between the government, the *Histadrut,* and the industrialists was capable of firmly restraining price rises. After a rise of 19.5 percent in November, the index was held to a rise of 3.7 percent in December and 5.3 percent in January 1985. The cooperation between the sides in reaching the agreement was institutionalized and stabilized. Nevertheless, without budget cuts, pressures to increase prices were created, as a result of rapid devaluation of the NIS, the raising of subsidy rates and high interest. This situation was exacerbated by the money flowing into the economy as a result of the need to finance government expenditure, and the growth of NIS credit, caused by expectations of new devaluations (*BI. 38:9*).

One of the main difficulties of the wages issue was the lack of a biennial framework agreement with various strong unions in the public sector. This was due to the fact that just before the elections to the Knesset, the *Histadrut* signed the framework agreement for the public sector with the government, but many unions did not add their signature. The agreement was, it is true, more generous than the one signed with the private sector, but did not meet the expectations of the strong unions (*HA., YA.* 24-26/6/84).

When the unions began negotiations for a framework agreement after the signing of the package deal which froze wages, the government declared that it was unwilling to ratify wage agreements. Thus, public sector workers, engineers, teachers, doctors, nurses and others, found themselves with no wage agreements. Keisar managed to persuade the unions not to wage an open struggle and strike, but rather to conduct peaceful negotiations behind the curtains, mediated by the *Histadrut* (*HB.* 22-26/11/84, 2/12/84).

The teachers were in a particularly delicate situation, as they had no framework agreement and pay assurances based on the Etziony Government Inquiry Committee Report had not yet been realized. Moreover, thousands of workers were threatened with dismissal. The Teachers' Association hastily accepted the framework agreement without the other labor organizations, receiving in return the support of the

Histadrut in its campaign against the firing of thousands of teachers (*HB.* 15/11/84, 16-30/12/84).

This case serves as an example of the policy developed by the *Histadrut* for all the public sector workers, in the new era of the NUG. Facing demands to reduce the public sector, the *Histadrut* offered to mediate between the workers and the government, so that the workers gave up wage demands in return for assurances of employment given not by the government, which continued to demand both wage erosion and mass dismissals, but by the *Histadrut*. This is the new face of split corporatism, under the conditions of the NUG, according to which negotiations are held, there being an indirect exchange of wage restraint in return for full employment. The bill is paid by the government. In this system, the *Histadrut* has, once again, a pivotal position, coordinating various demands through separate agreements with each side.

Along with the threat of unemployment, there were deep concerns that once the three months of the package deal ended, inflation would explode once more. To prevent this possibility, the *Histadrut* began negotiations with the *Lishkat Hateum* about the COLA, and after reaching certain agreements in the second half of December, demanded to begin tripartite negotiations on a new package deal ("B") immediately (*HB.* 17-23/12/84). Undoubtedly, the *Histadrut* was the most determined to continue the temporary policy of package deals and prevent real budget cuts which would mean, above all, sacking workers and reducing subsidies.

The *Lishkat Hateum* supported the demands of the *Histadrut* for another package deal, at least until after the elections, in exchange for which it was granted most of its requests. On the issue of prices, it was agreed to allow a controlled monthly rise, though the rate of increase remained unsettled. The conflict inside the *Histadrut* over this question was sharper than with the private industrialists. Keisar offered a rise of 3 percent per month, the heads of "Koor" demanded 7 percent and the Manufacturers' Association agreed to 5 percent-6 percent. (*HB.* 13-23/1/85). The proposal made by the industrialists for package deal "B" included two clauses omitted from "A": cutting the state budget and exchange rate policy. On the issue of the exchange rate, the demand was to have a clear government commitment to undertake a real devaluation of several percent per month. The main significance of this proposal was that the acute problem of the balance of payments and the dwindling of currency reserves could be resolved by massive support for exports. This support included generous compensation for the damage done to export subsidies by restricting government credits, as part of the restraint of inflation (Manufacturers' Association, 20/1/85).

Towards the end of January 1985 an agreement was reached between the *Histadrut*, the government and the *Lishkat Hateum*, to sign this second package deal. According to package deal "B," the employers were given permission to raise prices at a rate of 5 percent per month, the government was allowed to raise the prices of subsidized products. The *Histadrut's* main achievements were to prevent budget cuts in the sensitive area of dismissals and a 5 percent discount for employees on their income tax (Gatenio, 1986:63; *HB*. 24/1/85; Manufacturers' Association, 20/1/85). Although it was not part of the agreement, the exporters were, in practice, to benefit from a real devaluation.

Package deal "B" was an attempt to create another stop-gap until the *Histadrut* elections. Though it was valid for a period of six months, it was noted that each side had the right to withdraw from it from the beginning of July 1985. In fact, the adjustments in the prices of subsidized products was scheduled only until April, as it was generally assumed that the government would not raise prices a week before the *Histadrut* elections. Yet these efforts were in vain, as government expenditure was unrestrained. In March the government presented a relatively balanced budget, but during the months of April-June deviations from it reached the sum of about a billion dollars. None of the announced public sector dismissals were carried out. While the financial situation of the state deteriorated, the employers were still not asked to contribute to ending the crisis.

Package deal "B" expressed the ongoing situation characteristic of the period of Likud government, when private sector corporatism dictated an economic policy to the government, according to which the private sector was subsidized, thus harming the fiscal situation of the state. In the package deal, the *Lishkat Hateum* took the political needs of the *Histadrut* into consideration, which in return accepted a serious erosion of wages.

After package deal "B" was signed, prices went out of control, rising in February by 13 percent. Between February and June the monthly rate of inflation was 12 percent on average. The deficit in the balance of payments reached a high but stable monthly level of sixty million dollars and precipitated a drop in foreign currency reserves below the predetermined minimum level. Instead of a recession a considerable recovery occurred. Private and public consumption increased but investments fell (*BI*. 38:7). The *Histadrut* election campaign focused on developments in the sphere of prices and wages, necessitating close coordination with the government and industrialists. The day after the package deal was confirmed, the *Histadrut* fixed the exact date of its elections (*HB*. 6/2/85), believing that the issues of prices, wages and employment were already settled. When control over prices was lost, the *Histadrut* was obliged to run its election campaign against a background of overt and covert deals with its other partners in the political economy.

The Re-election of the Labor Party in the Histadrut

One of the most prominent features of the *Histadrut* election campaign was that though there was an electoral economic cycle, it differed from that of the Knesset elections, as this time wages were eroded significantly. The Labor party's representatives in the *Histadrut* (referred to below simply as the *Histadrut*) succeeded in mobilizing the support of the workers by presenting an image of independence from the party, by emphasizing their willingness to confront the government as well as the industrialists, by threatening strikes by those unions under their authority, and by conducting successful negotiations with strong workers' groups which took advantage of the situation to receive wage increases.

Despite the electoral system of proportional representation, the *Histadrut's* main problem was not competing with the rest of the parties for votes, but dealing with the labor organizations and placating their demands. The largest competing party (the Likud), gave up early on, leading an apathetic and unthreatening campaign. It may be that the explanation for this was the dire need of the Likud, at that time, for a political partnership with the *Histadrut*, within the framework of the NUG.[4]

One of the new tactics used by the trade unions to increase their wages during the *Histadrut* election campaign was the threat to create their own lists and run independently in the elections. The cardinal group which threatened to establish an independent list comprised five strong trade unions: The Engineers' Association, the Association of Humanities and Social Science Graduates, the Organization of Secondary Education Teachers, the Merchant Navy Officers' Organization, and the Pilots' Committee. This grouping already possessed the whole infrastructure necessary to compete in the elections (INT-LO). Its component bodies take part in the public sector wage negotiations, and its members are highly skilled, earning large wages. Their collective action began with a demand to open negotiation for a framework agreement, followed by covert bargaining which produced a secret agreement on wages. According to this deal, a new set of pay scales would be introduced, reestablishing the differentials between scales. Thus the higher ranks of the public service would receive approximately a 12 percent-24 percent increase in their salaries. The agreement was leaked to the press, apparently in order to sabotage it. The trade unions responded with their own leak, renewing their threat to run separately in the *Histadrut* elections. The threat was repeated periodically, only being completely withdrawn after the original, "secret" wage agreement, the one which had collapsed a month earlier after exposure in the press, was finally ratified. (This agreement, was deposited in a Bank Hapoalim safe [INT-LO; *HB*. 1/1/85, 16/17/3/85, 11/4/85]).

Shortly before signing the framework agreement for the public sector, the Technicians' Association, which is considerably less powerful than any of the five trade unions which had already acted early in January, also threatened to run separately in the elections (*HB*. 7/4/85). A closer look at their actions shows that each of the labor organizations understood the pivotal position of the *Histadrut*, as instead of threatening their employers (the government) with strikes, they came close to intimidating politically the "pivot" of the political economy—the *Histadrut*. It is interesting to note, therefore, that it was the political danger they posed to the *Histadrut* which made the desired wage agreement possible, because of the government's interest in reinforcing the *Histadrut*.

The possibility of the trade unions competing independently in the elections represented a serious challenge to the political authority of the *Histadrut*. The issue at stake was not the electoral strength of this or that labor organization, but the mere precedent which could be adopted by each group of well organized workers, undermining the whole political structure. The structural distance between the *Histadrut* and the representatives of the workers is what provides the *Histadrut* with its pivotal position in the political economy. Rather than being expressed by trade unions, the workers' resistance is "channeled" into political parties—which appoint the workers' representatives to the *Histadrut*. This mechanism makes the representatives of the workers dependent on the party apparatus responsible for their appointment, rather than on the support of the workers.

The establishment of electoral slates for the *Histadrut* elections, based on labor organizations which are directly elected by the workers, would have erased the gap between the economic and political organizations of the workers. This separation has contributed to the labor movement's success since its inception by giving priority to labor parties rather than trade unions. Ending the divorce between a faction in the *Histadrut* and a representative organization of the workers would simultaneously break the dependence of the workers on the parties. In the long term, such a change could alter the whole structure of the *Histadrut*.

During the election campaign, talks were held with the industrialists on three central issues—the COLA, wage erosion compensation in industry, and price controls. The *Histadrut* took advantage of its ability to raise wages in *Hevrat Ovdim* during negotiations with the *Lishkat Hateum* over the COLA. The industrialists were determined that the COLA of 12 percent should be paid in April, whereas the *Histadrut* demanded a COLA of 14.5 percent. The *Histadrut* ordered its factories to pay 13.2 percent, thus forcing the employers to fall in with its wishes, and sign an agreement for the COLA at the same level (*HB.* 18/3/85, Gatenio, 1986:32). Such a move was an alternative means to grant legitimacy to the *Histadrut* ownership of *Hevrat Ovdim*, demonstrating that with control of a significant sector of the economy, the *Histadrut* leadership would pressurize other employers to accept wage increases (Keisar, 1983). After a verbal confrontation between the *Histadrut* and the employers, an agreement on compensation for the manufacturing workers at a rate of 6 percent was accepted (*HB.* 8/3/85). What is relevant here is the fighting image with which the *Histadrut* leadership portrayed itself to win the elections.

The most complex deal, involving coordination of all sides, was on the issue of prices. In the middle of March package deal "B" expired and prices rose without control. The *Histadrut* leadership needed to demonstrate some success in halting inflation for at least the short period of the following two months. The difficulty was to ensure that individual industrialists not raise prices, in recognition of the political needs of the *Histadrut* leadership facing elections. After two weeks of negotiations an agreement was reached (called "B improved") to freeze prices for two months, following an increase of 6 percent in the price of 300 products. The agreement contained a secret clause, which was later leaked to the press, and confirmed by Keisar, providing for a 13 percent rise in prices after the freeze (*HB.* 28-30/3/85, 21/4/85; Gatenio, 1986:69).[5] The contribution of the government to the agreement was also significant. It refrained from raising prices of the subsidized products until after the elections, in spite of a clause in package deal "B" permitting it to do so. A combination of COLA agreements, erosion compensation, and the price freeze produced the conditions for real wages to rise, temporarily, to the peak achieved on the eve of the Knesset elections. Circumstances were particularly favorable in April, shortly before the *Histadrut* elections.

The results of the elections satisfied the *Histadrut* leadership and buttressed it for the difficult tasks ahead of it, implementation of the EESP and the war against inflation. The Labor party received 70 percent of the votes. To obtain these results, the *Histadrut* had been assisted by its political associates who required its victory: the *Lishkat Hateum*, for whom a stable *Histadrut* was the basis of the private sector corporatist partnership, and the government, in the form of the Labor party as the ruling party. The *Histadrut* was also vulnerable, being forced to compromise with strong labor organizations in the public sector and in *Hevrat Ovdim*. In spite of extensive wage erosion in the months before the elections, the *Histadrut* succeeded, with the help of the price freeze and the COLAs in April and May, in reducing the sense of crisis and conveying to the workers an image that it possessed the considerable power needed to face up to the struggles lying ahead.

Discussion: The Inflationary Significance of
Legitimation of the Histadrut

Between the establishment of the NUG in September 1984 and the *Histadrut* elections in May 1985, inflation was not halted in spite of repeated attempts by the three main factors in the economy. Periodically, in package deal "A" from November 1984 to January 1985, and "improved B," from April to May 1985, they reined in inflation with administrative measures: price controls. Yet at the end of each freeze there was a sudden surge in prices. Inflation was, and remained the most salient issue to be dealt with by the government, yet whatever drastic policy was needed required the *Histadrut's* consent. The *Histadrut* could not accept any such policy shortly before the elections, as it would undermine its legitimacy.

The political structure of the *Histadrut*, entailing legitimation of its leadership through factional elections, is what prevented wage restraint with correct economic timing. Thus both the government and the employers had to wait for the right political conjuncture in the eyes of the *Histadrut*. The period before the *Histadrut* elections, as before Knesset elections, is the worst time to seek concessions from strong labor organizations.

The election campaign transferred the *Histadrut's* strength into the hands of strong labor organizations because of the political structure of the organization. The main weakness of the *Histadrut* is to be found in the organization's structural disjuncture from the workers, and the dependence deriving from it on the workers' willingness to continue to acquiesce to the *Histadrut's* policy as well as its political structure. The cooperation of the strong workers is manifested: (a) by their organizations remaining within the framework of the *Histadrut*; (b) by their acceptance of the ruling parties heading its structure; (c) by their consent to the political control of *Hevrat Ovdim*; (d) by their compliance to

Histadrut mediation between them and their employers; and (e) in their willingness to refrain from collective action with other workers (for most of the time) which could culminate in the establishment of an alternative centralized labor organization. In this way, the strong labor organizations do not undermine the structure of the *Histadrut,* yet do demand rewards in the form of employment and wages. So the *Histadrut* makes a deal whereby the workers grant it political support in exchange for economic attainments. Deals of this type were prominent in the period prior to *Histadrut* elections.

In chapter 1, corporatist exchanges were presented as they appear in separate spheres on the political level, where the trade unions receive legitimation in return for the legitimacy they grant the government, as well as to the social order as a whole; and on the economic level, trade unions restrain their wage demands in exchange for an assurance of full employment. This research suggests that the exchange occurs across both levels, and that rank and file workers legitimate both centralized unions and the state in return for wage increases and employment security. This phenomenon was already noted in chapters 3 and 4, where it appeared that the strong workers received wage rises in exchange for quiescence in the *Histadrut.* In this chapter this need is clearly revealed as a phenomenon recognized by all the sides involved—the *Histadrut,* the government and the employers, and primarily, the workers.

These "political economic labor exchanges," whereby legitimation of the social order is translated into economic rewards for the workers, which are plainly evident in the Israeli case, can contribute to an understanding of the corporatist as well as of the dual pattern, and the common basis of both. From the moment that rank and file workers are ready to grant, in exchange for higher wages, legitimacy to centralized trade unions and through them to the social order, the unions' and the employers' elite become mutually dependent on each other to maintain their power. Union leaders need to cooperate with employers to fulfill their obligations in the eyes of the workers, who offer their acquiesence in return. A less flexible position on the part of the employers is liable to undermine the centralized structure of the trade unions, bringing chaos to wage bargaining. On the other hand, the employers will always prefer to negotiate with one responsible, centralized union, with whom they can conduct a steady dialogue. If bolstering the position of the unions' leadership entails concessions in wage increases at a certain stage, that would appear to be in the long-term interest of the employers.

The logic of exchange presented so far does not include the labor power structure and the role of the state. On the side of the workers, it is obvious that those who are unable to demand wage increases independently are those excluded from political economic labor exchange of legitimation for wages. Weak workers who do not pose a threat to the employers also present no danger to centralized unions. In economies with a fragmented labor market, exchange will occur only with the strong workers. Where there is a homogeneous labor market, a characteristic of the corporatist pattern, a similar logic operates: the capital-labor class conflict is regulated by "buying" the hearts of the workers with cash or standards of living. It seems that in democracy, for which legitimation is a key issue, this exchange is most likely to occur in states or segments of the labor market which are capable of financing the political-economic deal to conciliate strong workers. In regions and segments of the labor market where there is no possibility of "financing democracy," the capital-labor conflict is regulated by the competition between the workers themselves, which forestalls the organization of labor and its representation in a democratic struggle. Examples of this pattern are the political business cycle or different types of fragmented labor market.

The discovery of a political economic exchange with labor is not original to this research. It is clearly reminiscent of the neo-Marxist literature which explains the durability of capitalism as a result of the "embourgeoisement" of the working class. However, this discussion suggests treating the "exchange deal" as an analytical concept, rather than as a moral judgement decrying the absence of a proletarian revolution, or as an a priori truth requiring no proof. Following Bonacich (1979), this study suggests looking at the situation of the organized workers, in the world labor market, their conflict with capital, and competition with the disorganized workers. The definition of the "political economic labor exchange" as an analytical concept makes it possible to ask concrete questions and analyze changing situations and different patterns of the regulation of class conflict. These questions deal with the structure of workers' power and how it is reflected in bargains made with employers. Every society has its own specific pattern and characteristics which the scholar must discover. A central issue in every comparative study should be the specific organizational form of distinct labor groups, including questions such as by what procedure and how often their leadership is selected.

In these contexts the state appears to be interested in helping the employers and centralized trade unions to attain legitimation, while having its own interest as an institution in receiving legitimacy through them, and to ensure wage restraint as an employer. In the corporatist pattern the state mediates the dialogue between unions and employers, subsidizing its consequences, while in the dual pattern, it provides the legal framework for the discrimination between labor groups, subsidizing only the strong. Split corporatism in Israel is a combination of both patterns, in which the *Histadrut* (rather than the state) is the pivot of political-economic exchange, while the state subsidizes capital and strong workers and provides the framework to discriminate against workers in the secondary sector.

The pivotal position of the *Histadrut* is a consequence not only of its political structure, but of the structure of the fragmented labor market as well, which helps it to control weak labor groups without needing to represent them, directly or indirectly. The leadership of the *Histadrut* deals with a variety of labor groups, reaching (or not reaching) different agreements with them, based on their distinct positions in the labor market. In the exchange between the *Histadrut* and the strong labor organizations, it trades economic rewards for the workers in return for political support for its structure. Most of the members of the weak groups do not vote for the *Histadrut* leadership in any case. The noncitizen Palestinian workers are denied *Histadrut* membership; the Israeli citizen Arabs vote mostly for the anti-Zionist, left wing parties; and the Oriental Jews, inhabitants of the development towns, have a tendency to vote for the Likud and other right wing parties.[6]

The weak labor groups fail to organize themselves,[7] are incapable of threatening the political structure of the *Histadrut* and depend on it for their wages increases, won through agreements with the *Lishkat Hateum* in private sector corporatism. The weak workers are controlled politically by nondemocratic unions governed via the *Histadrut* by party cadres. The *Histadrut* does not even guarantee these groups full employment in this relationship, making them even more dependent on it. The dependent position in which Oriental workers and Israeli-Arabs are placed enables the complex *Histadrut* apparatus to mobilize support among them, especially in exchange for employment in its various institutions.

The form of the exchange, according to which the strong workers grant political legitimacy in return for economic rewards, creates a problem for the political economy in general, and the involvement of the government in particular. Wages and full employment in the primary (mostly public sector) segment of the labor market are provided in exchange for legitimation of the political structure of the *Histadrut*. That is to say, to make a bargain with the workers entails reliance on a powerful *Histadrut*, yet this power costs money.

The era of the package deals illustrates that cooperation with the *Histadrut* implies a state commitment to meet its needs, involved in the maintenance of its political structure. This commitment is financed by the state budget, and includes agreements to increase wages, continued subsidization of consumer essentials, but excludes public sector dismissals. Thus the re-election of the *Histadrut* leadership requires increased government expenditure, which fuels inflation. This, in a nutshell, is the inflationary significance of the *Histadrut* problem of legitimation. Only on the day after the *Histadrut* elections did the necessary conditions exist to take drastic measures to tackle inflation. These conditions were a NUG with wide parliamentary support, and a *Histadrut* leadership with a stable majority for a period of four years. This was the political conjuncture in which the government was free to dictate a comprehensive, anti-inflationary economic plan, to be discussed in the following chapter.

CHAPTER 6

DISINFLATION AND THE PROBLEM OF STATE AUTONOMY

This chapter discusses the closing period of this research, one characterized primarily by disinflation. Inflation fell from an annual rate of 466 percent, recorded in the months of February to July 1985, to 25 percent in the period of August 1985 to March 1986. This success was achieved as the result of government determination to enforce its decisions on both the workers and the private employers. Additional accomplishments of the EESP were a significant reduction of the balance of payments deficit, and an actual surplus in the budget. The EESP was implemented against the background of the package deals, which although ineffective for the task of disinflation, created a suitable environment for it. During their operation there was a real devaluation of the NIS, a drop in the real wage and a reduction of the budget deficit (BI. 39; Bruno and Piterman, 1987:97).

In order to tackle the issue of the political preconditions of disinflation, it is fruitful to turn to the literature on "state autonomy." Skocpol (1982) asks what it is that gives a state the ability to implement a policy opposed to the interests of powerful social groups—groups which in this case, as shown in the previous chapters, had decisive influence over all economic measures, their execution and results.

The generally accepted explanation of the Israeli government's success in putting into practice a radical economic program, which hurt broad segments of society, is that because of the crisis before this program, "the public" was willing to accept the edicts imposed on it. While the resolve of both the public and the government in the face of crisis are significant, that does not explain either the specific timing of the plan in July 1985, or the consequences of the policy. There had also been an atmosphere of crisis in 1980, yet the government was unable then to sustain a comprehensive policy to halt inflation and improve the balance of payments. The same can be said about October 1983, following the stock market crash, and September 1984, after the establishment of the National Unity government.

The aim here is to explain why and how things occurred as and when they did. Although economic facts and the "public will" must be taken into consideration the explanation relies on the same political and institutional analytical concepts as in previous chapters. The same concepts used before to describe inflationary constraints are relevant to explain disinflation too, because structures and institutions did not change significantly. From the economists' perspective, this lack of structural change was the main failure of the program. The political economic perspective adopted here will focus on the reasons for this resistance to change by examining the actions of conflicting groups and organizations, their contradictory interests, the fierce struggle which ensued over the EESP, and the successes and failures of that policy.

The analysis here concludes, in agreement with the economists, that the EESP did not guarantee that high inflation will not occur in the future. The explanation for this proposed here is that those social groups and organizations whose actions tended to cause inflation remained strong enough to resist structural change. Inflation had been avoided because of the legitimation of state power by the Labor party and *Histadrut*, but as that was a matter of political conjuncture rather than structure, the chance remained that economic crisis would recur.

However, there was some change within the prevailing structural stability: American aid was converted from loans into grants, and almost all large *Histadrut* enterprises were hit by economic crisis. The difficulties of *Hevrat Ovdim* are presented here as the counterpart to state power and autonomy, and a consequence of *Hevrat Ovdim* losing its former role as the articulator of PSC interests. The political ramifications of this, according to this line of analysis, were that the Labor party redefined its role in government as a procurer of subsidies for *Histadrut* enterprises. In long term, this behavior would undermine state autonomy and has inflationary potential.

The EESP First Steps

On the day of the *Histadrut* elections (in which the Alignment, headed by Keisar, received 69 percent of the votes and thus strengthened its position), a government panel to formulate the smallest operational details of the EESP was set up. The panel, headed by the director-general of the Finance Ministry, Emmanuel Sharon, also included representatives of the universities, Professor Michael Bruno and Professor Eitan Berglas, the prime minister's adviser Amnon Neubach, and a member of the research department of the Bank of Israel, Mordechai Frenkel (INT-NA).

The panel constantly coordinated its activities with the political echelon, especially with the prime minister, who at that time held repeated discussions with various groups at his home in the evenings (primarily with the industrialists and *Histadrut*), also consulting with teams of specialists on various sections of the program (INT-BM, NA, FA, BE, BU, and MM).

Among the panel's important activities was what we will call the "mobilization" of American pressure. Over a long period of time, the members of the team maintained contact with the American government and kept it informed of the main principles of the program. According to the key figures interviewed, the panel's members facilitated the exercise of American pressure in order to persuade the politicians that uncompromising action was necessary. Thus the Israeli group drew up a ten-point economic program, but presented it as a plan which the American government required as a condition for an extra grant one and a half billion dollars over two years (from 1985, the rest of the American aid was provided as grants rather than loans). There was a consensus among the interviewees that American pressure was crucial to the formulation, acceptance and implementation of the EESP, serving as a crutch in the face of opposition (INT-BM, BE, MM, and NA).

Throughout the month of June there was an atmosphere of a general breakdown of the system of price and wage control agreements, and of a governmental crisis. The labor organizations which were close to the leadership of the *Histadrut* declared labor disputes as a response to wage erosion and the nonpayment of compensation guaranteed before the elections (HB. 12-17/6/85).

The employers, well-informed of the government's intentions to implement a comprehensive economic program, expressed their opposition to the package deal, urging a price increase, so that they could begin the tough time ahead in good condition. They achieved their objectives by means of a total shutdown of the food industry, an

extreme measure designed to demonstrate the nonprofitability of production at existing prices. Two days later the government surrendered
and agreed to raise food prices. Four days later it gave its approval for
similar increases across the board (*HB*. 2, 3, 16, 17, 20, 21, 25/6/85).

The government was also in dire straits. Foreign currency
reserves, which had been dwindling for the last several months, fell by
28 percent in July, from two billion dollars to a billion and a half. With
inflation running at 10 percent per month, the tax system was in ruins,
deepening the budget deficit. From the government's point of view, this
was the time to act.

The Logic of the Stabilization Plan

It was obvious that the most convenient time for the government
to set its plan into action would be after the *Histadrut* elections. It had
already been written into the package deal of January 1985 that
although it was set to last until October, from July any partner could
decide to withdraw.

The committee drawing up the plan considered that it must simultaneously attack the problems of both inflation and the balance of payments. Accordingly, they believed that a significant cut in the budget
was necessary, as well as one of considerable devaluation of the NIS to
be immediately followed by the fixing of the major independent factors
determining price levels such as wages, products, and the rates of
exchange and interest. While they did foresee a need to compensate
employees, they did not envisage it at a generous level, as their intention was to stabilize wages at a lower level than the prior to the program. The planned level of wage erosion was of 10 percent, relative to
July 1985 wages, which were already comparatively low. Decreasing the
labor costs was expected to support export expansion.

The central issue that remained the focus of disagreement
throughout the panel's deliberations was the proposal to fix the
exchange rate. This was a cardinal question in respect of economic conceptions, subsequent developments, and attitudes towards the role of
the state. This issue connects the two central facets ("anchors") of the
EESP—the rate of exchange and wages (Bruno 1985:215). Those in favor
of fixing the rate, led by Sharon and Bruno, hoped to put an end to a
process which had already being going on for ten years, initiated by the
government and known in the Bank of Israel as "functional inflation."
This concept was developed in the Bank of Israel in 1974, after the Yom
Kippur War, as a means of coping with growing budget difficulties
caused by security costs. The supposition was that inflation, eroding

wages, and thus the domestic debts of the government, would function as a tax reducing private consumption. By putting more resources into the hands of the state, it would be able to extend public consumption proportionally, thus fulfilling security needs (INT-RA).

Devaluation was a significant factor in the idea of "functional inflation" as it both raised prices and ate away at wages. In fact, since 1975, the government had devalued the shekel by several percent each month. The effect of these creeping devaluations was sustained by reducing the COLA agreements (by 30 percent).

Inflation began to spiral when the devaluations and price rises were followed by labor demands for proportional wage increments. The government defended the employers by circumventing the primary sector workers' strength, by means of the rate of exchange. Each time the workers won wage rises, the exporters would claim that the profitability of exports had fallen which must concern the government as it is responsible for the balance of payments. Effectively responsible for the profitability of exports, the government committed itself to insure the exporters for the losses caused by the gap between the exchange rate and rising prices. This form of subsidy could be reduced only by means of a devaluation. The government's inflationary policy was one of the factors behind the crystallization of private sector corporatism, in which the common insistence of *Hevrat Ovdim* and of *Lishkat Hateum* that the government guarantee the profitability of exports led to a policy of devaluations and inflation.

From the issue of the rate of exchange, one can infer a broader picture of the relationships between capital, government, and the workers. The state is inevitably bound to the profitability of capital, yet it does not necessarily depend on it. The state does rely on export profits, being committed to support them, when it lacks alternative foreign currency resources, such as foreign aid or the proceeds of sales of raw materials. Dependence of the state on the wealth generated by capital in general occurs, when it cannot assure its independent income by direct ownership of assets, natural resources or taxation. An example of the conditional nature of state dependence on capital was seen during Aridor's period in office, when devaluations were curbed and local manufacturing was hurt. Aridor could afford to ignore the question of profitability of both manufacturing and exports thanks to the financial boom, mobilization of capital abroad, and bank shares regulation. There is thus no "structural necessity" for continuous support of capital by the state or vice versa. In a period of rapid inflation, capital flourished while the state suffered losses. The government was in effect subsidizing capital by both granting credit and the dissipation of income tax.

Obviously devaluations intensified inflation. At a certain level of hyperinflation, the point was reached where the conflicting interests of capital and of the government became clear. Once inflation went out of control it damaged the financial stability of the state by reducing foreign currency reserves and by deepening its budget deficit (INT-BE and RA). Those economists in favor of freezing the exchange rate (whose victory came only in 1986), argued that the government should cease to protect the private employers from wage claims because it was too expensive for the state. Thus part of the disinflation plan was intended to force the employers to stand up to the workers or pay the cost of not doing so.

The final result of the debate on the exchange rate, after ministerial consultation, was a compromise. It was agreed that there would be further devaluations should an increase of wages occur. It was determined that "the government will freeze wages, prices, the rate of exchange, and interest. The freeze of the rate of exchange is conditional on reaching the required level of nominal wages" (INT-BE and RA; Neubach, 1986:10). This compromise was interpreted by the industrialists as a government commitment to devaluate .

These are the main points presented by the planners to the government shortly before the decision to adopt it the EESP on 30 June:

a) *Timescale*. The program was to last one year, with an initial emergency period of three months.

b) *Goals*. A rapid reduction of inflation, raising of the foreign currency reserves, and improvement of the balance of payments. This would lay the foundations for renewed economic growth, and a restructuring of the economy.

c) *Measures*. A devaluation of 20 percent, cuts in subsidies of basic products and the budget. Freezing of wages, prices, exchange and interest rates.

d) *Means*. A Budget cut of 750 million dollars. Reduction of manpower in the public sector, and of subsidies on production and capital.

e) *Rate of exchange*. Should wages rise beyond the desired level, the exchange rate would be adjusted proportionally. Exchange rate insurance for exporters to be suspended.

f) *Wages*. Real wage to be eroded by 10 percent. Inflation compensation to be arranged with the *Histadrut*. Suspension of COLA during stabilization. Wages of the public sector workers to be reduced by 3 percent.

g) *Prices*. Permission for increases of 15 percent-20 percent to be followed by a freeze.

h) *Reform of the capital market*. Gradually, nonnegotiable bonds to become negotiable. To begin with, this principle to be applied to career advancement funds and savings programs. No more non-negotiable bonds to be issued. Bonds issued in the future to be index-linked for a period of two years only.

i) *Interest.* The Bank of Israel was to intervene only in the second month, should interest rates exceed 25 percent per month.

j) *Dynamics.* In the first stage, fixing the nominal wages should assure a steady rate of exchange and halt inflation. That would contribute to the budget and make it possible to reduce taxes. This move would help stabilize the real wage and the transition to an economy without price control.

k) *Projections.* The real test would be the curbing of inflation and growth of foreign currency reserves in the coming three months. Stabilization would be a precondition for renewal of growth, which would require a gradual disengagement of the government from the capital market.[1]

The government's decisions included several corrections to the panel's original program.[2] The reform in the capital market is not mentioned, nor is the suspension of exchange rate insurance.[3] The official devaluation was indeed of 18.8 percent, but taking into account the fluctuations of the next few days it was effectively 25 percent.

In order to make it abundantly clear that the government was unequivocal and resolute in its decision, ministers were given the authority to introduce emergency reforms to ensure price stability and the implementation of the rest of the plan.

Histadrut and Workers' Opposition to the EESP

It is important to note that the program met sharp criticism in the government and key Likud ministers voted against it. Likud minister David Levy expressed his outspoken criticism, insisting that the government had no moral right to decide on such a program. Levy's position strengthened the *Histadrut,* when an all-party coalition against the program was created (HA. 1-3/7/85).

Public reactions by workers' representatives to the plan were harsh. It should be borne in mind that the predictions of severe wage erosion followed the fall in the real wage in the period of the package deals. On 30 June the *Histadrut* assembled its Executive Committee (*Vaad Hapoel*) and established a special headquarters for the struggle against the program before its acceptance the same day. Although the heads of the *Histadrut* were already aware of the workers' distress, they merely made a moderate decision to arrange meetings of the labor councils to discuss plans for the expected struggle. These steps were agreed on in spite of the pressure of workers' representatives, union secretaries, and labor councils' chairmen to declare an immediate strike. Yet the tension was so high and bitterness so deep that the leadership of the *Histadrut* had no choice but to call a general strike for the very day after the government accepted the program. The extent of the strike was unprecedented and has not been repeated since then (*D., HA., YA.* 1-3/7/85).

It is reasonable to assume that the *Histadrut's* main aim was to assure control of the situation by negotiating, while holding the strike threats of the powerful unions and public sector workers' committees as a bargaining card. But in practice the strike broke out as a result of the pressure of the workers on their direct representatives in the biggest work places and on the heads of the labor councils in small settlements by weak labor groups. The strike was complete in the public sector, but only complied with by 60 percent in industry (*HA., HS., AM.* 1-3/7/85).

The general strike, backed by the threats of union committees and common workers to continue the struggle, gave the *Histadrut* a valuable bargaining chip in its talks with the government. Under conditions of economic crisis, eruption of class conflict between capital and labor threatened again, as it had done in 1980, including a clash of interests within the *Histadrut* itself. Keisar again developed a sophisticated strategy to regulate the conflict.

Keisar's strategy consisted of a return to Meshel's pact with the heads of the powerful workers' committees, with the essential difference that cooperation was open and there was no horizontal organization between labor groups. A controversy about how to wage their fight broke out among the workers' committees, some of them insisting on simultaneous strikes. Keisar backed those who accepted his leadership and a policy of dispersed strikes. Foremost among his allies was the chairman of the electric company's workers' committee, which had preempted other committees by declaring a separate labor dispute and beginning sanctions, thus forcing the others to follow suit and subordinate their actions to the directions of the campaign headquarters at the *Histadrut*. In accordance with these selective tactics, the telecommunications workers disrupted television broadcasts on the day the prime minister was supposed to present the economic program to the public (*YA., HA.,* 3, 4, 5, 8, 10, 11/7/85).

Once the leadership of the *Histadrut* had reasserted its authority, resisting the pressure for a general strike, it announced, ironically, that there would be a general strike within five days unless an agreement with the government about compensation was reached (*HA*. 10, 11, 14/7/85). At the time of the declaration, the *Histadrut* leaders knew that the situation was well under control. This was a threat that would never be carried out, but postponed repeatedly as negotiations continued, and then revoked. In the worst case, only the public services would be struck. Under the threat of a general strike, the government, the *Histadrut* and the *Lishkat Hateum* began talks on wages (originally scheduled for 14 July but postponed for several days), soon coming to a compromise.

However, the focus of disagreement in the public sector was not compensation for wage erosion but threats of dismissals. The confrontation between the workers backed by the *Histadrut* and the government on this issue lasted for one more month. In order to fulfill its obligation to cut its wage bill by 3 percent, the government threatened to sack 6 percent of the public sector workers by decree. The *Histadrut* objected, eventually accepting that some jobs be lost on condition that the government forego the use of decrees. The government also agreed not to sack anyone without giving about eighty days notice, as stipulated in labor agreements (*HA*., *YA*. 18, 19, 21, 24, 25, 29/7/85; 5, 7, 11/8/85) .

The case of the threat to jobs in the public sector highlights the differentiation between two levels of labor organization and struggle. On an economy-wide level, the tripartite negotiations led to an agreement on wage restraint alone. Yet in the public sector the *Histadrut* fulfilled an additional mediating function, when as in the period of the package deals, it successfully constrained the workers' protest by demonstrating its commitment to them in its opposition to dismissals. This is another example of an indirect deal whereby *Histadrut* involvement allows the government to restrain wages but prevents it from reducing public employment. The model for the whole public sector was set by the Teachers' Association, which agreed to a drop of 1.5 percent in wages in exchange for returning 700 teachers to work (*HB*. 1/9/85) .

The results of the economic program were impressive in several spheres. Its first and most conspicuous success was the reduction of inflation from a rate of 27 percent in July, to an average monthly level of 3.8 percent, from August to October 1985, followed after the price freeze by a further fall to a monthly level of 0.8 percent from November 1985 to March 1986. In addition, the balance of payments deficit improved, the income from tax collection grew, and the budget deficit turned into surplus. Foreign currency reserves also improved, and from October, an economic recovery was felt, including a drop in unemployment (*BI*. 39).

The erosion of the real wage during the first months of the EESP was severe, but the workers did not manage to organize an independent campaign against it. Later on, wages began to rise, mainly in the private sector, while in the public sector the wage freeze continued until April 1986. These wage increases puzzled the designers of the EESP, who expected precisely the opposite. Their confusion was partly the result of the industrialists' mistaken assumption that inflation would return and with it, devaluations. It was on the basis of this assumption that the industrialists had agreed to wage increases. The analytical framework adopted in this study provides another explanation, which requires an analysis of the changes occurring in the power relations between various labor groups and employers. The uncompromising attitude of the government towards the public sector employees was only partially effective in curbing the ability of the powerful workers in the private sector to win pay increases. As discussed earlier, private sector employers were accustomed to channeling the demands of labor organizations which are strong in the labor market to negotiations in the public sector. Once the government stood steadfast in its rejection of the workers' pressure, preventing a national increase of wages in the public sector, the engineers and graduates in the private sector began to act, and with success, to push up wages in manufacturing.

The strong workers of the private sector had not exercised their power in the past, but under the new circumstances, they acted according to their labor market strength. This strength was reinforced by the *Histadrut's* prevention of widespread dismissals in the public sector, thus averting unemployment in their segment of the labor market. From December 1985 until February 1986, most of the manufacturing workers received the pay increases provided for in the secret agreement signed on the eve of the *Histadrut* elections. It should be noted that these significant increases, estimated at an average of about 17 percent- 30 percent, were not paid to all workers but only to professionals in the higher scales, thus enlarging the differentials between scales (INT-LO, *HA*. 13-16/3/86). It is fair to assume that in manufacturing, this would push up the wages of the other workers as well.

The Histadrut Economic Crisis and Its Political Ramifications

Another major consequence of the EESP was the crisis into which economic sectors, companies and institutions were thrown, for three to six months after the disinflation. Foremost among those in difficulties were agriculture and construction, *Solel Boneh*, and *Kupat Holim*.[4] Each sector and institution had specific reasons for its crisis, but there were two common factors:

a) In the past, crises had been forestalled by the financial illusion creat-

ed by inflation, making it impossible to reveal the actual financial situation. (Bruno and Piterman, 1987:114).

b) Most of the institutions and companies were linked to the *Histadrut*,
and began to suffer as soon as the "financial program" of the *Hevrat
Ovdim* was rescinded in October 1980 (see chapter 3). However, it
was only after inflation had been halted that the extent of the damage was discovered.

The difficulties of *Hevrat Ovdim* became a focus of political relations between the Likud and Alignment, the *Histadrut*, and the Finance
Ministry. In reaction to the crisis, the Finance Ministry established two
commissions of enquiry to examine the states of affairs of *Kupat Holim*
and *Solel Boneh*. From a series of statements, the impression was given
that the Finance Ministry had no intention of acting magnanimously,
and that the *Histadrut* would have to sweat for government aid to save
its institutions (*HA*. 4, 6, 7, 27/3/86). It was only now that the Labor
leaders realized their lack of political foresight and poor understanding
of the labor movement's structure, manifested by their acceptance of a
Likud finance minister.

In response to the financial distress which its institutions were in,
the leaders of the *Histadrut* began to lobby within the Labor party to
urge the dismissal of the finance minister, claiming that his obstruction
of support for its institutions was politically motivated. The claim was
that the Labor party should threaten to refuse to honor the rotation
agreement of the NUG, according to which Shamir would replace Peres
as prime minister in October 1986. This bargaining card was particularly effective against the Likud leaders. Wage talks were linked to rotation
by an unprecedented demand to sign agreements for a period of no
more than a year valid until April 1987. The *Histadrut's* entire public
campaign against the finance minister was based on the economic
agreement claiming that after six months of restraint the time had come
for the next stage—growth (*HB*. 27-29/1/86; see articles written by
Judith Winkler in *HA*. 9/2/86-10/3/86).

The claim that renewed growth was necessary was in the direct
interest of the *Histadrut*, and was backed by its political ability to mobilize the workers, the employers, and the Labor party. Although the
EESP designated a future stage of anticipated growth, its timing was
never fixed. According to the economic conception of the Finance
Ministry, growth would come not as a result of active inducements but
as a consequence of the structural changes which would occur in the
economy following the EESP. However, these changes failed to emerge,
and in their place came pressure from the *Histadrut* and the industrial-

ists to restore the government protection they had enjoyed earlier, namely subsidies and devaluation.

In March and April the conventions of the two major parties of the government were held. The *Herut* convention ended with a disgraceful spectacle of physical violence caused by the inability to settle a dispute between Shamir the incumbent prime minister and his deputy, David Levy (YA. 10-14/3/86). That event created a very favorable public atmosphere for the Labor party, particularly for its hopes to disband the government (see Schweitzer article, *HA.* 17/3/86). In comparison with *Herut*, the order and unity of the Labor party appeared as the peak of political maturity and professionalism. The party conventions were held in the wake of two impressive achievements: the withdrawal of the Israeli army from Lebanon and the curbing of hyperinflation, both presented by Labor as the results of the failures of Likud government. Labor's only problem was thus to justify breaching the rotation agreement so that it would appear to be an act of public responsibility and not mere greed for power.

The debate over the government budget, particularly the sections concerning support for *Histadrut* institutions became the central bone of contention, overshadowed by the threat not to fulfill the rotation pact. The campaign against the *Histadrut's* and Alignment's demands for aid was led primarily by the official staff of the Finance Ministry rather than the minister himself. They constantly fed the media with estimates of the harm that would be done to economic stability if proposals requiring deviations from the budget were accepted (*HA.* 12, 17, 23, 24, 27/3/86). The acrimonious dispute between the Likud and the Alignment, conducted in the cabinet and the Knesset, aggravated the situation and generated a sense of crisis. Eventually, the government approved a budget which contained a significant proportion of the original demands for aid (*HA.* 30-31/3/86).

However, the confrontation between the *Histadrut* and the treasury officials did not come to an end when the government authorized the budget. Being well aware of the serious difficulties of both *Solel Boneh* and *Kupat Holim*, they later insisted that the assistance be conditional on the implementation of recovery programs and the mobilization of additional financial support from the resources of the *Histadrut*, the *Hevrat Ovdim*, and Bank Hapoalim (*HA.* 3/4/86). Moreover, their intention to make devaluations and budget adjustments dependent on the good behavior of the *Histadrut* in wage negotiations was leaked (*HA.* 2/4/86). The finance minister, Mr. Modai, vigorously expressed in several interviews his opposition to and criticism of the prime minister and the pressures brought to bear to grant the *Histadrut's* institutions with government aid under the slogan of renewed growth (television program "Moked," 2/4/86, YA., HA. and HS. 4/4/86).

Modai's media outbursts provided Prime Minister Peres with an excuse to fire the finance minister, whose dismissal he announced to the party convention. The excitement and loud cheers which greeted his statement diverted attention from the issues scheduled for the day to a coalition crisis over the appointment of a finance minister (HA. 9/4/86). By acting in this way, the prime minister succeeded in winning a renewed and firmer mandate to lead his party and determine its policy. At the time nobody would have predicted that the NUG would survive for another two and a half years, and that the Finance Ministry would remain in the hands of the Likud.

There were a variety of attempts to find a formula that would remove Modai from office without bringing down the government. The solution agreed to was that another Liberal, Moshe Nissim, then minister of Justice, and Modai would swap positions. This was a surprising end to the crisis, as the Alignment had accepted its resolution without exploiting its full potential to break up the ruling coalition, and, contrary to the labor movement's hopes, the Finance Ministry remained in the Likud hands. It appears that the Alignment accepted this arrangement in the expectation that a finance minister without economic experience and interest, yet politically astute, would be more suitable as an opponent and more amenable to compromises on issues of vital concern to the *Histadrut*. Yet by accepting this solution the Alignment lost its chance to prevent rotation.

The New Histadrut-State Balance of Power

In April it was not entirely clear what would become of the economic program and the power struggle between the *Histadrut* and the government. In the event, the appointment of a minister who was a lawyer by profession, and who understood nothing about economics, enhanced the independence of the Treasury officials. Minister Nissim's compliance and reliability made his officials a cardinal force in the economy, a position they had acquired nine months earlier, but had not fully expressed. Professor Bruno joined the staff of top economists, as the governor of the Bank of Israel, a move which in itself enhanced the status of the senior officials and strengthened the position of those rejecting devaluation as an antidote to wage increases.

It is astonishing perhaps, that when the day for rotation came, the premiership was handed over to the Likud without objection from within the Labor party, even though it was denied the Finance portfolio.

It seems that after the Modai crisis the chances of establishing a narrow government with the small parties headed by the Alignment were poor, while the option of going into opposition was abhorrent for the very same reason that induced Labor to bid for the Finance Ministry: the dependence of the *Histadrut* on government budgets. From the moment the Likud was granted the legitimacy to lead the government, the Alignment became its captive, because of the *Histadrut's* reliance on the government (INT-BU).

At this point it is worth taking a close look at the special nature of the rotation arrangement and its significance for the various parties. A government chosen by periodic elections every few years is subject to a structural compulsion to manipulate an "electoral business cycle." The rotation agreement produced its own unique cycle. The two biggest parties could each have established a narrow government under their own leadership, but were initially in need of one another, to implement the vigorous economic policy and withdraw Israeli troops from Lebanon. As soon as these two central problems were solved, both the Likud and the Alignment needed only the will and the right occasion to break up the NUG and form a new coalition, one excluding the other.

Yet the Alignment and Likud confronted different conditions while holding the premiership. For most of the time Peres was in office the government dealt with burning problems requiring the NUG. In contrast, Shamir's period of office was relatively "calm," at least economically speaking. The Alignment had only a short intermediate period in which it could "use" the premiership for its own benefit, in the first six months of 1986. The closer the date of the rotation came, the more tightly the Alignment became bound to the Likud. Whereas in April 1986 opinion in the Labor party and among the general public favored breaking the rotation agreement, it began to swing the other way from the middle of 1986. So by October 1986 the majority of party members supported the fulfillment of the agreement, the only real alternative being "to serve the people in opposition." This option would have seriously endangered the chances of resuscitating *Hevrat Ovdim*, thereby threatening the survival of the whole party, which relies very heavily on the organizational power of the *Histadrut*. Thus it was calculations of *Histadrut* interests that determined Labor's attitude to the NUG throughout 1986. At the beginning of the year the *Histadrut* was an active factor in favor of dissolving the government, but by the end of the year it was the main supporter of the Alignment's continued membership in it (INT-BM and BU). This unique conjunction was one of the political causes giving meaning to the relative autonomy of the state during 1986.

The new power in the hands of the state was expressed through-out 1986 by the firm resistance of the Finance Ministry to pressure from the industrialists and *Hevrat Ovdim* to devalue the shekel, and from public sector workers seeking to raise wages.

The industrialists took issue with the policy of the Finance Ministry to abstain from devaluations, contrary to the assurance written into the EESP that should nominal wages rise, the exchange rate would be adjusted accordingly. In fact, in the twelve months after the end of the freeze, wages rose by approximately 40 percent, and the consumer price index by approximately 15 percent, while the dollar rate remained steady. The government did not devalue the shekel throughout the whole year. The ability to sustain this policy derived primarily from the increase in the foreign currency reserves, which reached $5 billion in 1986, as a result of the improvement in the trade balance and the aid received from the United States (INT-BM). Furthermore, the strengthen-ing of the European currencies and the Japanese yen helped sustain the policy of freezing the dollar rate; by holding the dollar steady, there was a real devaluation of the currency basket. These developments in inter-national currency markets, along with a drop in oil prices, contributed to the government's success in maintaining the stability achieved as a result of the first steps taken in 1985 (*BI*. 40).

It was also no easy task to stand up to the pressure of the workers. Since the beginning of 1986 most public sector unions had been demanding increments to make up for erosion of their wages, which was relatively acute compared with the rest of the labor market. It is true that the engineers and other academic graduate workers had ben-efitted from their new pay scales stipulated in the secret agreement since April 1986, though most of their colleagues in the private sector had already received the payments through company agreements (INT-LO). Yet the government refused to grant any increase of wages what-soever beyond the COLA agreement signed between the *Histadrut* and the *Lishkat Hateum* (*HB*. 2-4/5/86).

The public sector framework agreement reflected the new power enjoyed by the government vis-a-vis the *Histadrut* and the workers. The new agreement granted no more than one pay scale increase during the following six months, which most of the workers were already due in any case (*HA*. 22, 24, 25/8/86). Soon afterwards another arrange-ment was reached between the *Histadrut* and the government, which appeared to be an integral part of the public sector contract: the recov-ery program of *Kupat Holim*, whose debts had reached $300 million (*HA*. 18-19/8/86). Apparently, a type of a package deal was made here, in which the *Histadrut* restrained the demands of the public sector workers in exchange for government aid for *Kupat Holim*.

In spite of the relative power of the state vis-a-vis the workers, the *Histadrut*, and the employers which was manifested in December 1986 and January 1987, it was forced to enter into a package deal, when a dispute arose over budget cuts, tax reform, and restructuring of the capital market. In the light of these events it appears that after the Likud took over the premiership, the relative autonomy of the state witnessed in the previous year and a half suffered a decline, as the balance of power shifted in favor of private sector corporatism.

Consistent with the approach that economic growth required the release of resources from the public sector to flow into the private sector, Treasury officials initiated a new series of economic measures as the new budget year approached, which were supposed to come into effect from January 1987. The program included a drastic budget cut, necessitating a public sector wage freeze of almost half a billion dollars and thousands of dismissals. The new policy also provided for a tax reform, reducing the top income tax scale to 45 percent but increasing the basic rate by revoking exemptions. Its third feature was a reform of the capital market, establishing similar competitive terms for the government and the private sector (*HA*. 4, 12, 15/12/86).

The *Histadrut* mobilized most of its available resources against the program. Within the cabinet the Labor ministers unilaterally blocked the program, urging that a package deal be made with the *Histadrut* and the employers rather than confronting them. So the government was forced to establish working committees to put the plan into operation. Nissim and Peres sat on both committees, one dealing with budget cuts, the other with tax and capital reforms (*HA*. 11, 16, 18, 22, 23, 25/12/86).

State-owned enterprises, the *Lishkat Hateum* and *Hevrat Ovdim*, acted to improve the profitability of exports by means of various subsidies and devaluations (*HA*. 12, 15, 19/12/86). The labor organizations were particularly concerned to prevent dismissals and taxation of the career advancement funds. The *Histadrut*, as the pivot of the political economy, supported the demands of the workers and of the employers, while representing its own interests in *Kupat Holim* and the pension funds. The bargaining process followed a similar pattern to that conducted in the past by Peres, at the time of the package deals. There were late night meetings at which Peres mediated negotiations between Treasury officials, leaders of the *Histadrut* and representatives of the *Lishkat Hateum*.

The final form of the package deal was far from the original intentions of the government, even if we assume that the Finance Ministry included several difficult conditions from the start which it intended to drop during the negotiations (*HA*. 14/1/87). Of the budget cut only the taxes and reductions of subsidies remained: whatever was easy to cut. The original plan to prune the defense budget by $150 million came to naught. The curbing of government expenditure did not diminish the state's involvement in the economy, nor did it lead to a reduction of manpower in the public sector. The employers benefitted from a 10 percent devaluation, 2.7 percent reduction of the COLA and reduction of national insurance payments and tax concessions. The *Histadrut* was granted aid for *Kupat Holim* and the pension funds. The tax reform was insignificant as the top scale was still 53 percent, while exemptions remained valid. Nor was a reform in the capital market expected. The journalist Nechemia Stressler succinctly expressed the view that the state was turning, once again, into a tool in the hands of private sector corporatism. He wrote "The *Histadrut* and the industrialists proved once again that there is no government in Israel. For a whole month they conducted negotiation as if they were an integral part of the government, as if it has been forgotten that they represent some very down-to-earth interests" (*HA*. 14/1/87).

Discussion: Structures and Conjunctures of State Autonomy

It was suggested that the government's de facto proinflation policy prior to 1985 indicated state weakness in the face of organizations representing powerful social groups which prevented the implementation of a policy of restraint. So a necessary condition for the success of the disinflation program was the ability of the state to take certain steps in spite of the objection of powerful groups in Israeli society. In brief, it was a question of power. What were the structural and conjunctural factors which gave the state the power to halt inflation?

The first structural change occurred on the political level: the establishment of the NUG and the effective neutralization of an opposition which could bring down the government or prevent the implementation of its policy by mobilizing powerful social groups. Most social groups and organizations of capital and of labor are represented within the Likud and Alignment, so that conflicts were conducted within the government itself. Resolving these conflicts through compromises and government decisions provided the greatest possible legitimation to sustain the economic program.

The second structural change was financial: the substantial aid granted by the American government to put the economic program into practice, including special supplements amounting to $1.5 billion over two years, and the conversion of loans into grants. This aid served as a "safety net" in the parlance of the program's designers, which was vital to the courage to undertake the project (INT-BM, BE, NA, and MM).

Skocpol (1982) has argued that the state's financial resources are the key to its autonomy, along with the existence of a professional bureaucracy formulating a policy strategy determined by the interests of the state. This study concurs with that view while also indicating a further condition, at least in reference to governments selected by periodic elections, which is the existence of a political configuration in which support and legitimacy are mobilized for the state. Because of Israel's party structure, in which each of the two biggest parties primarily represent different classes, only a government including both could have adopted an autonomous policy, able to withstand the pressures from various social groups, while also being the policy adhered to by the civil service. Yet these conditions held only for a short period of time, as Skocpol (1982:14) warns.

In dealing with the issue of state autonomy, a sharp distinction must be drawn between capital and the state. The state ceases to be dependent on capital if it has alternative resources available, such as external capital or local resources. What the state generally depends on the workers for is their support and provision of legitimacy, through parties and unions. If the workers' vote is split between the two biggest parties, as in Israel, the participation of both in the cabinet is necessary for the implementation of an autonomous policy, if the danger of delegitimation is to be averted.

The conjunctural factors operating primarily consisted of the fiscal crisis into which the state was thrown, compelling it to take drastic, independent steps. In this regard, the senior state officials played a crucial role. The best timing for such a policy in a political system of periodic elections, would seemingly be immediately after the government has been elected, when its legitimacy is at its peak. Central to the success of the plan was the officials' understanding of the Israeli polity, which dictated that they wait for the *Histadrut* elections before undertaking a radical economic program.

On the financial level too, there were several external circumstances which assisted the state in its confrontation with the employers pressing for a devaluation and subsidies. One of these factors was the strengthening of the European currencies and the yen in comparison with the dollar, which effectively devalued the shekel while the government froze the dollar exchange rate. Another was the reduction of world oil prices. Together with American aid, these conditions made the government iess dependent on exports to finance the external debt, and was thus less susceptible to exporters' complaints about declining profitability. If this had not been the case, it is possible that the state would have devalued the currency, thus restarting the inflational spiral.

Schmitter (1985:49) has also theorized a number of conditions for the autonomy of the state, including the inability of the other corporatist partners to agree between themselves. Being more acute than it had been in 1980, the conflict between capital and labor was not susceptible to Israel's traditional corporatist solutions. Economically, this was because of the serious injury done to the ability of the state to continue subsidizing capital and labor. Politically, it resulted from the inability of the Histadrut to find a compromise between the needs of labor and the employers. This was the most suitable time, from the point of view of the state, to implement a policy unaffected by the demands made by organizations and social groups which now depended on its decisions. Yet it is important to grasp that this conjuncture was contingent and unstable and not a structural, permanent pattern in which both labor and employers depend upon the mediation and subsidization of the state. Such a pattern may be what is most compatible with the corporatist ideal type.

Although the state possessed the strength to execute and sustain its autonomous policy for a year and a half, the long-term goals set by the planners were not achieved (i.e. curbing the involvement of the state in the economy by reducing employment in the public sector, and reforming the capital market). These measures were supposed to have led to the desired stage of renewed growth, which proved to be short-lived. Crucially, real wages did not fall as planned. The explanation for this failure suggested here is that while the cardinal social and political groups were weakened for some time, relative to the state, they were not powerless. They successfully prevented structural changes which could impair their power. A conspicuous example of this is dealt with in the following discussion about employment and wages.

Economists (Bruno and Piterman, 1987; Artsteinn and Sussman, 1988; INT-BE and MM) locate the major failure of the stabilization program in the sphere of employment and wages, in contrast to its startling achievements in the fields of inflation and the balance of payments. As mentioned above, the goal of cutting public sector employment was unfulfilled, as was the target of the erosion of real wages by 10 percent (which was defined as "a new balancing point of relative prices"). Behind the professional terminology of such economic analysis lie basically political explanations. The heart of the issue is the balance of power between social groups and institutional influences on the market. Some blame the employers, as it was they who awarded wage increases in the private sector, in the partially founded but mistaken expectation that the government would devalue the currency. Some consider that the government was responsible, because it did not carry out a devaluation, or perhaps misled the employers by agreeing that the exchange rate would be linked to adjustments in wage levels. Another argument is that the government, concerned with wages only on the national level, ignored the specific difficulties of sectors where severe wage erosion had occurred, and misperceived the differential capacities for restraint existing in the public and private sectors.

While there is some truth in all of these arguments, the present analysis suggests that some further distinctions of a political economic nature must be drawn. Firstly, it is essential to take the structure of the labor market into consideration. This entails a distinction not only between the sectors of the economy, but also between the power of different groups of workers. Secondly, there was a significant post-EESP change in the rules of the game, whereby the government ceased to surrender to the main powerful groups of split corporatism: private employers and public sector unions. As a result the existence of another powerful group was discovered: professional workers in the private sector.

The structure of Israel's fragmented labor market consists of several layers. It was noted earlier that primary workers in Israel are directed, by their employers, to bargain over wages within the framework of the public sector. The reason for this is political: it enables private sector employers to avoid a confrontation with their professional employees. Thus, in the past strikes by professional unions, such as the engineers or graduates, usually took place in the public sector alone. The private sector employers relied on the ability of the government to stand up to the workers, steering clear of disputes which could disrupt production. The agreements signed in the public sector were mimicked also in the private sector.

Yet as soon as the government launched a frontal attack against the public sector workers, the power of the private sector's professional workers was manifested in their attainment, in industrial enterprises on a local level, of wage increases stipulated in the secret agreement. It is no wonder then, that the employers hoped for government compensation in the form of a devaluation. The success of the private sector workers is surprising only if wages are considered an issue of economic equilibrium, and not of power relations. Workers in the primary segment of the labor market were and remained powerful because of the structure of the labor market. Their relative impotence was temporary, a consequence of the obstinate position of the government in the public sector.

The ability of the public sector workers to prevent dismissals also contributed to the private sector workers attainment of pay rises. If thousands of public sector workers had been thrown onto the streets, unemployment would have been created in the primary sector of the labor market, undermining the bargaining strength of the manufacturing workers.

The changes which disinflation introduced in the power relations between social groups and economic forces were not confined to the workers. Foremost among these changes, which became apparent when the key links of PSC loosened, and also the one with the most bearing on the continuation of inflation, was that which befell *Hevrat Ovdim*. While inflation lasted, the effect of cancelling *Hevrat Ovdim's* financial program was barely felt. Later on though, everything began to collapse. The most momentous consequence of the EESP for Israel's political economic pattern was the metamorphosis of *Hevrat Ovdim* into a body dependent on the state, and hence the debilitation of private sector corporatism. This, it appears, turned the *Histadrut* into an organization permanently interested in the existence of the NUG even though that injures the Alignment in elections (as in 1988). The political structure of the *Histadrut* was converted from being an asset of the Israeli labor movement in the 1950s and 1960s, into a liability by the end of the 1980s. Yet the vast apparatus of the *Histadrut* clings to its power, and has to date successfully steered the Labor party in the direction which suits it. *Hevrat Ovdim* itself appears to have undergone a change of position from one of relative independence during the Likud government, to one of dependence upon the state, the government and its ability to mobilize the whole Alignment to maintain its position.[5]

An additional change occurred which was related to the capital market. One of the proclaimed goals of the EESP was to remove government intervention and the index-linking of interest rates from the capital market. At first the *Histadrut* supported the reform, which appeared to offer a way to regain control over pension funds capital that had been loaned to private manufacturers at favorable rates when the government was trying to restrict credit. Yet when the *Histadrut* institutions found themselves in economic difficulties, concern arose, justifiably, about the possible collapse of its financial institutions, especially the pension funds. With this in mind, the *Histadrut* adjusted its thinking, demanding a politically guaranteed rate of return on pension assets invested in government bonds. This guarantee had the effect of preventing the government from withdrawing from the capital market.

Ironically then, the failure of the second structural reform planned as part of the EESP, was partially caused by the reversal of the power relations between the government and private capital. It is now the government which is believed to offer the best assurances of monetary value. From a historical perspective, it is fair to say that it was the rise of the Likud that led, paradoxically, to the broadening of the state's involvement in the capital market. The first stage of this process occurred when Finance Minister Horowitz effectively nationalized the deposits of the pension funds by means of refusing to renew the pension fund agreement. The second stage came when, as a result of disinflation, the pension funds preferred to insure their monetary value by investing in index-linked government bonds.

Nevertheless the essential features of the political economy for the sphere of labor relations—the split structure of the labor market and the political structure of the *Histadrut*—have not changed, although the pattern of class conflict regulation did alter. The main changes were *Hevrat Ovdim's* loss of status as a mediating factor between capital and labor, and the intensification of the salience of the role that Labor party representatives play in the government as agents for the *Histadrut* in its dealing with the state. When Labor governed alone, the tension between the *Histadrut* and government representatives within the party grew to the point where the party could no longer act as intermediary. Once the Likud took over, the leadership of the *Histadrut* was in a considerably stronger position. Its policy followed a line independent from the government and obviously from the party, while *Hevrat Ovdim* mediated between it and the private employers, completely coordinating its policy with the powerful labor organizations. These organizations successfully pressurized the Likud government to increase subsidies to capital so that even the losses caused by the cancellation of the *Hevrat Ovdim* Program were swept under the "inflationary carpet."

Yet in the long run, the state was thrown into a crisis, to be followed by all of the social groups and economic organizations which benefit from its favor. When the state began to implement its autonomous policy, the representatives of the Alignment in the government became key mediators between the state, the *Histadrut* and the employers. The *Histadrut* did remain in a pivotal position in the political economy, with its particular functions in respect of the government, the private sector and the public sector workers, but it became more dependent on government aid. In this respect, The *Histadrut* is obliged to rely on party representatives to protect its interests. The analysis presented here suggests that the establishment of the National Unity government and formulation of an autonomous policy created a new political economic pattern in which the *Histadrut* and the government became mutually dependent upon each other's cooperation. At the same time, the Likud and Alignment were bound to each other, as only in alliance could the government mobilize the support and garner the legitimacy required to put the economic policy into effect.

EPILOGUE

The aim of this study was to combine neocorporatist and dual labor market theories while analyzing Israeli society, and to demonstrate that this combination is a better framework for analysis than the two theories taken separately.

The *Histadrut* is the focus of this study because of its historical and theoretical relevance. The *Histadrut* embodies within its structure both corporatist and dual patterns. Corporatist patterns are formed by the business considerations of *Hevrat Ovdim* enterprises and the political interest of *Mapai* (the ruling Labor party). Dual patterns were due to the Zionist aim of Arab-Jewish economic segregation. Corporatist and dualist policies were developed and executed by the dominant Labor party in both *Histadrut* and Zionist institutions.

In chapter 1 the common theoretical concepts and patterns that should be explored were commented on. The overlap between the theories is based on a feature shared by both patterns, the need to repair the damage to labor and capital caused by the business cycle. Both patterns allow for this redress through collective bargaining, the transfer of class conflict in the economic sphere to politics, and interclass compromise.

Corporatism and dualism are two patterns of the transformation of class conflict into forms of politically controlled conflict. In this light corporatism is seen as the transformation of labor-capital class conflict into political exchange and power relations between their elite, collaborating in the allocation of resources through state intervention. The problem of legitimation is transferred to centralized trade unions, backed by the state and employers, in their relations with the rank and file.

Dualism is characterized as the transformation of class conflict into the segmentation of the working class and discrimination in the allocation of resources within the legal framework of the state. The employees' weakness in the international labor markets is transformed into capital's local strength. The legitimation question is transferred to national, racial, or ethnic relations and competition within the working class.

The Israeli pattern of political economy, as revealed in chapters 2-6 in an analysis to be expanded on below, is complex. In brief, it can be said that corporatist wage restraining agreements are usually reached in the secondary sector, while conflict in the primary sector remains a structural problem for the Israeli political economy. Secondary sector workers in the private sector are subject to wage restraint not because they are represented by centralized trade unions but because of their weakness in a split labor market, which enables the *Histadrut* as a non-democratic, political, centralized trade union to impose restraint on them. The economic interests which the *Histadrut* shares with the Manufacturers' Association and its comprehensive structure including quasi-welfare state capacities constitutes a pattern of private sector corporatism (PSC) in which the *Histadrut* mediates between capital and workers. This peculiar Israeli pattern has provided certain conceptual and theoretical insights applicable beyond the case.

This study suggests that the coexistence of corporatist and dual patterns must be recognized as a concrete historical pattern to be found in specific cases. The importance of dualist and corporatist theories is their deep insights to actual developments in political economy. It seems that one of the difficulties in combining both analytical frameworks is methodological, lying in the tendency to regard them as ideal types.

Ideal types are based on concrete patterns that fit either of the two theories extremely well (usually the U.S. for dualism and Sweden for corporatism). The ideal type methodology of research directs the social investigator away from discovery of the most interesting, complex, and significant aspects of the historical "raw material." Instead, the researcher tries artificially to fit the society in question into a previously defined model.

If this research had started from a dualist or corporatist "ideal type" perspective it could describe Israel in either way, at the expense of grasping the essence of its political economy. The fact that the Israeli experience does not fit either of the two ideal types might lead the researcher to interpret Israel as a "unique case." The alternative approach proposed here to these two flawed approaches is to apply both theories' analytical concepts and questions in order to define the specific Israeli pattern of political economy. The specific political economic pattern of the transformation of class conflict described here originated in the case study itself. This purpose was served ˡ⁻ ⁻st by a long range historical perspective.

The labor movement became the leading force of Ziˑ.ₐₐₓᵢ because it succeeded in developing a policy to confront the cheap Arab labor force (Shafir, 1989) and to create an economy controlled by and oriented to the Zionist political goal (Kimmerling, 1982). The World Zionist Organization financed the labor movement through the *Histadrut* because otherwise private capital business interests could have lead to the creation of a binational society characterized by Jewish capital and Arab labor.

The *Histadrut's* principal aim was to provide work for Jewish immigrants and to assure their absorption into the country. In the absence of a Jewish state the British Mandate allowed the labor movement to develop its own quasi-state institutions within the Mandate framework. The *Histadrut* was the recipient of an influx of Zionist public capital and used it to create its own economic enterprises *(Hevrat Ovdim)*, providing jobs only for Jews. During the pre-state period the *Histadrut* performed almost all state functions: defense, finance, health, education, housing, trade, industry, agriculture, colonization, jobs, and social security.

The establishment of the State of Israel in 1948 created a new structural and institutional situation in which *Mapai* remained the ruling party in both "governmental" institutions: the state and *Histadrut*. The *Histadrut's* political structure and status of PIG reinforced *Mapai* during the first period of mass *aliya*, "absorbing" new immigrants into the highly developed political institutions. The crisis in political and economic control began after the waves of immigration ceased, and when accelerated industrialization and growth occurred. The position of rank and file workers was strengthened, so they won pay awards despite *Histadrut* and government opposition. This crisis threatened the collapse of *Mapai's* political and economic domination.

The 1967 occupation of the West Bank and Gaza Strip provided the labor institutions, paradoxically, with a structural solution to their relations with rebel rank and file workers. Weak Jewish and Arab workers became the secondary sector, employed by private and *Hevrat Ovdim* employers. The centralized wage negotiations were mediated by *Hevrat Ovdim* institutional connections with the *Histadrut* and business connections with private employers. In this sector the government did not interfere, but provided the legal framework for discrimination.

Strong workers, including professionals of the private sector, negotiated their wage agreements with the government, mediated by the *Histadrut.*

In the Israeli complex pattern, combining dualist and corporatist features, the original economic class conflict is transferred to the political arena and transformed into national conflict between Jewish and Arab workers or an ethnic split between Jewish workers supporting rival parties.[1]

Class Power and Weakness

Following the historical analysis of the patterns of the Israeli political economy and an elaboration of its conceptual implications, this epilogue returns to the original theoretical discussion. The central argument of this study which has yet to be developed fully is that corporatism and dualism are two typical answers to the same question: how is the eruption of the capital-labor conflict transformed within the political framework of the state?

Goldthorpe's (1984) argument that corporatism and dualism are divergent tendencies of alternative working class or capital power is based on an ideal type interpretation of both patterns, and two assumptions objected to here. The first assumption is that there is a direct relation of political and economic to class power. The Israeli case shows that during the pre-state period (working) class weakness in the economic sphere was transformed into the strength of class organizations in the political sphere. The significance of my objection is that a more dialectical relationship between class strength and weakness should be conceptualized theoretically.

The second assumption is that class strength and weakness is a matter of capital-labor power interrelations within the framework of a single state. Following Maier's (1984) view of corporatism and Bonacich's (1979) view of dualism, this study suggests that capital and labor power is also dependent on their international position within their respective classes. This means that local capital power is also dependent on its ability to compete in international goods and capital markets and working class local power is also influenced by the international labor market.

In contrast to Goldthorpe's interpretation of class power, corporatism may be understood as capital weakness and dualism as workers' weakness, each in their own international markets. If so, there is no contradiction between corporatist and dual patterns, because capital's and labor's international weakness may coexist within the framework of a single state. This is the case in Israel.

In the first period of Zionist history the Jewish workers were weak in the labor market but politically powerful, whereas the employers were strong in the market and weak in politics. A superficial analysis of this period might lead to the conclusion that corporatism and dualism were alternatives, but in fact they coexisted. It is true that despite the *Histadrut's* efforts to achieve corporatist agreements with the employers, promising wage restraint in return for full employment, it was unsuccessful until the second World War (Shalev, forthcoming). Its failure does seem to be connected with the employers' ability to obtain cheap, unorganized labor in a dual market. Yet the corporatist tendency was not entirely suppressed, as it developed in a complex form within the *Histadrut*. It consisted of a special connection between the *Hevrat Ovdim* funded by the Zionist capital subsidy, and two forms of labor organizations: the political, centralized trade union department of the *Histadrut*, and the economic, decentralized cooperatives.

Although dualism and corporatism coexisted, they were split by the labor market. Private Jewish employers were not committed to full Jewish employment, often preferring Arab labor. The *Histadrut* guaranteed Jewish employment by using the funds of the national subsidy and restraint was imposed on the workers by means of their weakness in the labor market. This explains the opposition of the labor movement to the unionization of the workers, as it threatened the power of the *Histadrut* parties, signalling a decline of the workers' dependence on the politically controlled and allocated subsidy.

The theoretical implication of this is that working class power relations are shaped not only by the structures of labor markets and capital, but also by the institutional pattern of the political and economic labor organizations controlling the workers. The subsequent pattern of political control must be investigated through the conceptualization of the relationship between the workers' power based on the market structure and their political organizations' action and structure.

The Israeli case provides empirical support for those who argue that the threat of full employment to the employers is crucial to the formation of the corporatist pattern (Panitch, 1977). The historical illustration of this is the first corporatist agreement in the Second World War. The sudden industrialization which began then, accompanied by an economic boom, strengthened the working class economically. They became more independent of the subsidy coming via the *Histadrut* and organized at plant level. This happened after a period of separation between the Jewish and Arab economies (1936-39) and the concomitant homogenization of the Jewish labor market, which also enhanced the rank and file workers' position. Another factor creating difficulties for capital was competition with neighboring countries producing for export to the British Empire. As the colonial government was interested in industrialization and increased production, it protected local producers against both external markets and working class militancy.

In these historical developments the main characteristics of capital's interest in corporatism are revealed. There was fierce competition between the employers for labor under conditions of full employment and a homogeneous labor market, pushing wages up. Centralized corporatist agreements could moderate the costs of competition. Capitalists are also weakened by international competition, which is affected by production costs, including wages. Corporatist wage restraint would help local producers on the international market. All these considerations in favor of collective bargaining and political exchange are groundless without the state. The state has a monopoly on legality, being the only institution which can provide a legal framework for political exchange, and the only one able to protect local interests from external pressures.

The question to be asked here is related to the origins of the relative weakness of capital in corporatism: is this weakness rooted in the power of the working class, or in the competition of employers in the labor market and of producers in international markets? Unlike the workers, however, capitalists are not seeking an arrangement which would completely eradicate competition between them, simply because competition is their raison d'etre. They organize to alleviate some harmful effects of the market, in public, nonmarket forms of political intervention.

Dualist and corporatist theories share the assumption that class power relations are a matter of struggle between labor and capital. The argument presented here is that at least in one state there are another two economic factors determining political class power relations, which have been discussed above. They are competition between the workers, and competition between the employers. Taking this line of reasoning a step further, it follows that if corporatism is a response to capital's relative weakness caused by internal class competition, and if dualism is based on labor's weakness resulting from competition between workers, then a combined pattern of dualism and corporatism will develop where both classes are weak in these ways.

Israel is a good example of a labor force constantly threatened by competition and weak capital. It is not the only society possessing these features, though perhaps they are most clearly defined in Israel. In each case where the combined pattern appears it is related to some historical peculiarities. The intention behind this study was to derive some conceptual distinctions from the Israeli case which would help in the analysis of other societies containing a combined pattern.

Capital and labor differ in their capability to transform their weakness in the labor market into political strength. While capital is able to transfer its weakness to labor within the framework of the state, labor depends on the availability of resources for distribution to convert its economic weakness to political strength. In the corporatist pattern, capital threatens labor with unemployment, on a general or national level. Labor's self-reinforcement through politics requires that the state be able to finance the interclass compromise. In dualism, capital transfers its vulnerability to fluctuating demand to a certain group of workers. These latter are differentiated from other workers by their less fortunate market position, and only the strong workers benefit from political distribution and improved incomes, in part from the welfare state and in part from the employers.

Processes of Legitimation

Legitimation is an issue of class power relations and political regulation. Corporatism and dualism are two different patterns in both of which problems of legitimacy are transferred to the internal relations of the working class. In the corporatist pattern, based on institutions, it is the trade union elites who must be legitimated in the eyes of the workers. The dualist labor market structure constructs the issue along national, ethnic, and racial lines, splitting the workers. In both cases strong labor groups or organizations may ally politically with employers, parties, and the state apparatus in order to maintain their position and exchange legitimation. In both cases there are institutional and structural limitations to the egalitarian democratic political game. In dualism the state provides the structural framework for weak workers' segregation, and in corporatism the state attributes public power to centralized unions.

Thus the possibility of authoritarian corporatism must be considered in the theoretical discussion. In this pattern the workers lack rights and political representation, and their acquiescence is imposed by force, without them recognizing the regime as legitimate. Rather than treating authoritarian corporatism as a deviant case, I prefer to conceptualize it at a level which encompasses both authoritarian and democratic features (Crouch, 1983). Thus corporatism should be considered not only as a system for mediating interests when the workers are strong, but as one form of political intervention needed by capital to compensate for economic competition, which is a flaw in its strength. Thus the segmented labor market may provide an excellent opportunity to impose corporatist policies on weak workers.

The Israeli case demonstrates that the nondemocratic, partially corporatist agreements in the private sector, made within the secondary labor market on behalf of the unrepresented workers through the *Histadrut's* political mediation, are more stable than those reached with the democratically elected representatives of the strong public sector workers.

Employers and the state have a deep concern that union elites be considered legitimate by the rank and file, as only when these elites have a fairly free hand can they make concessions on their constituents behalf in centralized negotiations which ensure control of the economy. To ensure legitimacy they not only offer the unions recognition, legal or otherwise, but also provide the workers with economic gains. This pattern of legitimation was conceptualized in chapter 5 as the "political economic labor exchange." In this exchange, economic rewards are traded for political support. Public and private employers are prepared to grant workers pay rises in centralized bargaining with unions representing them. In the eyes of the workers this legitimates the social order, perceived as responsive to their needs and which gives recognition to labor organizations, which they are therefore prepared to support. The workers that the corporatist elite fear and must pay off if necessary are those that are strong enough to challenge the centralized unions' monopoly as labor representative. It is because of the different impact of weak and strong workers in the whole political economy that it is important to include the structure of the labor market in any analysis, addressing the variations conceptually.

The *Histadrut* elections of 1985 offer substantial evidence of the state's and employers' concern for the legitimacy of this centralized trade union, and of how strong workers can threaten to withdraw their recognition of the elite's legitimacy in order to attain wage increments. The pre-election period provides indications of both the success and failure of the EESP:

a) The firm support the *Histadrut* received from the workers made it possible to implement a very unpopular plan with the *Histadrut's* cooperation. This was the key to the success in halting inflation and extracting the state from its fiscal crisis.

b) The government's and *Histadrut's* promises of wage increases to strong workers after elections established the legal basis for pay raises, despite state pressure on employers to freeze wages. This was the main failure of the plan, brought about by the planners themselves.

Because of the centrality of legitimation, the examination of ruling parties and opposition parties is essential to political economic analysis. What is in question is the ruling party's ability to coordinate interests and mediate legitimation, and the opposition's ability to obstruct state policies. Chapters 3 and 4 analyzed the shortcomings of the Likud as the sole ruling party because of its detachment from labor and capital organizations. This was a period of private sector corporatism growing power and split corporatist processes, with concomitant spiralling inflation. The disinflation process and state capacity to impose autonomous economic policies analyzed in chapter 6 were possible thanks to the broad government coalition including both the Likud and Labor parties.

In fact, because the *Histadrut* is governed politically by parties, the ruling party in it, Labor, was a vital member of any government seeking economic stability. But the same political structure later became and had previously been the principal cause of the delegitimation of the Labor party. Since 1967 the Labor party has found itself in an insuperable dilemma. The 1967 War had produced a new labor market structure, which facilitated Labor rule of the *Histadrut*, as the working class had to be protected from the effects of the influx of noncitizen workers. However, the party's government of the state was delegitimized, as there was no ideological justification either in socialist terms or according to the original national idea of exclusive "Jewish labor" for occupation of the West Bank and discrimination against Palestinians. The evidence for this delegitimation is that while Labor's control of the *Histadrut* has continued and increased from 1967 to 1989, its hold on government has diminished.[2]

Institutions and the Political Allocation of Resources

Democracy is a means for legitimating interest representation in capitalist society, but the cost of the interclass consensual compromise is high. Thus the importance of resources available for political allocation to finance it should be emphasized. The analysis of the institutionalized form of allocation is crucial to an understanding of the specific pattern of a political economy.

The main questions to be asked about the form of political allocation are: What is the role of the state in the process of political allocation? Which organizations or institutions control or influence the allocation process? How does allocation of resources bridge between political and economic structures? What material resources are available for allocation? What are the dynamics in which different social groups receive their allocation?

Political allocation of resources is crucial for the Israeli pattern, being peculiar in terms of its sources and size. As the most important sources are external, it makes more sense to refer to allocation as subsidy.[3] Without external subsidies, given to help the recipients attain their goals, the existing structure of the Israeli political economy would collapse. At first Jewish donations from abroad were given without consideration of financial return. Later, German and American aid were made partially conditional on purchases in their own industries.[4] This "disinterested" form of subsidy reinforced the public economy and the political forces governing it. The most recent change in the source of the subsidies was the sharp increase in U.S. aid grants since 1985.

Once subsidies are obtainable, the dynamics of political power are related to the strategies of various social groups for the control and distribution of the subsidies. In split corporatism, *Histadrut* and private employers on the one hand, and public sector workers on the other, were part of an institutionalized pattern in which they managed to receive large subsidies. The role of the state was to mobilize external sources for these subsidies on their behalf.

The National Unity government's EESP policies altered some aspects of the split corporatist pattern. With expanded foreign aid and the backing of both major parties, the state was able to resist demands of private sector corporatism and the workers. After the *Histadrut* economic enterprises suffered serious injury, the Labor party delegation in the government, worried about the future of the *Histadrut,* assumed mediating roles formerly performed by *Hevrat Ovdim.*

There is a difference between institutional and structural political allocation of resources. The strength of different social groups in the economic sphere depends on their ability to translate it into political power. If successful, the organized groups will try to organize their power in a stable, secure form—a structural one. The best way to solidify power is through legislation; state authority is invoked to define political strength. In this sense, certain forms of legislative action should be regarded as structural, such as the establishment of a welfare state which is hard to dismantle. Corporatism, on the other hand, is an institutional arrangement, being more flexible, relying on long-term yet temporary agreements, which arise from a constant dialogue reflecting power relations and changes in them. Dualist patterns of political economy are more stable, depending on both labor markets and state structures.

The state has both structural and institutional features. The structural role of the state lies in its monopoly of legality, and is not necessarily connected to its active intermediary role between labor and capital as an institution. In fact, all forms of subsidy are conditional upon the state providing a legal framework, but this does not mean that as a matter of course the state monopolizes its distribution. The institutional relations between the state and private interest governments (PIGs) are central to the question of state autonomy (Schmitter, 1985).

The *Histadrut* is an excellent example of a private interest institution that controls distribution. The Labor party's historical success was grounded in legal recognition of the *Histadrut's* comprehensive structure and the governmental functions it performs. Thus the party regulates a great deal of subsidy distribution, subject to far less supervision than in the state.

The *Histadrut's* pivotal position in the political economy is based on its distributive role, which allows it to penetrate into other areas of society. An example of the complex inter relationship of *Histadrut* and state is the so-called *Hevrat Ovdim* program. This agreement was not determined by legislation, but was constantly revised by the government. It was first made at a time when *Mapai* (Labor) controlled both bodies and allowed the *Hevrat Ovdim* to distribute 50 percent of the pension fund's capital as free credit for investment (Grinberg, forthcoming). As the whole private sector required this capital, its investment program gave the *Histadrut* enormous influence in trading capital subsidies for corporatist agreements.

Even so the *Histadrut* political economic structure rests on the state's legal framework. This is why the state has threatened it several times with legislative changes, such as a law for compulsory arbitration in labor disputes, and the nationalization of its health service and pension funds. Although the *Histadrut's* legal dependence on the state provides the latter with a bargaining card to counter the demands of the former, the state is unwilling to play this card. There are two main reasons for this. Firstly, the card can only be played once. Secondly, once it has been played, it would result in unknown changes in the whole political economic game. This was the case of Horowitz's cancellation of the *Hevrat Ovdim* program in 1980. The long range results of this step were: an intensification of the state's intervention in capital markets; ongoing bargaining between the *Histadrut* and government about the rate of interest to be paid on the pension funds; *Hevrat Ovdim's* economic crisis and interminable negotiations about state subsidies to rescue it; and the new pattern of the NUG in which the Labor party government members represent the *Histadrut's* interests.

Despite all these changes the *Histadrut* still maintained its pivotal position. The reason for this unaltered outcome is that the state has an interest in the legitimation of the existing social order, and as the

Histadrut is a keystone in it, the two remain mutually dependent.

While the relative autonomous capacity of a strong, quasi-statist institution to allocate resources is remarkable in Israel, it is not exceptional. There are other states where employers and trade unions play distributive roles, contributing to particular political economic patterns. The theoretical implication of this is that the institutional form of political allocation and its structural connections with the state are crucial issues for analysis.

This is particularly true of Israel, where historically the *Histadrut* was the main institution of the "state in the making", the *Yishuv*. When the state of Israel was established, *Mapai* (Labor) intended to control it as well as the *Histadrut*, dividing state functions between the two and ensuring its strong position on the basis of the *Histadrut's* capacities. Relations between *Histadrut* and the state, the partition of roles between them, their mutual dependence and conflict are essential to an understanding of Israel's peculiar political economy.

Structures and Conjunctures

The structural bases of the Israeli political economy are a labor market which is split along national and ethnic lines, the *Histadrut's* political mediation of capital and labor interests, and the state's provision of a legal framework for both, while mobilizing the resources for subsidies through foreign aid. There are two main conjunctural features of the political economy. These are the economic fluctuation of demand and political changes in degrees of legitimation. The pivotal position of the *Histadrut* is related to both structures and conjunctures. The *Histadrut's* peculiar political structure is dependent on the split labor market and state subsidy. The *Histadrut* is also a prominent broker of political legitimation of the social order and coordinator of the economic demands of capital and labor.

Perhaps this study's most significant finding is that the processes of change did not alter institutions and structures. In fact, crises were overcome by complex adjustments in the political economy that conserved the essential elements of the existing pattern. The lack of any secure basis for collective bargaining from 1966 to 1970 was made good by the agreement in 1970 to divide the bargaining process, and hence the workers, into sectors representing labor groups' market strength. The crisis between the state and the *Histadrut* which echoed in the ruling party from 1974 to 1977 was resolved by the new balance of power, leaving Labor in control of the *Histadrut* and putting the Likud into government. This partition of power made possible the permutation in the political economy, which emerged between 1977 and 1983, the split corporatist pattern.

In split corporatism the differentiated strength of groups of workers in the labor market was channeled by private sector corporatism into two levels of wage restraint and two sets of collective bargaining, divided between the public and private sectors. There was also a political understanding that the state would subsidize both private sector corporatism and public sector employees. The split corporatist pattern had inflationary consequences, as a result of which the state experienced a fiscal crisis. Finally, to resolve this crisis a broad national unity government coalition was established.

The NUG's foremost task was to strengthen the state's capacities in relation to other social forces, so that it could stabilize the economy that was plummeting into alarming hyperinflation. The disinflation policy put an end to large state subsidies of capital and plunged almost all the *Histadrut*-linked economic institutions into crisis. Once the budget deficit was wiped out, the fiscal crisis of the state was transferred to the *Histadrut's Hevrat Ovdim*. It then became the Labor party representatives in the government who demanded capital subsidies. This stabilized the apparently contingent Likud-Labor party coalition, making it an important feature of the new political economic pattern.[5]

The relevant question to be asked here is why was each crisis resolved by a more sophisticated adjustment of the political economy? Is it a matter of functional adaptation by the system? Bearing in mind that each solution cost money, which some generous donor had to provide, they clearly involved a different process to functional adaptation. Yet in my opinion there is an additional crucial factor at work. Each of the main structural bases of the political economy has powerful social forces and political organizations behind it. The Labor party, strong workers, and their organizations support the *Histadrut's* political structure. The Likud, Jewish employers of Palestinian labor, and weak Oriental workers uphold the split labor market.[6] Obviously both parties, along with a large majority of Israeli Jewish organizations and citizens, approve the use of foreign aid to subsidize the state.

If structural factors are backed by strong, organized groups, then the spontaneous organizations and forces thrown up by the fluctuating processes are not powerful enough to change them. This was the case of the Forum in 1980 and the EESP in 1985, when class conflict between capital and labor threatened to erupt.

In 1980 the contradiction between labor and capital prevented the *Histadrut* from mediating the interests of each. The managers in the *Hevrat Ovdim* supported the government and private employers' policy of dismissals, whereas the labor representatives demanded full employment and wage increases. In the absence of representative trade unions and exclusive working class parties and under conditions of a split labor market, the general weakness of the working class affected strong labor groups too. This was the first time these groups had been directly threatened by employers. Yet the Forum rejected a strategy to change the *Histadrut's* internal corporatist structure or to abolish the split labor market. As their strategy was defensive, once the crisis was over the Forum became redundant and each workers' committee returned to its previous, strong position in the split corporatist pattern. In this sense the establishment of the Forum and its action was a pseudorevolt. The Forum awareness of their inability to change structures meant that the strategy chosen by them was pragmatic, and the most appropriate to their interests. It also explains why the *Histadrut* secretary-general regarded the Forum as a positive initiative: he saw its potential for extracting the *Histadrut* from its crisis and rescuing it from its internal labor-capital contradiction. That is precisely what the Forum did.

In 1985 the state was in a crisis that had to be ended by any means. The top Treasury officials formulated the new EESP policy with the aim of altering the political economic pattern of state involvement in the labor and capital markets. This policy was backed by massive American economic aid and across the board political support. Nevertheless, structures were not transformed. On this occasion the strong workers did not organize separately but played an important role in obstructing government officials' plans for structural change: they launched a campaign immediately after the program's contents were disclosed which helped the *Histadrut* win some wage concessions; they fought against dismissals in the public sector; and they obtained high wage increases in the private sector. But it was the *Histadrut* itself that primarily coordinated the activities against structural change, while attempting to maintain its pivotal role in the political economy. In addition to aggregating the workers' demands, the *Histadrut* collaborated with its private sector corporatist partners to pressurize the government to renew the devaluation policy and mobilized the Labor party delegation in the government to obtain state subsidies for its enterprises. All these efforts did not avert the *Hevrat Ovdim* crisis, but preserved the intervention of the state in the economy, its subsidization of capital and labor, and its own pivotal position in the political economy. Even *Hevrat Ovdim's* economic crisis seems to be a logical outcome of the state's autonomous EESP, as previously this body was the political center of PSC whose demands caused the state's fiscal crisis.

The structural aspect of politics, solidified by legislation and centered on the state's legal monopoly, is much more easily understable than its flexible, conjunctural facet. Political fluctuations are mainly attributable to the actions of parties, not only at elections and periodic changes of government, but in the everyday struggles that occur between the ruling and opposition parties. Party political processes, which are integrally involved with the legitimation of the state and social order, have been misestimated by corporatist scholars and ignored by dualist theorists. The ruling party is able to determine the specific form of distribution performed by the state or other institutions. It is also able to change the role of the state in a dual labor market and the extent of its mediation between labor and capital.

Thus the conceptual differentiation proposed by Schmitter (1985) between governments and state administrations is essential to an understanding of the state's autonomous capacities. The Israeli case study shows that to the three conditions of state autonomy listed by Skocpol (1982)—a crisis situation, strategies developed by skilled officials, and availability of financial resources—a fourth should be added: political institutions mobilizing support and legitimation.

Conclusion

Corporatism and dualism were useful theoretical frameworks for understanding the complex pattern of the Israeli political economy. Their use lies mainly in their conceptualization of typical patterns of class conflict regulation in capitalist societies. These approaches led this study to address key questions, generating fresh discoveries. The effectiveness of applying both theories in combination emerges when they are rejected as ideal types and a historical methodology is adopted. The approach developed in this study emphasizes the compatibility of both patterns which focus on different aspects of the political economy: corporatism on institutionalized political exchange, and dualism on structural economic divisions within the working class.

Two principal aspects of political economy demand more sophisticated analysis, research, and theoretical conceptualization: the state and ruling parties. The main shortcoming in dualist and corporatist theories requiring elaboration is the question of the legitimation of power relations and their coordination by political parties within the framework of the state. Dualist theory clearly pays little attention to politics, but even corporatism, which focuses on legitimation and political exchange, has not yet sufficiently developed these themes in its research and theory.

The role of the state in political power relations, legitimation, and political allocation of resources is crucial but far from simple. In each political economic pattern the transformation of class conflict and the transference of crises of that conflict take place in the legal framework of the state. But the specific mode of operation of the state, its intervention, control, or domination of the economy and politics, is not constant. The fluctuation in all of these factors should be included in theories seeking to explain political exchange and economic structure.

Israel seems to be a very peculiar case, but not unique. The "unique" approach induces research to focus its analysis on national characteristics of the Jewish people and the conflict with Palestinians. From this perspective the more typical social models and theories are disregarded as irrelevant to the unique case. This study set out to demonstrate the value of a contrasting approach: Israel's complex peculiarities make it a very fruitful test case for theories and patterns which have been developed by social scientists, as the confrontation with its idiosyncrasies fertilizes theoretical refinement and evolution.

The characterization of Israel's political economy as split corporatism should not be misinterpreted as the theoretical goal of this work. Every society develops its own concrete political economic patterns, be they complex or simple. The common features of each pattern are the subject of social theory, generating questions which help the researcher to identify specific patterns. In this sense the combination of corporatist and dualist approaches is an improvement compared to the use of both separately. Yet this does not imply that there is a tendency of advanced capitalism to converge in a combined pattern. Such convergence only seems likely from a perspective in which the combination of both patterns is a matter of structural-functionalist adaptation. This study intended to demonstrate the contrary: the specific pattern of each political economy is fashioned continuously by social struggles centered on class conflict. Its changing features are shaped by structures and institutions, backed by powerful social forces. But the outcomes of these clashes of forces are unpredictable, and therefore logically undetermined. What can be done is to analyze and explain changes after their occurrence. The constant fluctuations of the Israeli case support this modest but cautious approach.

APPENDIX OF SOURCES

DOCUMENTARY SOURCES
(AND THE ABBREVIATIONS USED IN CITATIONS)

Newspapers

Davar	D.
Ha'aretz	HA.
Maariv	MA.
Yediot Aharonot	YA.
Hadashot	HS.
Al Hamishmar	AM.
Hahistadrut Bahadashot	HB.

Archives

Labor Archives (Lavon Institution)	LA.
Histadrut Central Committee Minutes	CC.

Bank of Israel

"Last Month's Economic Developments,"	
Research Department Report.	BI. (No.)

List of Interviewees

The following list indicates the informant's position during 1980-1987, and the abbreviations by which they are cited in the text (linked to "INT").

Avitan, Shlomo, chairman, Graded Seamen's Association.   AS
Ayash, Matti, chairman, Ashdod Port Workers' Committee.   AM
Bar'am, Uzi, secretary-general of the Labor party.   BU
Ben Menahem, Eli, member, El Al ground crew committee.   BME
Berglas, Eitan, EESP programming team member. Bank
   Hapoalim chairman.   BE
Blumenthal, Naftali, chairman, Koor board of directors.   BN
Bruno, Michael, EESP programming team member. Bank of
   Israel governor from 1986.   BM
Fogel, Aharon, chairman of the budget division in the
   Ministry of the Treasury.   FA
Gavish, Shaike, Koor general manager.   GS
Horovitz, Yigal, finance minister, 1980.   HY
Keisar, Israel, chairman, *Histadrut* trade union department.
   Histadrut secretary general from 1984.   KI
Knafo, David, chairman, Dead Sea Works Committee.   KD
Liram, Oded, chairman of the wage committee of the
   Engineers' Association.   LO
Mandelbaum, Moshe, Bank of Israel governor until 1986.   MM
Meshel, Yeruham, *Histadrut* secretary general, 1977-84.   MY
Modai, Itzhak, finance minister, 1984-1986.   MI
Neubach, Amnon, Prime Minister Peres' economic advisor.   NA
Overkovitz, Yoram, chairman, Electric Company Workers'
   Committee.   OY
Rubin, Amos, Prime Minister Shamir's economic advisor.   RA
Shavit, Abraham ("Buma"), chairman of *Lishkat Hateum* and
   Manufacturers' Association. El Al board of directors.   SA

Other Abbreviations Used in the Text

Cost of Living Allowance.   COLA
Emergency Economic Stabilization Plan.   EESP
National Unity Government.   NUG
Private Interest Government.   PIG
Private Sector Corporatism.   PSC
World Zionist Organization.   WZO

NOTES

PROLOGUE

1. See the Appendix for further details concerning the sources, including the abbreviations used in the chapters which follow when citing newspaper articles, interviews, and archival materials.

2. Some of the documents which we received from anonymous sources are cited in the text. This refers primarily to internal memoranda of the Manufacturers' Association, referred to only by date.

3. This phrase is the literal translation of the Hebrew term for what is generally understood as the private sector. The reason for the idiosyncratic Israeli term is that it is used to include *Histadrut*-owned enterprises as well as privately owned firms. Hereafter I shall use the term private sector to include the *Histadrut* enterprises.

4. This contention is "opposite" only in terms of the possibility of synthesizing dualism and corporatism, but is merely the other side of the coin in relation to the significance of the synthesis. While Goldthorpe maintains that the working class will become apolitical, I contend that from the capitalist point of view this is an overly ambitious goal.

CHAPTER 1

1. My own view is that Israel is neither an advanced capitalist country nor a developing country, and, as shall be demonstrated, Israeli corporatism fits neither the democratic nor the autocratic pattern, but is rather a combination of the two.

2. The term "fragmented" is not intended as a fourth, additional concept,

but is rather presented here as a neutral approach to the three existing ones. It is important to mention this since I see the existing concepts not as alternatives, but rather as models that can be synthesized into a broader theoretical framework. The concept "dual" was chosen as a heading because of its chronological primacy, and not out of any theoretical preference. The intent was rather to comprise within this concept the problematic aspects of the origins of nonuniform markets.

3. What is referred to here is the importing of products manufactured in developing countries with low wage scales, which forces the developed country's companies to lower the cost of labor in order to successfully compete with the imports.

4. This workers' strategy can suit that of the employers who seek to maintain depressed pockets. This combination also approximates the approaches of the two previous theories.

5. Furthermore, a central criticism of Bonacich's theory is that state intervention is needed to keep the two labor markets separate (Peled and Shafir, 1987; Peled, 1990).

6. The Zionist consensus on full employment for Jews did not evolve without internal conflict, involving a struggle in the formative period that will be examined in the following chapter. The agreement to employ high-priced labor was achieved with the help of national subsidization, through Jewish funds raised abroad. Furthermore, the full employment agreement applied only to Jews.

7. The Hebrew concept *(Hameshek)* refers in a generic way to the economic system, but inside the *Histadrut* it is also the everyday name for the *Hevrat Ovdim*.

8. On the nonprofitability of Zionism in economic terms, see Kimmerling, *Zionism and Economy* (1982).

9. Most Israeli capital, whose source is foreign aid, is concentrated in the hands of the public employer.

CHAPTER 2

1. For explanations of Hebrew words, concepts and details of Israeli personalities, see glossary and interviewees list.

2. "Self-contained labor economy" refers to the companies and plants owned cooperatively by groups of workers, labor parties, or the *Histadrut*. WZO public capital investments are usually involved. In order to create jobs not subject to the profit motive for Jews, management, labor, and ownership are placed under labor's control. Organized under a roof company called *Hevrat Ovdim*

and controlled by the *Histadrut*, these firms play an important role in the Israeli economy (see Horovitz, 1948).

3. On the problematic aspects of the labor market, its threat to Zionism, and the manner in which the Second *Aliya* period labor parties dealt with it, see Shafir (1989).

4. On the organization of groups of workers aiming to prevent market competition and to exclude "other" workers, and the significance of cooperatives see Weber (1978:339-343).

5. The *Histadrut* leadership had clashed with the construction workers in the leftist opposition as early as 1921. Construction was a rapidly growing area that absorbed many workers, who wished to organize as a labor union. The *Histadrut*, however, demanded that they organize as a cooperatively-owned construction contracting company. The construction workers' organization was paralyzed for two years, until a compromise between the two positions was formulated. See Studni (1975). The cooperatives embodied a certain form of internal corporatism within the structure of the *Histadrut*, in the sense that capital-labor conflict was subsidized and politically mediated.

6. It was not only the opposition of the Jewish political bodies that caused the failure of joint Jewish-Arab labor organization; even more important were the market conditions that drove workers of various ethnic groups and wage levels to compete with each other for jobs. On the differences in labor and commercial cooperative activity, see my monograph (1986) "The Jewish-Arab Drivers' Association Strike of 1931," unpublished paper.

7. "Labor economy" is the term popularly applied to the network of enterprises amalgamated as the *Hevrat Ovdim*.

8. Ben Gurion saw the labor movement not only as a representation of the workers' interests, but also as a factor of prime importance for most of the Jewish population, including the bourgeoisie (Ben Gurion, 1974:205).

9. The labor councils are the local branches of the *Histadrut* executive committee. They are also chosen by proportional party elections, but the labor councils are more open to the workers' influence simply because of their proximity to them.

10. Local unions represent the compromise between the workers' demand for trade unions and the *Histadrut's* efforts toward party control. They function as embryonic labor unions, dealing with the problems of an economic branch and individual plants, but are under party control.

11. *Hashomer Hatzair* began as a Zionist socialist youth movement with its own collective settlement groups. The *Histadrut's* party structure and the confrontation over ideological and political issues prompted *Hashomer Hatzair* to start defining itself as a Marxist-Leninist group (without abandoning its

Zionism) and to join the urban workers' protest movement (see Margalit, 1971).

12. *Histadrut* membership was the condition for membership in *Mapai*. *Histadrut* membership, however, did not depend on the member's work, but rather on his interest in the *Histadrut's* services. *Kupat Holim* made new immigrants dependent on *Mapai*. Also the urban middle class could be members of the *Histadrut* through *Kupat Holim*.

13. The *moshav* is another type of cooperative agricultural settlement, which includes more private features than the kibbutz and was therefore considered more suitable for the Oriental "mentality." Oriental refers to Jews originating in Asian and African countries, also referred to in the literature as Sefardim or Easterners.

14. In 1954 there was a new split when *Achdut Ha'avodah* left *Mapam*.

15. In 1951, *Kibbutz Hameuhad* split between its *Mapai* and *Mapam* supporters. In 1954, *Mapam* split between the founders of *Achdut Ha'avodah* (who came from *Mapai*) and *Hashomer Hatzair* veterans, who continued to be called *Mapam*. In 1955, after years in the opposition, *Mapam* and *Achdut Ha'avodah* joined the government. Both changes in the composition of the work force and the kibbutz movement's dependence on government subsidies had far-reaching effects on both parties.

16. Action committees are horizontal associations among workers' committees, principally in the Tel Aviv area (Gush Dan).

17. The Liberal Party has traditionally represented private capital—merchants and industrialists formerly called "General Zionists." *Herut* was the nationalist opposition body that united the underground movements that had withdrawn from the *Haganah* (the *Yishuv's* defense force) during the mandate—*Etzel* and *Lehi*. *Herut* also had a following among the veteran Sefardi community, and benefitted from the frustrations of a growing number of Oriental immigrants who had undergone a process of proletarization under *Mapai*.

18. It is important to distinguish between trade unions and the trade union department. The former are labor groups that represent economic branches or specific trades—government employees, teachers, engineers, etc. Some were established by the *Histadrut*, which controls them through party elections, and others were able to "liberate" themselves and conduct nonparty workplace elections. The trade union department, on the other hand, is the political body appointed by the *Histadrut* executive committee to deal with the *Histadrut's* trade unions' affairs, and symbolizes the centralist attempt to impose discipline over the workers without their participation in the processes of bargaining and exchange.

19. Military industry represents an intermediate sector which is partly government owned and partly in partnership with *Hevrat Ovdim* and the pri-

vate sector. This sector is dependent on government demand, that is, on the defense budget. It also represents an intermediary area in respect of its work force and their organizational level.

20. On the connection between voting for Alignment and *Histadrut* membership, see Arian (1973). Bahat (1979) conducted a comparative analysis of the tie between membership in the Labor party and membership in the *Histadrut*, showing that this tie is more prominent in Israel than in other countries.

21. The Likud representatives (headed by *Herut*) in the *Histadrut* "parliament," the Executive Committee, followed a "worker-oriented" line that opposed the *Histadrut* leadership's tendency to compromise with the government. The Likud representatives in the Knesset, particularly the Liberal leaders, demanded a less interventionist economic policy in subsidies, foreign currency, and other areas.

22. After strong labor groups managed to contravene the centralized policy and receive increments in irregular agreements, partial COLA payments became a wage restraining tool for the *Histadrut* and the employers (Leviatan, 1982).

23. This gap is even more significant if we take into account that fewer voters are eligible to participate in *Histadrut* elections than in Knesset elections, and that the proportion of voter participation is lower in the *Histadrut* elections.

24. The WZO is politically funded and supported.

25. Shapiro (1984) discusses the role of the the large Jewish bourgeoisie's non-*aliya* in the formation of the political elite.

26. The Hebrew concept for private sector is "business sector." This term was coined in the 1970s when the *Histadrut* owned enterprises passed from the public to the private sector. The "business sector" including private and *Histadrut* employers is here called the private sector.

27. The Civil Servants' Association did make some attempts to express the power of certain strong groups of workers through workers' committees in the workplace. The workers, however, are divided between strong and weak groups (the latter known as "unprivileged"). The unprivileged workers, who are the majority, are those who failed to obtain increments or special benefits for their work. Attempts to organize a nonparty list to control the union failed, chiefly because the *Histadrut* loyalists have been able to exploit the controversy between the strong workers, who seek independence, and the weak, who depend on the *Histadrut* as a mediator. The Clerks' Association is the union controlled to the greatest degree. This group represents clerks working for large nongovernment public institutions, chiefly the *Histadrut* and various municipalities, where party control is highly centralized. The technicians' organization is a somewhat stronger and more independent group because it represents skilled workers in all the sectors, but this group is nevertheless under the *Histadrut's*

ruling party control through the elections system—an expression of its weakness in the labor market in relation to the professional groups. Another group notably under party-*Histadrut* control is the nurses, most of whom work for the *Histadrut Kupat Holim*. This control disintegrated in 1986, when the less dependent nurses, those working in hospitals, withdrew from the nurses' organization and established an independent organization based on personal election of committees in the workplace (see chapter 6).

CHAPTER 3

1. The arrangement in which a comprehensive pension plan was traded for cheap credit came to my attention through a student who worked as a bank clerk responsible for pension funds. Since he was not willing to be quoted, I had to seek other sources. The existence of the deal was confirmed in interviews with Manufacturers' Association head Shavit, Koor management council chairman Blumental, and then Finance Minister Horowitz. However, none confirmed the student's contention that the agreement was a condition for continuation of COLA payments. There is, nevertheless, a correspondence in time between the months when the COLA was not paid (May and June) and the signing of the pension agreement (the beginning of June).

2. The *Histadrut* changed its position within a day, between one meeting of the Central Committee and another. The moderate decision that followed the Finance Ministry's announcement of its policy on 20 November 1979 was adopted almost without discussion. The next day a long debate took place, during which hundreds of workers' committee members packed the Executive Committee. It was only then that a strike was called. It is worth noting that the *Histadrut* secretary-general was absent from the first meeting and that it was he who strongly urged a strike at the second, with broad hints that trade union department chairman Israel Keisar was responsible for the lukewarm reaction to the Finance Ministry (CC., LA. 20-21/11/79).

3. The El Al ground crew committees initiated the first meeting, during which the Forum was established. The two committee leaders—Alignment activist Eli Ben Menahem and Likud activist Eitan Rozenman—expressed a political formula that held for the Forum as well.

4. It is important to understand the contention that the weak workers are dependent on the *Histadrut*. The trade union department controls the "strike fund" designed to provide the workers with a wage during their struggles. The *Histadrut* uses these vast sums to create workers' committee dependence on the centralized trade union department. Any committee wishing to strike must first obtain the authorization of the trade union department in order to receive the financial support of the strike fund. The strong labor groups are those that can do without the strike fund and thus conduct unauthorized strikes.

5. In Israel there was still only one state television channel.

6. The Alignment's meteoric rise in the public opinion polls is undoubtedly attributable to the Likud government's economic failures. During the period in question, the government scored an impressive foreign policy gain in the form of the Camp David Israel-Egypt peace agreements.

CHAPTER 4

1. Aridor was the first *Herut* finance minister since the Likud had come to power in 1977. His predecessors came from other Likud factions: Erlich was a member of the Liberal party and Horowitz of *Rafi*, a faction that had originally supported Ben Gurion and withdrew from *Mapai* in 1965. (Horowitz's labor movement background may have influenced his approach and his closeness to the *Histadrut* and *Hevrat Ovdim*.) Prior to 1977, Aridor had been active in the Likud faction in the *Histadrut*, which he led together with David Levy. At the time of Aridor's appointment, the two were very close, and both were keenly aware of the need to renew ties with the Likud constituents of the lower socioeconomic strata.

2. The finance minister's proposal of a monthly COLA payment of 100 percent was unquestionably much more generous than the COLA payment agreed on by the *Histadrut* and the *Lishkat Hateum*, which was paid every three months at a rate ranging from 80 percent to 90 percent of the price rise index. However, the *Histadrut's* demand for monthly updating of the tax scales also entailed an advantage for the government included in this proposal. If the COLA were paid every month, but the income tax grades were not updated, the increments would cause both a rise in the workers' real wage and a concomitant increase in taxes paid by the employer. The *Histadrut* did not agree to this, and the proposal became a bone of contention from the time Aridor took office until the beginning of 1983.

3. With the outbreak of the war, the public sector trade unions stopped their sanctions and plans to strike in an expression of willingness to contribute to the war effort.

4. Despite the *Histadrut's* control over the union organization, the negotiations were the occasion for several strikes, the first for forty-eight hours and later ones held on individual union level. The *Histadrut* was able to decentralize the strikes and prevent the unions from intensifying their collective action by means of those unions in which its control was greatest—the government workers' organization, the clerks, and to some degree the technicians. In all these unions leaders were elected in proportional elections of party lists. When the professional unions demanded a general strike of all the workers, the *Histadrut* leadership outmaneuvered them by "sending" the clerks and government employees out on separate strikes (*HA.* 9, 16, 21, 27/12/82).

5. The COLA arrangements were almost always ratified as an addition to the wage agreements, after negotiations between the *Histadrut* and the *Lishkat Hateum*. This agreement was usually automatically extended to the rest of the economy. This system was generally acceptable to the finance minister because of the ability and desire of private sector corporatism to restrain wages.

6. This was proposed during a period of 6-9 percent monthly inflation.

7. 85 percent was the rate stipulated in the previous agreement, and was determined by anticipated inflation.

CHAPTER 5

1. The bank shares crisis in October 1983 was the inevitable outcome of the banks' policy of regulating their shares, initiated in the 70s. The selfregulation allowed share prices to reach inflated levels by 1981, and in October 1983 crisis the bank shares lost 50 percent of their value. The government intervened to end the crisis, by undertaking to redeem the stocks at their dollar value in October 1988. Thus the state saved the banks from bankruptcy at the cost of practically "nationalizing" them.

2. Labor party 44; Likud 41; Religious parties 13 (Mafdal 4, Agudat-Israel 2, Morasha 2, Shas 4, Tami 1), Center parties 7 (Weizman 3, Horovitz 1, Shinui 3); extreme right wing 6 (Techia 5, Kahane 1); left wing 9 (Ratz 3, Progressive 2, Communists 4).

3. In the second unity government established after the elections in 1988 the picture was clearer, so that few doubt that the main group interested in this coalition was the *Histadrut*, which was a crucial factor in the battle within the Labor party over the question of the establishment of the NUG (INT-BU).

4. This does not mean that the Likud always has an interest in a NUG, as conjunctures are constantly changing. Chapters 3 and 4 discuss the maintenance of the *Histadrut's* structure in spite of the existence of a government headed by the Likud and without the Labor party.

5. In fact, this rise was of 14 percent (*HB*. 28/5/85).

6. For the labor market motives which push Oriental workers to support the right wing parties, see Peled, research report for the Sapir Institute (1989).

7. The political organization and revolt of the Palestinians towards the end of 1987, including the proliferation of strikes and their effect on the Israeli economy, deserve serious attention within the conceptual analysis proposed here, but is beyond the scope of this research.

CHAPTER 6

1. This is Neubach's (1986) version of the proposed plan.

2. These are seen in the comparison of the panel's plan and the Government Resolutions (number 707, 30/6/85-1/7/85).

3. The previous exchange rate insurance arrangement with the government was replaced by a blanket payment of 11 percent of the value of exports (INT-FA). Thus the exporters became very interested in a devaluation, since in any case they would have received the 11 percent.

4. Later on, in a period beyond the scope of this research, the "Koor" company joined this list and thus it would be fair to say that the whole of *Hevrat Ovdim* was in a state of crisis, excluding Bank *Hapoalim*.

5. An example of the *Histadrut's* ability to manipulate the Alignment can be seen in the establishment of the NUG in 1988 and in particular the allocation of the Finance portfolio to a Labor minister, which above all was a response to the needs of the *Histadrut*. The new economic policy, which accepts the demands of the employers for further devaluations, also caters more to the dictates of PSC than to the considerations of the state.

EPILOGUE

1. The general tendency of Jewish low-paid workers, originating mainly from Arab countries, is to support the right wing anti-Arab and anti-*Histadrut* Likud party. Well-paid and skilled workers, originating mainly from European countries, tend to support the *Histadrut* ruling party, now called the Labor party.

2. At the time of writing in 1989, the total length of time in which there has been a national unity government was eight years. The two periods of unity government differ in that in 1967-70 the Likud (as *Gahal*) was a marginal coalition partner, not needed to form a majority, whereas the 1984-88 coalition was an equal partnership. The government coalition since 1988 is led by Likud but with almost a fifty-fifty division of power.

3. In other societies, too, resources for political allocation originate in international exchange, such as commercial trade, dependence of underdeveloped countries, or colonialism. The broad question of the influence of particular forms of international exchange and their impact on the political economic pattern is beyond the scope of this study.

4. In this sense, Israel indirectly subsidizes American and German industries.

5. It is probably not coincidental the Likud's aim in the 1989 *Histadrut* elections is to form a coalition like that of the government. This would add complexity to the political economic pattern.

6. The support of the Orientals is the least comprehensible aspect here. It is expressed primarily by voting for the Likud. After 1967 the segmentation of the labor market raised the employment status of certain groups of Oriental Jews, while the Likud's ideological commitment to retain the occupied territories offered a guarantee of their new position. But after the deterioration of the economic crisis, their attitudes seem to have moved closer to split labor market exclusionist strategies of the extreme right, although they still vote Likud (see Peled, 1989).

Achdut Ha'avodah: a) majority political party in the *Histadrut* founded in 1919 by Poalei Zion and unaffiliated workers. In 1930 merged with Mapai; b) minority splinter party from *Mapai* in 1944, rejoining *Mapai* for the 1965 elections, and together with Rafi forming the Labor party in 1968

Aliya: (literally, "ascent") Zionist ideological concept for Jewish immigration to Israel

Aridor, Yoram: Likud Finance Minister 1981-1983

Bank Hapoalim: *Histadrut*-owned bank

Begin, Menachem: *Herut* leader since 1948, prime minister from 1977-1983

Ben Aharon. Yitzhak: *Achdut Ha'avodah* leader and *Histadrut* secretary-general from 1969-1973

Ben Gurion, David: *Mapai* leader and prime minister 1948-1953 and 1955-1963

Eretz Israel: biblical concept for the land of Israel, but also Hebrew term for the geographical area of the British Mandate

Erlich, Simha: first Likud finance minister from 1977-79; leader of the Liberal party

Etzel: Hebrew acronym for National Military Organization. A right wing military underground group led by Menachem Begin, and basis for the *Herut* party

Framework Agreements: biennial collective wage agreements reached separately in the private and public sectors. These agreements are merely the basis for further industrial, professional and enterprise-level negotiations.

Gahal: *Herut*-Liberal bloc, formed in 1965, merged with other small parties to form the Likud in 1973

Gdud Ha'avodah: Zionist, cooperative-based labor organization in the 1920s with a communist ideology opposed to the *Histadrut* leadership

Hagana: official pre-state underground defense forces under Jewish Agency command

HaKibbutz Hameuhad: The largest kibbutz association, affiliated with *Achdut Ha'avodah* and *Mapai*

Hapoel Hatzair: Zionist centrist Labor party founded in 1905, merged into *Mapai* with *Achdut Ha'avodah* in 1930

Hashomer Hatzair: Zionist socialist youth movement at its inception, later turning to Marxism-Leninism, and in 1948 founding the *Mapam* party

Herut: right wing party led by Menachem Begin. Majority party in the Likud list established in 1973 and during its 1977-1984 period in power

Hevrat Ovdim: holding company of all *Histadrut*-linked economic enterprises

Histadrut: the General Organization of Hebrew Workers in the Land of Israel, founded in 1920

Jewish Agency: the primary organization of Zionism in the pre-state era, implementing policies of the WZO

Knesset: the Israeli Parliament

Koor: *Histadrut* holding company for manufacturing enterprises

Kupat Holim: the *Histadrut's* health service and medical insurance fund

Lavon, Pinhas: *Histadrut* secretary-general during 1956-1960

Lehi: Small right wing military underground during the *Yishuv* period

Levinson, Yaakov: Bank Hapoalim Chairman during 1967-1982

Likud: right wing unified electoral list established in 1973 by *Gahal* and other small parties. Majority party in 1977 and 1981 elections

Lishkat Hateum (or *Teum*): coordinating bureau of economic organizations. Established in 1965, effectively active since 1970 Package Deal Agreement. Represents all private employers' associations headed by the Manufacturers' Association

Maki: Israeli Communist Party

Mamlachti: Hebrew term for the priority of national goals

Mapai: *Eretz* Israel Workers' Party. Established in 1930 by *Achdut Ha'avodah* and *Hapoel Hatzair*. Ruling party during 1948-1968 and main force in the merger with *Rafi* and *Achdut Ha'avodah* into the Labor Party in 1968. In government until 1977

Mapam: United Workers' party. Left wing Zionist-Socialist party rooted in *Hashomer Hatzair* movement. Established in 1948 together with *Achdut Ha'avodah*, merged with Labor party in 1969 Alignment, and participant with Labor party in government

Palmach: pre-state underground military strike force committed to Zionist institutions and linked to Labor movement

Poalei Zion: Zionist Socialist party founded in 1905. Central party of *Achdut Ha'avodah* foundation in 1919

Rafi: electoral list led by David Ben Gurion after split with *Mapai* in 1965. Joined *Mapai* and *Achdut Ha'avodah* before 1969 elections to form the Labor party

Solel Boneh: *Histadrut's* building company

Va'ad Ha-Leumi: National Council, the governing body of the Jewish community during the British Mandate

Weizman, Haim (Dr.): second chairman of World Zionist Organization and first president of Israel

Yerida: literally "descent," Zionist ideological concept for Jewish emigration from Israel

Yishuv: pre-state Jewish community in Palestine, refers also to the pre-state period

BIBLIOGRAPHY

Arian, A. 1973. *The Choosing People: Voting Behavior in Israel*. Cleveland: Case Western Reserve University Press.

Arnon, Y. 1979. "The Israeli Economy 1953-1978 and Forecast for 1979." *Economic Quarterly*, 100:27-45 (Hebrew).

Artstein, Y. and Z. Sussman. 1988. "Wage Policy During Disinflation: The Israeli Stabilization Program of 1985." Discussion Paper 88.07, *Bank of Israel Research Department*.

Baharl, E. 1965. "The Effect of Mass Immigration on Wages in Israel." Jerusalem: Falk Project.

Bahat, S. 1979. *Structural Relations Between Trade Unions and Labor Parties: A Comparative Study*. Unpublished M.A. thesis, Department of Labor Studies, Tel Aviv University (Hebrew).

Bauboeck, R. and H. Wimmer. 1988. "Social Partnership and 'Foreigners Policy': On Special Features of Austria's Guest-Worker System." *European Journal of Political Research*, 16: 659-681.

Ben Gurion, D. 1974. *From Class to Nation*. Tel Aviv: Am Oved (Hebrew).

Ben Porat, Y. 1975. "The Years of Plenty and the Years of Famine—A Political Business Cycle?" *Kyklos*, 28:400-403.

———. 1982. "The Conservative Turnabout That Never Was. Ideology and Economic Policy in Israel since 1977." *Economic Quarterly*, 115:325-33 (Hebrew). English version: *Jerusalem Quarterly*, 115:3-10.

Blumenthal, N. 1984. "The Influence of Defense Industry Investment on Israel's Economy." in *Israel Security Planning in the 1980s*, ed. E. Lanir. Tel Aviv University: Praeger Publishers. Pp. 166-180.

190   Bibliography

Bonacich, E. 1972. "A Theory of Ethnic Antagonism: The Split Labor Market." *American Sociological Review*, 37:547-559.

——— . 1979. "The Past, Present, and Future of Split Labor Market Theory." *Research in Race and Ethnic Relations*, 1:17-64.

Brodet, D. 1979. "Subsidizing Capital and Return of Capital." *Economic Quarterly*, 101/102:200-212 (Hebrew).

Bruno, M. 1985. "Economic Stabilization: The Emergency Plan in its Early Phase." *Economic Quarterly*, 126:207-223 (Hebrew; for English version see next).

——— . 1986. "Sharp Disinflation Strategy: Israel 1985." *Economic Policy*, 2:380-402.

——— . and S. Piterman. 1987. "Two Years after the Stabilization Program: Israel 1985-1987." *Economic Quarterly*, 133:95-120 (Hebrew; for English version see next).

——— . 1987. "Israel's Stabilization: A Two Year Review." Discussion Paper 87.05, *Bank of Israel Research Department*.

Cameron, D. 1978. "The Expansion of the Public Economy—A Comparative Analysis." *American Political Science Review*, 72:1243-1261.

Crouch, C. 1982. *Trade Unions: The Logic of Collective Action*. London: Fontana.

——— . 1983. "Pluralism and the New Corporatism: A Rejoinder." *Political Studies*, 31:452-460.

——— . and Pizzorno, A., eds. 1978. *The Resurgence of Class Conflict in Western Europe Since 1968*. London: McMillan.

Dan, H. 1963. *On an Unpaved Road*. Tel Aviv: Shoken (Hebrew).

Dror, D., ed. 1983. *Collective Agreements Establishing Labor Relations in Israel: 1953-1982*. Tel Aviv: The Institute for Labor Relations (Hebrew).

Esping-Andersen, G., Friedland, R. and C. Wright. 1967. "Modes of Class Struggle and the Capitalist State." *Kapitalistate*, 4/5:188-220.

Galin, A. and Y. Taab. 1971. "The 'Package Deal' as a Turning Point in Labor Relations." *Economic Quarterly*, 69/70:106-113 (Hebrew).

Gatenio, Y., ed. 1986. *Collective Agreements Establishing Labor Relations in Israel*. Labor Productivity Institute (Hebrew).

Goldthorpe, J. 1984. "The End of Convergence: Corporatist and Dualist Tendencies in Modern Western Societies." In *Order and Conflict in Contemporary Capitalism*, ed. J. Goldthorpe. Oxford: Clarendon Press. Pp. 315-343.

Gordon, D., Reich, M. and R. Edwards. 1982. *Segmented Work, Divided Workers*. Cambridge: Cambridge University Press.

Gorni, Y. 1973. *Achdut Ha'avodah: 1919-1930*. Tel Aviv: Kibbutz Meuhad Publishing House (Hebrew).

Grinberg, L.L. 1986. "The Jewish-Arab Drivers' Association Strike of 1931." Unpublished paper, Department of Sociology, Tel Aviv University (Hebrew).

————. forthcoming. *The Crisis of the Israeli Labor Movement: 1957-1970, the Political Economy of the Relations Between Mapai, the Histadrut and the State*. Unpublished Ph.D. dissertation, Tel Aviv University (Hebrew).

Gross, E. 1983. "On Wages in the Public and Business Sectors." Pp. 157-172 in *Iyunim Bekalkala 1981*. Jerusalem: Falk Institute (Hebrew).

Gross, N. 1984. "The Economic Policy of the Mandatory Government in Palestine." *Research in Economic History*, 9:143-185.

Halevi, N. 1979. "The Economic Development of the Jewish Community in Palestine, 1917-1947." Jerusalem: Falk Institute, Discussion Paper No. 79.14 (Hebrew).

Harel, A. and A. Galin. 1978. *Developments and Changes in the Israeli Labor Relations System*. Ramat-Gan: Massada (Hebrew).

Horowitz, D. 1948. *The Palestinian Economy in Development*. Tel Aviv: Dvir for Mossad Bialik (Hebrew).

————. 1970. "Guidelines for an Economic Policy Today." *Economic Quarterly*, 65/66:3-8 (Hebrew).

Horowitz, D. and M. Lissak. 1978. *Origins of the Israeli Polity: Palestine Under the Mandate*. Chicago: University of Chicago Press.

Keisar, I. 1983. "The Histadrut and The State." *Economic Quarterly*, 116:507-516 (Hebrew).

Kimmerling, B. 1982. *Zionism and Economy*. Cambridge, Mass.: Shenkman.

Kleiman, E. 1967. "The Place of Manufacturing in the Growth of the Israeli Economy." *Journal of Development Studies*, 3:226-248.

Klinov-Maloul, R. and N. Halevi. 1968. *The Economic Development of Israel*. New York: Praeger.

Klinov, R. 1976. "Changes in Labor Force—Professional and Industrial Structure, 1960-1974." Pp. 11-18 in *Iyunim Bekalkala 1976*. Jerusalem: Falk Institute (Hebrew).

Korpi, W. and M. Shalev. 1980. "Strikes, Power and Politics in the Western Nations, 1900-1976." *Political Power and Social Theory*, 1:301-334.

Lange, P. 1984. "Union Democracy and Liberal Corporatism." Ithaca, N.Y.: Cornell University, Western Societies Program Occasional Paper No. 16.

Lehmbruch, G . and P.C. Schmitter, eds. 1982. *Patterns of Corporatist Policy Making*. Beverly Hills and London: Sage Publications.

Leviatan, O. 1978. "Is Capital Import to Israel Exceptional?" *Economic Quarterly*, 96/97:51-61 (Hebrew).

——— . 1982. *Developments in COLA Agreements and Wage-Prices Correlation*. Jerusalem: Bank of Israel Research Department, Discussion Paper 82-89 (Hebrew).

Maier, C. 1984. "Preconditions for Corporatism." In *Order and Conflict in Contemporary Capitalism*, ed. J. Goldthorpe. Oxford: Clarendon Press. Pp. 39-59.

Margalit, E. 1971. *Hashomer Hatzair—From Youth Community to Revolutionary Marxism, 1913-1936*. Tel Aviv: Tel Aviv University and Kibbutz Meuhad Publishing House (Hebrew).

——— . 1976. *Anatomy of the Left: Left Poalei Zion in Palestine (1919-1946)*. Tel Aviv: Peretz Publishers (Hebrew).

Medding, P. 1972. *Mapai in Israel: Political Organization and Government in a New Society*. Cambridge: Cambridge University Press.

Neubach, A. 1986. "Conclusions after one Year of Economic Stabilization Program Implementation." Prime Ministers' Office, 29/6/86. (Hebrew).

Ofer, G. 1976. "The Characteristics of Israel's Industrial Structure in an International Comparison." In *Iyunim Bekalkala 1976*. Jerusalem: Falk Institute (Hebrew). Pp. 19-35.

Offe, C. and H. Weisenthal. 1980. "Two Logics of Collective Action: Theoretical Notes on Social Class and Organizational Form." *Political Power and Social Theory*, 1:67-115.

Offe, C. 1985. "The Attribution of Public Status to Interest Groups." In his *Disorganized Capitalism*, Cambridge: Polity Press.

Panitch, L. 1977. "The Development of Corporatism in Liberal Democracies," *Comparative Political Studies*, 10:61-90.

——— . 1981. "Trade Unions and the Capitalist State." *New Left Review*, 25:21-43.

Peled, Y. 1989. "Socio-Economic Factors and Support for the Radical Right: The Case of the Kach Movement in Israel." Discussion Paper No. 9/89, *Sapir Center*, Tel Aviv University.

————. 1990. *Class and Ethnicity in the Pale*. London: McMillan.

————. and G. Shafir. 1987. "From Caste to Exclusion: The Dynamics of Modernization in the Russian Pale of Settlement." *Studies in Contemporary Jewry*, 3:98-114.

Peres, Y. and S. Shemer. 1983. "The Ethnic Factor in Elections." In *The Roots of Begin's Success: The 1981 Elections*, eds. D. Caspi, Diskin, A. and E. Guttman. London: Croom Helm. Pp. 89-112.

Piore, M. 1979. *Birds of Passage: Migrant Labor and Industrial Societies*. New York: Cambridge University Press.

————. 1980. "Dualism as a Response to Flux and Uncertainty." In *Dualism and Discontinuity in Industrial Societies*, eds. M. Piore and S. Berger. Cambridge: Cambridge University Press. Pp. 23-54.

————. and S. Berger. 1980. *Dualism and Discontinuity in Industrial Societies*. Cambridge: Cambridge University Press.

————. and P. Doeringer. 1971. *Internal Labor Markets and Manpower Analysis*. Lexington: Heath.

Pizzorno, A. 1978. "Political Exchange and Collective Identity in Industrial Conflict." In *The Resurgence of Class Conflict in Western Europe Since 1968*, ed. C. Crouch and A. Pizzorno. London: McMillan. Pp. 277-298.

Portugali, Y. 1986. "Arab Labour in Tel Aviv: A Preliminary Study." *International Journal of Urban and Regional Research*, 10:351-375.

Razin, A. 1979. "Israel: The Economic Crisis." *Economic Quarterly*, 103:341-346.

————. 1982. "Israel's Economy: 1981." *Economic Quarterly*, 112:6-11 (Hebrew).

Reshef, Y. 1981. "The Impact of Political Change on Patterns of Political Exchange." Unpublished M.A. thesis, Tel Aviv University (Hebrew).

Rosenberg, Y. 1980. "Offer Shock and Unemployment Rates," *Iyunim Bekalkala 1979*. Jerusalem: The Israeli Economists Association (Hebrew).

Rosenfeld, H. and S. Carmi. 1976. "The Privatization of Public Means, the State-Made Middle Class, and the Realization of Family Value in Israel." In *Kinship and Modernization in Mediterranean Society*, ed. J. Peristiany. Rome: Center for Mediterranean Studies. Pp. 131-159.

Sabel, C. 1981. "The Internal Politics of Trade Unions." In *Organizing Interests in Western Europe: Pluralism, Corporatism, and the Transformation of Politics*, ed. S. Berger. New York: Cambridge University Press. Pp. 209-248.

Schmitter, P.C. 1974. "Still the Century of Corporatism?" *The Review of Politics*, 36:85-131.

————. 1985. "Neo-Corporatism and the State." In *The Political Economy of Corporatism*, ed. W. Grant.. London: MacMillan.

————. and G. Lehmbruch, eds. 1979. *Trends Towards Corporatist Intermediation*. New York and London: Sage Publications.

Semyonov, M. and N. Levin-Epstein. 1985. "Non-Citizen Arabs in the Israeli Labor Market: Entry and Permeation." *Social Problems*, 30:56-66.

————. 1986. "Ethnic Group Mobility in the Israeli Labor Market." *American Sociological Review*, 51:342-351.

————. 1987. *Hewers of Wood and Drawers of Water. Non-Citizen Arabs in the Israeli Labor Market*. New York: ILR Press.

Shafir, G. 1989. *Land and Labor in the Making of Israeli Nationalism*. Cambridge: Cambridge University Press.

Shalev, M. 1982. "The Israeli Experience of Wage Restraint and Political Business Cycles—Reflections on Some Current Paradigms and Perspectives." Working paper presented to the Annual Conference of Europeanists, Washington, D.C.

————. 1984. "Labor, State and Crisis: An Israeli Case Study." *Industrial Relations*, 23:362-386 .

————. 1989. "Jewish Organized Labor and the Palestinians: A Study of State/Society Relations in Israel." In *The Israeli State: Boundaries and Frontiers*, ed. B. Kimmerling. Albany, N.Y.: SUNY Press.

————. Forthcoming. *Labour and the Political Economy in Israel*. Oxford: Oxford University Press.

Shapira, A. 1977. *Futile Struggle: Jewish Labor, 1929-1939*. Tel Aviv: Tel Aviv University and Kibbutz Hameuhad Publishing House (Hebrew).

Shapiro, Y. 1984. *An Elite Without Successors: Generations of Political Leaders in Israel*. Tel Aviv: Sifriat Hapoalim (Hebrew).

————. 1989. *Herut: on the Road to Power*. Tel Aviv: Am Oved (Hebrew).

————. and L.L. Grinberg. 1988. "The Full Employment Crisis: 1957-1965, a Chapter on Israeli Political Economy." *Golda Meyer Institution*, Discussion Paper 45, Tel Aviv University (Hebrew).

Shirom, A. 1983. *Introduction to Labor Relations in Israel*. Tel Aviv: Am Oved (Hebrew).

Shteier, H. and Levin-Epstein, N. 1988. "The Sectoral Structure of Israeli Labor Market." *Megamot*, 31:111-132 (Hebrew).

Skocpol, T. 1982. "Bringing the State Back In: Strategies of Analysis in Current Research." In *Bringing the State Back In*, eds. P. Evans, D. Rueschemeyer, and T. Skocpol. Cambridge: Cambridge University Press.

Streeck, W. and P.C. Schmitter. 1985. "Community, Market, State—and Associations? The Prospective Contribution of Interest Governance to Social Order." In *Private Interest Government*, ed. W. Streeck and P.C. Schmitter. London: Sage Publications. Pp. 1-29.

Sussman, Z. 1974. *Wage Differentials and Egalitarian Ideology of the Histadrut.* Ramat Gan: Massada (Hebrew).

————. and D. Zakai. 1983. "Changes in the Wage Structure of the Civil Service and Rising Inflation—Israel: 1974-1981." Jerusalem: *Bank of Israel Research Department* (Hebrew).

Swirski, S. and D. Bernstein. 1982. "The Rapid Economic Development of Israel and the Emergence of the Ethnic Division of Labour." *British Journal of Sociology*, 33:64-85.

Temkin, B. and U. Ben Hanan. 1986. "The Overloaded Juggler: The Electoral Economic Cycle in Israel, 1951-1984." In *The Elections in Israel—1984*, eds. A. Arian, and M. Shamir. Ramot: Ramot Publishing Company. Pp. 15-36.

Tokatly, R. 1979. "Political Patterns in Labor Relations in Israel." Unpublished Ph.D. dissertation, Tel Aviv University (Hebrew).

Tzaban, Y. 1977. "The Strike—An Analysis," *Emda*, 27 (Hebrew).

Weber, M. 1978. *Economy and Society.* eds. G. Roth and C. Wittich. Berkeley: University of California Press.

Weiss, S. 1979. *The Turnabout.* Tel Aviv: Am Oved (Hebrew).

Yishai, Y. 1978. *Factions in the Labor Movement: "Siah B'" in Mapai.* Tel Aviv: Am Oved (Hebrew).

Zandberg, M. 1970. "Security and Standard of Living." *Economic Quarterly*, 65/66:9-14 (Hebrew).

INDEX